GONE
with the
BREEZE

A TRUE STORY ABOUT THE *Spirit of Ontario 1*

LARRY DICKENS

Sulind Hill Press

ISBN-13: 9780978724405
ISBN-10: 0-9787244-0-2

Cover concept by Larry Dickens
Cover design by Sue Larysz, S&G Imaging and Susan Dickens, Spyglass Studio
Front and back cover photographs courtesy of Austal Ships, Henderson, Australia

Sulind Hill Press
PO Box 535
Canandaigua, New York 14424

Visit www.LarryDickens.com

For my loving wife, Sue, who lived
through every single up and down moment.

ALSO BY LARRY DICKENS

Forever Ten
Mrs. McGillacuddy's Garden Party
Hillary's Wish
Tropical Depression

GONE

with the

BREEZE

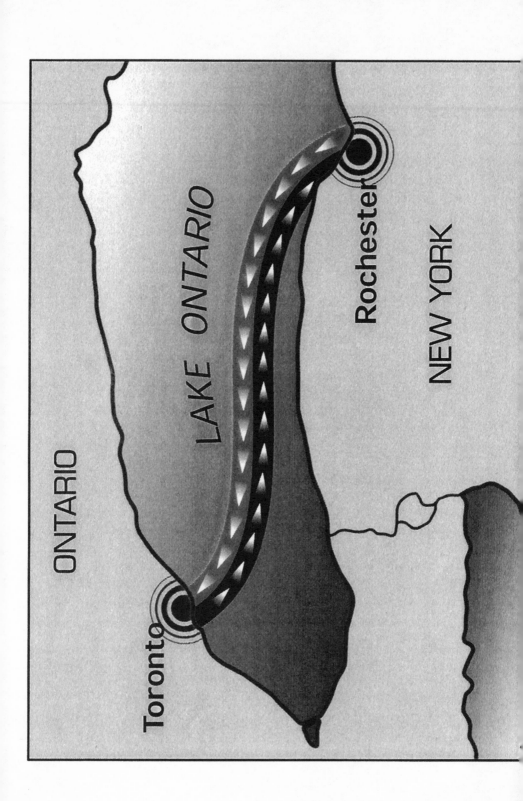

CONTENTS

The *Spirit of Ontario's* navigation bridge
Photo courtesy of Petr Chudoba, copyright 2005

Preface

This story is part crew tribute, part memoir, and part history. Those looking for a financial thriller which follows the money trail should look elsewhere.

Oddly, this story may also serve, in a unique way, as a training guide for *anyone* planning to work aboard a fast ferry or contemplating the start of such a business. The book is filled with many lessons on what could go wrong, and right, on any fast ferry.

Regarding CATS founder Dominick DeLucia, he started it and in 2004 he shut it down. Credit must be given where credit is due. Former CATS president Cornel Martin would say to me months after the September 2004 shutdown, "They got it to Rochester. They get zero credit for it."

It is sad, but true. After decades of talk, no one else stepped up to the plate and made this remarkable addition to our community happen. Mr. DeLucia and his associates did.

The *Spirit of Ontario 1* project created a great deal of pent up malevolence, anger, and frustration for those who lost money and jobs. To some degree, those emotions represented the passion that the project evoked, the passion that we all shared to make this work. Almost *everyone* wanted to see this project succeed. It was the most unique project to come to the area in years.

"They should have had more cash," many have said.

It seems to me that the CATS fast ferry was a project that was brought to its highest pinnacle, and then ran out of resources needed to sustain it at the wrong time. Undercapitalization, the experts said. In the end, it may have been a case of buying your dream car but having no money left to purchase gas, insurance, or a garage.

CATS did everything first class, but ran out of steam before the job was done.

The City of Rochester would learn the same thing a year later, but the lessons would be much harsher. It would hire a foreign operator, observe an extremely high turnover in American licensed officers, cause foot-dragging in the reflagging of the ship to the United States, and helplessly stand by as the operation plunged deeper into debt. In addition, the city would have to deal with a fuel oil problem which nearly resulted in the explosion of an engine room in late September and could have injured passengers and crew and left the ship disabled.

As with any major undertaking that involves hundreds of individuals and millions of dollars, thousands of stories can resonate from the operation. What I present here is only a fraction of those experiences. I do think I have captured the overall operation and the fine efforts of the crew. This story is primarily written with the crew perspective in mind since very little has been said about them in the press. Also, I was a crewmember, one of the ship's three chief mates during both years. For the layman, the chief mate is the second-in-command of the vessel.

This handpicked and dedicated, patient and loyal group of men and women made the *Spirit of Ontario 1* the success it was in the eyes of the riding public. They were responsible for the rave reviews and accolades the ship received from the 133,000 passengers it carried during the brief eighty-day period between June 18th and September 7th, 2004 and, again, from the 110,000 passengers it carried between June 30th and December 12th, 2005.

For the sake of their privacy, some of their names have been changed. Those whose real names are used either gave me permission, or their position in the company or on the ship was so high profile that fabricating a pseudonym for them was pointless.

To all of the people who were associated with the *Spirit of Ontario 1* project, many of whom have long since moved onto other ventures, I wish them all well. They are now an ingrained part of Rochester's ferry history.

Larry Dickens
June 2006

"What have you been doing since stepping down as CEO and president?"

"Working on the second boat, dude."

—CATS founder, Dominick DeLucia, in response to an author's question on August 28th, 2004.

Ten days later the *Spirit of Ontario 1* was shut down.

"Fast ferries...they're real heartbreakers."

- Rob Hamilton, a longtime, fast ferry chief engineer

Part I
The CAT'S in the Hat

Chapter 1
The End of the Line

Clank-clank! Bang-bang!

It was the day after Labor Day, Tuesday, Sept. 7th, 2004, and the high-speed ferry *Spirit of Ontario 1* had just docked starboard side to near the Cherry Street container port in Toronto, Canada. The weather was mostly clear with light winds, and temperature in the mid-seventies. The *Spirit*, nicknamed "The Breeze," was a huge 284-foot long, Australian-built catamaran. Nearly a football field in length, it stood five stories tall, and 78 feet wide. The twin-hulled, aluminum craft was light: it weighed only 1,059 tons; 1,529 tons fully loaded. Driven by four 11,000 hp (each) MTU diesel engines and four waterjets, it was capable of whisking 220 cars and 774 passengers across the fresh waters of Lake Ontario at an incredible, breath-taking 50+ miles per hour.

It was our last trip of the day, our second from Rochester, New York. The ship's bow ramp was down and cars were rolling off the main deck in rapid succession. They were being directed by car-meister second mate Chris Coleman and his crew of five skilled deck hands. The uniformed ship's officer—dressed in black slacks, black shoes, white short-sleeved shirt with shoulder epaulettes—rhythmically moved his hands much like a symphony conductor, quickly pointing and waving, back and forth, as if directing a great orchestra through an arpeggio. His staccato-like movements signaled the drivers, one at a time, that sat at the head of each of the nine short columns of autos that stretched aft on the ferry's vast aluminum car deck. It was a light trip, vehicle-wise. Only 31 cars.

The vehicle numbers had dropped dramatically from the four previous days which made up the Labor Day weekend. From Friday through Monday the ship had carried 1,522 vehicles, plus two buses; an average of 96 per each of the 16 legs. From Friday through Monday 9,378 passengers were carried, an average of 586 people per leg. It had been an excellent weekend.

Yesterday there had been lots more noise; lots more cars. There was the roar of auto engines, the squeal of tires, the rumble of cars driving down the massive aluminum ramp from the second vehicle deck, known on the ship's plans as the mezzanine deck.

Car-miester Coleman had been incredibly busy directing traffic.

Left lane. Right lane. Middle lane.

Zoom-zoom!

1

Clank-clank! Bang-bang!

The noise was sharp and loud. It was the sound of the autos driving over the bow ramp door's hinge plates. Every axle rolling over the plates caused it to clank and bang sharply. This was only one of the many sounds heard on the great ship's car deck. There was the shouting and echoing of human voices as the deck crew directed drivers, most of them bewildered by the sheer size and scope of the immense operation going on around them. Drivers turning their wheels to make the sharp, 180-degree turn at the top of the mezzanine ramp. Tires squealing, rubber against aluminum deck, in discordant harmony with the excruciating screeching sounds of overstressed power steering.

Collision avoidance was the game here: Don't hit the ship's support posts, and don't hit anything or anyone else.

Screeeeeeech!!

ROAR!!

The deck hands barked out assistance.

"Turn it sharp! More! More! Keep going! Keep coming! Okay, you're clear of the post, sir. Go!"

Down the ramp and through the center lane the cars would go.

Second mate Coleman waved them on while alternately funneling in cars from the sides. Over the hinge plates the cars flew and then bursting from the cave-like darkness of the car deck and into the bright sunlight, their drivers suddenly free to feast their eyes on the spectacular Toronto skyline. The first thing their eyes saw was CN tower, the world's tallest free-standing land structure, piercing the sky and the busy, vessel-laden, blue water Toronto harbor glistening in the foreground. Managing the car deck was an exercise in precision, coordination, and choreography, the likes of which were known only to the world's best figure skaters.

Zoom-zoom!

Clank-clank! Bang-bang!

Though today's numbers were much lighter, still, there were a lot of noises. I watched the operation from my position near the bow ramp. As the *Spirit of Ontario 1's* chief mate—or, 2nd in command—my job, among many other things, was to make sure the passengers disembarked safely. One hundred forty-one passengers were disembarking. I was to help with their wheelchairs, strollers, take an elderly person's arm and provide support walking down the ridged bow ramp. Toronto did not have a proper terminal. Instead, they provided a makeshift facility made up of several trucked-in office modules band-aided together. Unlike the state-of-the-art Rochester terminal which the city had spent $19 million

2

renovating an old warehouse, there was no gangway in Toronto that connected directly to the ship's starboard side door through which travelers could exit the vessel in style from the passenger decks.

Instead, the passengers were required to walk down two flights of stairs, pass through the busy car deck, and disembark down the vehicle ramp. The walking area for the passengers consisted of a small narrow section on the right side of the bow ramp which was marked with bright orange road cones.

At that moment, it was my job to keep them in the marked area and not allow them to stray into the path of an overwhelmed, nervous, or inattentive driver.

For the passengers disembarking, the activity on the car deck was just as overwhelming as it was for the drivers. Even on a day such as this, with only 31 cars, they were astonished by the sight of so many vehicles in motion and the sounds.

Disembarking down the ship's bow ramp wasn't the best way to say goodbye or welcome people. The car deck reeked of exhaust fumes and it was deafeningly noisy as the powerful ventilation fans roared to push out the bad air and replace it with fresh. Despite these irritants, passengers found the activity fascinating. Many would stop to take pictures of themselves in front of the fast ferry as cars poured out. Judging by their excitement, you'd think they were disembarking the *Titanic*.

For many of the passengers and drivers it was sensory overload. Everyone knew the *Breeze* had broken the 100,000 passenger mark in early August. She was already well on her way toward the 150 point. All of this—the numbers, the buzz, the sights and sounds on the car deck—all of it set a grand stage. It was a bright, intoxicating picture of a hugely successful operation that had tossed sand in the eyes of its eternal doubters, and doubters there were many. The populace of the entire Rochester community and the region surrounding the Flower City were split over the wisdom of investing large sums of public money in this questionable ferry project. Either they loved the *Breeze* or they hated it. There were few, if any, in-betweeners.

"If only the naysayers could see us now!" someone in the office had said.

If only...

My neighbors, John and Jane Bowler from Canandaigua, New York, were disembarking. They had just taken the *Spirit* over from Rochester and were planning to return on the ferry the next morning. As I

3

helped people off the ship, they stopped to express their praise and excitement over their first voyage.

"It was a fantastic trip! We truly enjoyed it."

"I'm glad you had a good time," I said loudly, attempting to be heard above all of the noise. "I'll see you both tomorrow."

Just then a voice crackled over my belt-mounted radio. It was Captain Danny's voice. Despite all of the noise on the car deck, Captain Winston Danny Aycock's Texas twang was unmistakable.

John Bowler patted me on the arm and said cheerfully, "You're busy. I'll let you go. See you tomorrow."

Jane waved and my two friends melted into the seemingly endless stream of departing passengers. The Bowlers, like so many other ferry passengers, were doing an overnight stay. I wished them well and then turned my attention to my radio.

Captain Danny had two messages. The first was to all of the ship's crew.

"As soon as the passengers are off the ship, I want all crew members to please report to the atrium."

The second message was to the Toronto ferry terminal. He said to the terminal manager, "There will be a brief delay before we backload PAX and cars."

"Roger," the terminal manager replied without—oddly enough—asking why. In this fast-off, fast-on business, delays without reason were uncommon.

When the last car and passenger had left the ship, all hands headed to the atrium.

The atrium was the center of the ship and was the first place the excited passengers would see. It was where every passenger, rich or poor, famous or unknown, boarded our magnificent place of work. It was where all walks of life crossed paths as they entered through the sideports from the terminals.

Through the sideports on each side (well, not the Toronto side due to the lack of a proper terminal that first year) this was where passengers were warmly greeted by our attractively uniformed and polite crew. They would cross the threshold from shoreside and willingly place their trust and safety into our capable hands.

Their curious eyes had a tremendous amount to absorb. The atrium was a wide open space. The warm, simulated wooden deck was light and inviting. The large, blue and red Maplestar logos—a half

Canadian maple leaf merged with a half U.S. star—imbedded in the deck at each entranceway proclaimed "Welcome." Two, thick columnar support posts with a veneer of marble supported invisible beams above the ceiling. The centerpiece was the large, grand staircase ringed with shiny curved and round chrome railings and glass connecting the two passenger decks. Travelers thought of it as a scaled down, modern-day version of the grand staircase aboard the *Titanic*.

Above it all was a huge skylight. A huge rectangle made up of space-age looking, lightweight aluminum frames and 12, large 4 x 8-foot windows made of Plexiglas. The atrium was the place where the deep blue sky pushed its way through and into the ship; where the outdoors came indoors.

Beneath and forward of the grand staircase was the concierge desk. It buzzed with a hub of activity where passengers could have questions answered by the knowledgeable staff and pick up maps of and/or literature about the intended destinations, Rochester or Toronto, and their attractions.

From the atrium, passageways radiated forward and aft, leading to other places on the ship which they could explore on their own and discover the ship's fine amenities.

The atrium was more than the center of the ship. It was the *heartbeat* of the *Spirit*.

The entire crew was assembled beneath the massive skylight. A mixture of blue sky and white cumulus clouds hovered over us.

That evening the crew consisted of one purser, two catering staff, and eleven cabin staff; three engineers, two mates, and five sailors. With the master, 25 in all.

Captain Danny was waiting. A jovial man in his early 30s, he was of average height and wore his black hair crew-cut short. He was overweight for a young man. The front of his white uniform shirt overhung his belt and hid his buckle. The crew liked and respected him. He was a down-to-earth fellow who was not the type to be self-absorbed in the fact that his shoulder epaulettes boasted four gold stripes. At that moment, with the crew assembled, the usually gregarious skipper was uncharacteristically subdued as he held a sheet of white paper in his hand.

"Folks," he began. He then let out a deep breath. "I don't like this. I don't like this at all. I'm sorry, but I've been told CATS is suspending service after today."

CATS stood for Canadian American Transportation Systems. This was the American company that owned and was operating the fast ferry.

"I just found out ten minutes ago myself. When we return to Rochester, the company is going to suspend the operation."

There was a sickening silence. Not even the sound of a jaw hitting the vinyl wooden deck could be heard.

The captain continued. He held up the white piece of paper and said, "This press release just came in from the office. I'm just gonna read it."

"Canadian American Transportation Systems announced today that it will stop operations Wednesday of the high-speed ferry between Rochester and Toronto, due to accumulating debt that has made it unable to continue service. This is a very difficult decision, but until the other parties involved fulfill their promises and obligations, we have no choice. Signed, Cornel Martin, president, CATS."

Captain Danny looked up from the paper and said, "I'm just as pissed off as you are. It's something political. I don't know much about this stuff. I just drive the boat."

The silence in the atrium turned into mumbles and whispers.

He then lowered the paper and looked at every person in the room. "I don't know for how long this is going to be, folks," he continued. "However, we have more than one-hundred people out there waiting on the dock. We need to carry these passengers back so I want everyone to be professional. I don't want any displays of anger or slackness. I want everyone to do their jobs as best as always and be professional."

The meeting was over. The crew dispersed to prepare for the returning passengers.

The crew, loyal and hardworking, was assembled from all over the country, drawn to Rochester to serve on this fantastic, one-of-a-kind in the United States ship. The fine, young captains were from Corpus Christi and Austin, Texas. The second mate from Coos Bay, Oregon. The chief engineer from Split, Croatia, by way of Houston, and the assistant engineer from Oswego, N.Y. Crew members came from Long Island, the Thousand Islands, Rochester, and myself, the chief mate, from Canandaigua. Most of the cabin staff was from the region surrounding Rochester.

We all went quietly to our duty stations.

Mine was on the starboard stern that evening. Since there was no proper ferry terminal in Toronto and no gangway to allow people to enter

6

through the starboard sideport and into the atrium, either the bow ramp or the stern mooring station was used. Passengers would then walk through the car deck and up the stairs to the passenger areas. The access to the stern mooring station was by a large stair and platform structure constructed of pressure-treated wood and beams. The link between this shoreside jungle gym arrangement and the ship was a small, narrow, one-person wide, 10-foot long aluminum gangway.

The passengers were standing on the pier at the foot of the pressure-treated stairs waiting patiently to board. They were held back by a span of chain between the stair's wooden railings. Without a permanent terminal, the passengers had checked-in and passed through a handful of bandaged housing modules and gathered on the narrow pier. With only 138 passengers boarding that night, I could see the end of the line. On days when we carried over 700 people, I could never see the end of the line as it snaked around the corner and into the make-shift terminal.

If one has never seen 700-plus people standing in one long, narrow tight place at one time, well, that is a LOT of people, waiting with no shelter from the sun or the rain.

One may ask, what about the people who traveled the ferry on days when it rained?

They got wet.

Today was a nice day.

As I checked over the tiny, one-person wide gangway, making sure its lines were secure and the safety netting beneath was in position, I wondered if these people knew they were taking a one-way trip to Rochester? Did they know they were possibly going to be taking their last ride on the *Breeze*? Had any of them considered an alternate way to return home to Toronto? At that moment, the most prominent worry that weighed heavily on my mind was whether or not to tell them as they stepped aboard. Or should I be a company rat, polish up my acting skills, and play dumb?

I had to do neither.

As the passengers crossed the little gangway, many expressed their deepest sorrows and sympathies to me.

"That's terrible you're shutting down," said one elderly lady as I took her arm and assisted her off the gangway.

"I hope you're not down for long," said another with warm encouragement.

"I'll miss you. I hope you're back soon."

In some ways I felt like I was participating in a wake for a lost relative. It was like being at a funeral.

I am sorry for your loss.

Be strong. You'll get through it.

I asked one grieving passenger, "How did you know, sir?"

"It was on television earlier," he answered. "You guys didn't know?"

I lowered my eyes and shook my head in response.

The man was astonished. So was I.

Apparently, we were the only ones in the entire metropolis of Toronto who didn't know we were just one return-trip away from the unemployment line.

"Your management sure knows how to treat its employees," the gentleman said as he followed the long line of people deep into the ship.

Another nice elderly lady asked me as I took her arm and helped her step off the gangway, "What will you do now, young man?"

I hadn't thought about it until she asked. After a moment, I finally said, "I guess I'll be looking for another ship."

Amid these concerns, a little girl of about 5 years old with long, wavy blonde hair and blue eyes stepped aboard holding her mother's hand. She looked up at me, her head tilted, a question mark evident on her pretty face. She was puzzled about something. She asked with some wonder, "Do you drive the fast ferry?"

I looked at her and smiled. Nodding warmly, like a proud little boy who knows he does the coolest thing in the world, I answered, "I do. I do drive the fast ferry."

The little girl smiled and nodded back at me. She, too, knew that it was a cool thing to do.

As she disappeared into the car deck, I wondered when I would get a chance to drive the fast ferry again after tonight.

Just then, a loud compressed air starter in one of the two engine rooms was turned on. Beginning with low, deep octaves and instantly soaring through and beyond the highest-pitched ones, it created an ear-piercing sound much like a jet engine starting up. Moments later, the other three air starters turned on. The 40 bars of compressed air they each produced then kicked over, one by one, the ship's four massive and powerful 44,000 total horsepower diesel engines and they thundered to life like a group of train locomotives. The last trip of the year was about to begin.

When would any of us ride the ferry again?

Chapter 2
Their Dream Became Ours

I'm sure I had thought about driving the fast ferry long before most anyone else in our region, if not the entire country.

For the previous 25 years, I had been a deck officer in the United States Merchant Marine. My career on ships began when I graduated with an unlimited third mate's license from the Massachusetts Maritime Academy. During the early years, I sailed on a variety of vessels, including a self-propelled suction dredge with the Army Corps of Engineers operating in New York harbor, several coastwise tankers carrying everything from tallow to jet fuel, and a freighter carrying military cargoes to Europe and the Orient. I spent the last 19 years of my career in the Orient aboard liquefied natural gas (LNG) carriers. These gigantic, three-football-field-length ships hauled liquefied methane to utility companies in Japan. Our loading ports were located on the Indonesian islands of Sumatra and Kalimantan (Borneo). Incidentally, our loading port in Sumatra was located just around the corner from Banda Aceh, 124 miles to the east, near the town of Lhokseumawe. Banda Aceh was one of the hardest hit cities by the December 26th, 2004 devastating tsunami.

As is common with men and women in my field, I raised my license over the years and finally acquired a "Master of Steam or Motor Vessels of Any Gross Tons upon Oceans" license. In short, an unlimited master's license. This license would allow me to be captain of any size ship in the world and sail it on any ocean. My assignment prior to the fast ferry had been as chief mate aboard an LNG ship.

The life of a mariner could be compared, to some degree, to an actor's. Shipping companies come and go (with surprising regularity), much like acting jobs, and much like out of work actors, we mariners are always looking for our next assignment. It is a difficult field in which to find job stability.

It is also a difficult field in which to have a stable home life with a wife and kids. The time a mariner spends away from home has been the death of many seagoing marriages which were initially filled with love and dreams. Only the lucky ones survived (I was one of the lucky ones, I'm happy to say).

One of the few advantages of a seagoing career is that mariners and their families can live almost anywhere in the world they choose. When a shipping assignment comes up, most mariners commute to work via their nearest airport. From there, they are dispatched to any port on the planet to meet a ship. The Rochester/Finger Lakes region had been my home base for two decades and the Rochester International Airport my departure point.

As a longtime resident of the western Finger Lakes, my interest in the ferry began in 2001. The stagnant ferry project had been in the news for years. The Lake Ontario Fast Ferry Company was the original company that attempted to launch a ferry service between Rochester and Toronto, but it never got off the ground. Interested in the idea, a new group entered and replaced it: Canadian American Transportation Systems, or CATS. Suddenly, there was some substantial headway being made. The project began to look like it was actually going to be a reality and, due to my unique qualifications, I thought it would be a perfect fit for me and my career.

When it appeared that a shipping company was about to be dropped on my doorstep, I wasted no time in letting those in charge know of my existence. I began calling the CATS office on River Street every few months just to keep my name in front of them and to keep up on developments.

The idea of a ferry service connecting the two cities of Toronto and Rochester had been in the minds of many people for decades.

Toronto, the Queen's City, a city of 2.5 million people, offers shopping, a world-class theater district, museums, cultural center, and a vast variety of restaurants. It is one of the world's most multicultural and ethnically diverse cities and would serve as a gateway to points north.

Rochester, the Flower City, a city of 214,000 people, offers its own cultural attractions which include the Strong Museum, the Rochester Museum & Science Center, the George Eastman House, and the world famous Eastman Theatre, home of the Rochester Philharmonic Orchestra. Rochester hold many popular annual events, including the Lilac and Jazz Festivals, and the High Falls Film Festival.

Rochester's Port of Charlotte was the gateway to points south and to the beautiful New York State Finger Lakes region with its rich variety of wineries, lake and outdoor sports, golf courses, and ski centers.

It should be noted here that the core of the City of Rochester, unlike Toronto, is not situated on Lake Ontario. Downtown Rochester is actually seven miles inland. The city limits do extend to the great lake by way of the community of Charlotte. On a map, Charlotte appears as a narrow, elongated stretch of land which borders the west side of the north-flowing Genesee River. It is Rochester's only beachfront neighborhood. In addition to the Erie Canal, Charlotte is the city's only other connection to the maritime world.

The ferry project would assist in reducing the congestion at the U.S.-Canada border bridges during the summer. It would provide an alternate way to avoid the dreaded Queen Elizabeth Way, the narrow and bumpy paved corridor that links Buffalo, New York and the Niagara Peninsula with Toronto. Commonly referred to as the QEW or Queen-E, the freeway starts at the Peace Bridge in Fort Erie, Ontario, and continues 86 miles to Toronto. The QEW is one of Ontario's busier highways with over 200,000 average trips per day.

Development of the service began in the mid-1990's when a commercial real estate salesman by the name of William Wilkinson and a wealthy businessman named Leo Smith joined forces and formed a company called Lake Ontario Fast Ferry (LOFF). Wilkinson is considered the fast ferry's godfather as he originally took the idea to Mr. Smith.

An excellent article about the history of the fast ferry project appeared in the June 11th, 2003 *Rochester Business Journal*. As journalist Will Astor wrote, "they (Wilkinson and Smith) formed a business plan and set about lining up financing for what they estimated would be a $100 million to $120 million project."

The project was to have two 300-foot, Austal-built fast catamarans. One would be based in Rochester; the other in Toronto.

Along the way the project ran into numerous financial hurdles. In 1999, Rochester businessman and Charlotte resident Tom Riley introduced Dominick DeLucia and Brian Prince to the project. Both men were native to the area and had successful careers in the investment and banking fields. In 2000, Canadian American Transportation Systems (CATS) was formed and took the ferry project over from LOFF. As Mr. Astor wrote in the *Rochester Business Journal*, LOFF sued CATS, DeLucia, Riley, and others "in a province of Ontario court in 2000, claiming CATS used business plans given to its principals in confidence to unfairly take the project from LOFF." Continuing, he wrote, "In April 2001 CATS and LOFF announced an agreement to settle the Ontario lawsuit."

CATS was free to proceed to develop the project. It would be three years before the ship would arrive on Lake Ontario.

It is not the intent of this book to examine the marketing studies that were completed which led to the "green-lighting" of the fast ferry project. A review of the November 18, 2004 Rochester Port and Ferry

Authority business plan lists seven studies that were done between 1997 and August 2002. Some of these studies estimated the annual demand to be as high as 1.7 million passengers and 1 million cars.

An article written by Rick Armon and Gary Craig in the Rochester *Democrat & Chronicle* on September 17, 2002, reported that,

> "CATS commissioned a study to try to determine ridership from both sides of the lake. The study was conducted by The Centre for Spatial Economics in Waterdown, Ontario. The center based its analysis on a Harris Interactive poll that showed 1.7 million people in the United States and Canada would ride the ferry annually, with more Canadians using the ferry. Harris conducted the poll for CATS.
>
> The company needs about 650,000 people to ride the ferry annually to succeed, city officials estimated.
>
> Dominick DeLucia, president of CATS, said that Harris interviewed 1,000 people in Canada and 1,000 in the United States by telephone for the poll, which was conducted from April 30 to May 6, 2001. The margin of error was 2 percentage points. "

After all of the studies were taken into account, CATS adopted a business model which assumed roughly 670,000 passengers per year, growing at 2% per year.

There were high hopes in the community that the ferry project would assist in bringing about revitalization to the area.

This would not be the first time that a ferry operation would be coming to Rochester and the Port of Charlotte. The last ferry service to run into the Port of Charlotte was the Ontario Car Ferry Company, otherwise referred to by locals as the Charlotte-Cobourg ferry. It operated for 43 years from November 14, 1907 until April 30, 1950 and consisted of two ferries whose primary occupation was the transportation of railroad coal cars from Rochester to Cobourg, Canada. Cobourg was forty-eight miles to the northwest of Charlotte. The ships were named the *Ontario No. 1* and the *Ontario No. 2*. These conventional steel ships each carried 1,960 tons of coal and, during the summer, they also carried 1,000 passengers per trip at a speed of 13 knots.

Fifty-four years later, a brand new, technology-laden, twin aluminum-hulled high-speed ferry would make its debut on Lake Ontario. The ferry would be an Australian-built, Austal 86-meter (284 feet) craft that was capable of carrying 774 passengers and 220 cars each way at a speed of 46 knots (50+ mph).

Railroad cars laden with coal were not going to be a part of this new, modern day picture.

Ontario No. 2 departed Charlotte for the last time on April 30, 1950. Since then, the Port of Charlotte had remained silent of ferry traffic.

CATS placed the order for the huge fast ferry with the Austal shipyard in Henderson, Australia, in September 2002 with the hope of launching the service in August 2003. The launching would be postponed until the spring of 2004. The silence of ferry traffic would soon be broken.

For the community and the future crew members and employees, the visionaries' dream would become theirs.

Chapter 3
Early Training Concerns

After repeated communications with the office, finally, in late May 2003 I was invited to visit CATS for an interview. At this time the office was located above the Scuttlebutts Bar and Restaurant on River Street in Charlotte.

This short, one-block stretch of River Street contained the names of pubs that could have been lifted from a typical red light district in any of the globe's seaports. They possessed all the worldly charm of a typical deep sea sailor's port. Besides Scuttlebutts, there was the "Driftwood Inn," the "CPO Club," and the "Charlotte Social Club." Railroad tracks and an old abandoned and decaying train station depot sat quietly across the street. On the other side of the depot lay the murky waters of the Genesee River, constantly flowing into Lake Ontario. Every now and then a CSX freight train slowly rumbled by. All that was missing from this section of Charlotte was a massage parlor.

To assist in making this ferry vision a reality, CATS had hired an Australian fast ferry consultant by the name of Tony White to be chief operating officer.

"Aussie is top gun in world of fast ferries," declared Rochester's newspaper, the *Democrat & Chronicle,* in their February 26, 2003 edition. White had an impeccable reputation and more experience in the fast ferry business than anyone around. Among his remarkable accomplishments, he had been technical and operations director of Condor Ferries in Guernsey, Channel Islands, when they introduced car-carrying wave piercer ferries in the early 1990s (The wave piercers were a new design in fast ferries. They had a middle hull which made the ride smoother in rough seas, thus improving passenger comfort). He had been managing director of Condor Marine Services in England, operating and chartering high speed ferries in about seven countries with crews of nine nationalities under about nine different flags.

As Mr. White would tell me, "That operation was the cutting edge of fast ferry operational development."

He had been chairman of the International High Speed Ferry Operators Association and brought together operators from all over the world. He was also involved in building and refitting ferries in Sydney for the 2000 Olympic Games.

Walking up to the third floor of CATS' modest digs, I met Mr. White. The youthful-looking 55 year-old was a tall, slender, and athletic man, clearly from Australia judging by his accent. He was gracious, courteous, and disarming. The meeting went well and I felt warmly welcomed. He expressed interest in my qualifications; in particular, my unlimited master's license and the fact I had worked on liquefied natural gas ships. The LNG ships, as they were known, were a highly regulated breed of tank vessels where safety and training were paramount, perhaps, more so than on any other type of tank vessel afloat. My association with such a vessel immediately told him that I had a great respect for and knowledge of safety.

I explained to Mr. White I wanted to contribute my skills to help this become a successful and safe operation for my community. The plan called for a two-ferry operation, with a second vessel coming online six months after the first. His commitment to the project was to see it through the start up of the second vessel and then hand the reins to someone else and move on to his next project.

My biggest concern about joining this operation was making the jump from conventional ships to a high-speed catamaran.

The LNG ships were over 900 feet long, weighed 100,000 tons (fully loaded), were sluggish in handling, and had a maximum speed of 20 knots (23 mph). They were powered by a 43,000 shaft horsepower steam turbine engine turning a single 26-foot diameter propeller. Docking one of these behemoths required the assistance of two pilots and four powerful tugboats.

In drastic comparison, the sleek, high-tech, Austal catamaran was just under a football field in length, weighed a scant 1,529 tons (fully loaded), could twirl on a dime and walk sideways. It had an unbelievable and incredible operating speed of 46 knots (53 mph), powered by four, huge, MTU 11,000 horsepower diesel engines driving four LIPS waterjets. Docking the fast ferry required no tugboats or a pilot. However, it did require deck officers that were skilled in the use of the LIPS joystick controls to maneuver the vessel. The acquisition of these fine skills could come only from hands-on experience which I did not have.

I told Mr. White of my concern.

White had been involved with the development and start-up of nearly a dozen of these fast ferry operations throughout the world and he, more than anyone, knew of the problems associated with deck officers going through the transition from conventional ships to an HSC (high-speed craft). The fast ferries were a relatively new breed of vessel in the maritime community, especially in the United States. The one planned for Charlotte would be the first one of its size in the entire country.

Most deck officers, like me, came from conventional ships. Unconcerned, White explained to me his extensive training plan.

It called for the deck officers to fly to Europe for four weeks to observe and train on fast ferries similar to the one Rochester was receiving. Two United Kingdom HSC companies were to train three of our captains in waterjet maneuvering. Then, we would be flown to Australia and train for two more weeks in an HSC navigation class in Fremantle, as well as spend some time at Austal Ships. The engineers would be sent to MTU in Germany and LIPS in Holland.

Afterward the crew would be split in half. One would be part of the delivery crew and ride the ship up from Australia for familiarization purposes while being trained by an Austal master and chief engineer. Once the ship arrived in Panama, the first crew would swap with the second crew which would then receive the training and bring the ship the rest of the way up to Rochester. There would be plenty of time for hands-on training for everyone.

I liked the sound of the plan. I knew it was just what I would need to build my confidence and help me to master this new maritime slick machine with its LIPS computer-operated, joystick-controlled, waterjet maneuvering system. The only way to be trained on this type of craft was by people who knew it. I eagerly looked forward to the training and I wanted to know when it would begin. White was planning to send a group to Australia in January.

Due to my interest, Mr. White gave me an open door policy at the River Street office during the late summer in 2003. He allowed me to come in anytime I wished and to look over any of the ship's plans. I did so on several occasions.

A sudden and disappointing change in CATS management occurred in late August 2003.

I stopped by the office on August 20th to look over ship plans and, to my astonishment, discovered that the River Street office above Scuttlebutts Bar was in disarray and barren—nearly emptied out. All but a desk or two remained; the file cabinets were missing. Tony White was sitting at his desk quietly working when I arrived. When I asked what was happening, he explained that the office was being moved closer to downtown, to Commercial Street in Rochester's High Falls district.

The second piece of news, however, was the real shocker. White told me he was resigning from CATS. I also learned that CATS's founding chairman Tom Riley was leaving the project as well.

17

This stunned me because it had been reported in the press—and White had told me during our first meeting—that White was going to be with the operation until about six months after the first ship set sail and as the second ferry went into service. He then was planning to give the title of chief operating officer to someone else and move on to his next project.

When I had asked him why he was leaving, he paused for a moment and only offered, "I don't like the way they treat people here."

He left it at that and said no more. He barely knew me and found no reason to share anything more, nor leave the potential for rumors to run amuck in his wake as the result of telling a potential employee stories that I would not fully understand. White said he was leaving for various professional reasons and that a company named Hornblower Marine Services (HMS) would be stepping in to manage the operation.

Hornblower Marine was an Indiana-based company which had just entered into a three-and-a-half year contract with CATS. Hornblower was the only American company that had experience with large, Austal high-speed ferries. It was currently operating one called the *Westpac Express* for a Marine Corps charter based in Okinawa. Hornblower had been involved in that ship's reflagging to the United States. They also operated casino boats and small, conventional ferries in various parts of the United States. This new division would now be called HMS-CATS.

A week later on August 28, 2003, I arrived at the new CATS office on Commercial Street. It was Tony White's last day and he wanted to introduce me to the new director of marine operations.

I encountered White in the parking lot. He wore a hardhat and was just returning from the construction site that was the Charlotte terminal. One last inspection of the $19 million dollar terminal, perhaps, but more likely saying goodbye to those he had worked so closely with over the last few years as the new facility was being completed.

The CATS office had moved to the top floor of 4 Commercial Street in Rochester's High Falls district. A renovated six-story building that stands like a lone monolith perched high atop a sharp precipice at the edge of the city's largest waterfall, it was reminiscent of the world famous "Balanced Rock" in the Arches National park in Utah. One look and you might think the slightest shudder from an earthquake would cause the narrow structure to topple over and into the falls.

We rode the elevator up to the 6th floor and the doors opened to the office. It was hot that day. For some reason, the air-conditioning was not working.

18

With its various rooms and occupied partitioned cubicles, the place was a hub of activity. At one point we passed through the coffee area on the northeast side. There, I looked out the large plate glass windows. From this spectacular vantage point, the office looked down on what is known in Rochester as the "High Falls of the Genesee River." The falls plummets nearly 100 feet. Rochester is one of the few cities in America with a waterfall located in the heart of its downtown. This corner coffee area provided a fantastic view of the rapidly moving Genesee River. I noted that several logs had built up along its banks and lodged at the top on both sides of the falls. Occasionally, gigantic logs, some weighing possibly half a ton, floated straight down the center of the waterway and toppled over the edge.

I suspected logs would present problems later on down the road for the ferry itself since the river was flowing northward toward Charlotte and into Lake Ontario. I would not be proven wrong.

White quickly introduced me to the new director of operations. His replacement was a large, tall man in his mid-40s by the name of Bill Annand. Annand was a friendly, folksy fellow who was a native of Michigan. He possessed a 1,600-ton master's license which would allow him to pilot small casino boats and ferries, but not large, deep sea vessels or fast ferries of the *Spirit's* size.

White left me with Mr. Annand and he took me into the office's sole conference room where we sat down to talk.

We talked briefly about ourselves, our families, and our dogs. I then asked about the training plan and what would be the program.

He chuckled warmly and said he hadn't formulated his plan yet.

This basically told me they, Hornblower Marine, might not be implementing the Tony White plan.

I told Annand about Marine Institute of Technology and Graduate Studies (MITAGS) and Marine Safety International (MSI), two advanced maritime studies institutions with HSC courses and bridge simulators. He hadn't heard of either one. I offered to provide some information on these schools. He then handed me an employment application to fill out and that was the end of the meeting.

Afterward, I found Mr. White in another section of the office and bade him farewell. I would not see him again until January 2005.

The next day, I sent in my HMS application and resumé. I also provided Annand with information about simulator training at both MSI and MITAGS. MSI was in Flushing, New York, and had been conducting a fast ferry program for several years. MITAGS, located near the Baltimore-Washington International Airport, also offered a program.

With HMS and Bill Annand now in charge, the open door policy I had enjoyed at CATS was quickly shut.

In Henderson, Australia, work continued on the ship. By now, the fast ferry was 96% completed. The Rochester community was being treated to weekly pictures of the ship's construction progress on the local newscasts. The community's anticipation and excitement was slowly building. The terminal in Charlotte was taking shape.

During September, I spoke to Annand on a couple of occasions and continued to inquire about the upcoming officer training. White had told me that part of the training would have to take place in January because of tight scheduling and the limited number of seats available in a high-speed navigation class in Australia. I needed to know what the date was going to be so I could plan ahead and mark my calendar. I also wanted to know if I was still going to be hired now that there was a new management team in town. I had not yet received a formal offer, nor, for that matter, the hint of one.

The director of marine ops told me he still had not formulated a training plan at that time, but assured me he was working on it. He said he was talking to MITAGS about the use of their bridge simulator. I thought this was a good sign, though I had not heard anything more about observing or training on similar ferries in Europe or making the delivery trip from Australia. A red flag popped up in my mind. I was becoming concerned that perhaps the training plan that Mr. White had left behind was now being discarded.

I did not ask about his plan because I didn't understand the nature of the politics behind his sudden departure and I did not wish to ruffle any feathers with the new management by asking questions aimed in that direction. Besides, Hornblower Marine was a proclaimed industry leader in the operation of large fast ferries in the United States. Granted, they had operated only one large high-speed vessel prior to the *Spirit*, but that was one more than anyone else in America. I assumed they had a template for such training since all fast ferries have to comply with the strict rules of the IMO HSC 2000 code. The High Speed Craft Code is a book of internationally mandated regulations. It is very specific in its training requirements.

I did wonder. Why not use a sound training plan that your predecessor, a known leader in the field, had spent valuable time putting together?

Sometimes new companies spend so much money getting started that they don't save enough to conduct a proper training program or to provide an adequate cache of stores and spare parts for a new vessel. Like an independent film company that blows its entire budget to get the picture in the can but leaves not a dime for post-production costs like processing, editing, making prints, and marketing. When you can't cut the cost of the hardware—like the ship—where do you cut costs? With your employees and their training, of course.

I was eager to train, to observe, and to jump headfirst into this new cutting-edge operation. I couldn't contain my enthusiasm and I sent a few more emails to the office inquiring about the training program. Though I offered to help the marine ops director in any way I could, I never received a reply to my queries.

The following month, on a windy Wednesday, October 15th, 2003, CATS founder and president Dominick DeLucia was a guest on a Rochester radio afternoon talk show. On public radio WXXI, he was answering caller's questions about the fast ferry. The winds in the region that day were gusting up to 46 mph from the west. They were blowing as fast as a, well, a fast ferry.

A caller asked Mr. DeLucia if our fast ferry would be able to dock on a day like this.

Without hesitation, he answered, "Yes, absolutely."

At first, I thought DeLucia might be overstating this. I was skeptical because of the ship's large amount of wind surface and its incredibly light weight. When coupled with the narrow, 350-foot wide Rochester jetties, only 200 feet of which are deep enough for the ferry, there wasn't a whole lot of room to maneuver for set and drift; especially with winds from the west which blow across the jetties.

Tony White's partner was an Englishman by the name of Bob Mansfield. He was serving as CATS's technical director. He had a large role in the ferry's design and was currently in Australia overseeing her construction. I emailed him, questioning whether or not the catamaran could be handled with 46 mph winds on the beam.

Mr. Mansfield emailed back that an experienced master could handle the ship in force 8 conditions. On a Beaufort scale that means 34-40 knots (39-46 mph).

He wrote, "The wind factor would need to be coordinated with the captain's experience." He added, "The problems we will encounter is training officers like yourself to be confident in the use of the vessel."

In short, training was imperative and should not be shortchanged.

Ironically, two-and-a-half hours after DeLucia answered the caller's question, a 310 foot-long, orange Staten Island ferry carrying 15 crewmembers and 1,500 passengers struck a maintenance pier in Staten Island. It was the worst disaster in the history of that ferry service. Eleven passengers were killed and 70 people were horribly maimed and injured. The winds in New York City were blowing 40 mph, too; however, it was eventually determined they were *not* a factor in the tragedy.

Instead, a single captain who suffered a blackout was the cause. There had been no other officers skilled in the control of the vessel in the wheelhouse.

On October 3rd, 2003, the fast ferry saw sunlight for the first time in Henderson, Australia, when it was moved out of its cavernous construction warehouse. On October 5th, it was floated for the first time.

Traditionally, when a ship is launched, it is welcomed by her owners and christened with a bottle of champagne. The new ferry bound for Rochester was not greeted by either of her owners. Neither DeLucia or his partner, Brian Prince, had traveled to Australia to see their new lady.

Some seasoned mariners thought this was a sign of "bad luck" or a "bad omen." I've never been a superstitious sailor. When things go wrong, human beings usually don't have to look farther than themselves to find the cause. By the end of the next two years, the "omenists" would find plenty to support their case.

In mid-December the ferry was given its official name. It would be known as the *Spirit of Ontario 1*.

I knew a lot was going on with the marine ops director, Hornblower Marine, and the CATS office team and I did not take their lack of response to my training and employment queries too much to heart. Things were ramping up.

It was time. A ship had just been born and CATS was now moving into the hiring phase.

Chapter 4
We Came from Everywhere

"Local workers sought for ferry"
"Rochester is the 'priority hiring area'; 100 or so jobs envisioned"

As the cool, fall weather began to ease into the region, the above headline that appeared in the October 25, 2003 *Democrat & Chronicle* triggered a flood of resumés, letters, and telephone calls into the CATS Commercial Street office. The selection process had begun. The jobs offered included bartenders, wait staff, servers, concierges, pursers, car marshals, baggage handlers, and ticketing staff. CATS Human Resources Director Glenn Gardner, a former Xerox HR person, found himself suddenly inundated.

The resumés from hopeful applicants across the region for these service-oriented positions contained backgrounds as broad and diverse as the colors of the changing fall leaves.

Some of the former occupations included waitress, marketing director, drug addiction counselor, caterer, neuro-psychologist, retail clerk, Xerox tech support, Russian language instructor, flight attendant, mother, software engineer, hockey player, student, bartender, restaurant manager, congressional aid, graphic designer, manufacturing executive, computer networking engineer, and a teacher of autistic children.

Many college degrees were represented. Over 1,500 applications were received. Some were from people who desperately needed jobs, while others were from those who wanted a career change in their lives. Some wanted to be a part of history.

Gardner and his assistants spent countless days reviewing resumés, returning calls, and making choices.

The fast ferry had been named the *Spirit of Ontario 1* because the long range plan, which mirrored the original LOFF plan, called for the addition of a second ferry that would be based in Toronto. The numbering of the two ferries reminded some people of the old Cobourg ferry days when those two ships were named *Ontario No. 1* and *Ontario No. 2*.

There was great optimism in the region for a Charlotte renaissance. At the end of the 19th century, Charlotte had been advertised as the "Coney Island of the West." It had been a flourishing beach community and summer retreat complete with boardwalk, amusement park, and hotels. Vacationers came from all over the state.

23

The air in this western New York region was buzzing with the increase of recruitment news. Over the last three years, there had been a tremendous amount of media attention, both newspapers and television, covering this new and unusual project. Now with the ship actually a reality, separated by only 15,000 nautical miles, many of the area's residents were beginning to take the project seriously. People were being hired for the fast ferry and they would become part of this history-making operation. It would be the first of its kind, and a lot of firsts it would bring, too. This would be the FIRST major ferry service on Lake Ontario in 54 years. The ship would be the FIRST fast ferry of its size to enter the United States. The powerful, new MTU engines would be the FIRST of their generation. The new service would create the FIRST new border crossing in a post-9/11 era.

This group of women and men, this first wave of hires, would be the "pioneers." With so much media spotlight focused on this high speed, twin-hulled ferry, it made everyone proud to be a part of it.

It was going to be cool to be a part of the fastest ship on the Great Lakes!

When you are a shipowner, where in the world do you find seamen?

I had been a longtime resident of the western Finger Lakes region and had made a living sailing as a deck officer on commercial ships for nearly 25 years. I had followed the fast ferry project in the news since the late 1990s. In January 2004, the call for marine crew applications went out internationally. Applicants to fill the *Spirit's* licensed and unlicensed deck and engine positions were sought. In that month's issue of *Marine Log* magazine, Hornblower Marine Services ran a hiring ad. *Marine Log* is an internationally recognized publication devoted to reporting on marine business and technology.

"Join Our Team and Hang On!" declared the caption beneath several splashy pictures showing shiny new, Austal-built, twin-hulled fast ferries. The Hornblower advertisement announced that they were seeking applicants for the fast ferry not only in Rochester, but for the new *Lake Express* project which they also were managing. The *Lake Express* project would connect Milwaukee, Wisconsin, with Muskegon, Michigan, shuttling passengers and autos across Lake Michigan aboard a smaller, scaled-down version of the *Spirit of Ontario 1*. Masters, chief mates, deck officers, able-bodied seamen, chief engineers, and engineering officers were being sought for both endeavors.

The ad also stated in bold letters "IMO HSC (High Speed Craft) training provided."

I still hadn't heard from the director of marine ops about how this "IMO HSC training" would be conducted, but I was happy to see that Hornblower was announcing to the world that it was going to provide it. If it was in *Marine Log*, then it must be so. Maybe Mr. White's training plan wasn't entirely dead.

During the second week in January, the *Spirit of Ontario 1* broke speed records during sea trials in Australia when it reached a top speed of 47.2 knots, or nearly 55 mph. With its four MTU 11,000 horsepower engines and their total number of 80 cylinders pumping away at the speed of light, this made it the fastest vessel ever built by Austal Ships at the time.

Excited by the news, I called the CATS office and asked to speak to the director of marine operations. The receptionist informed me that he was not in the office, but was in Australia riding the ferry during sea trials.

To this day, I still don't understand why the director of marine ops was sent down for sea trials while not a single ship's deck or engine officer was sent. After all, he was not going to be driving the boat when it arrived on Lake Ontario. He did not possess the certification that would allow him to hold a licensed position on the *Spirit of Ontario 1*. I was disappointed I wasn't called to go. I live here and assumed that I would be a candidate. Heck, even local television newsman Berkeley Brean of Rochester's Channel 10 news team was allowed onboard for the sea trials.

In early February, a young, soft-spoken man by the name of John Williams became the first master and deck officer to be hired by CATS for the *Spirit of Ontario 1*. A graduate of the Merchant Marine Academy at Kings Point, New York, he and his young family lived in Corpus Christi, Texas.

He had been with HMS for two years and was currently sailing as chief officer on the *Westpac Express* which HMS managed for the Marine Corps. The *Westpac Express* operated in the western Pacific shuttling Marines and their equipment between Japan, Korea, and a slew of other Far Eastern ports. It was on a long-term lease to the U.S. military's Pacific Command (PATCOM). The duty kept the 34-year-old Williams overseas a good deal of the time and, like all merchant mariners, he missed his wife and child. When Hornblower Marine approached him with the offer of becoming captain of the *Spirit,* he was greatly interested. He had been eager to return to the States and find a seagoing job that would bring him closer to his family. The Rochester project seemed to be the perfect solution. He had never had a seagoing assignment before that would enable him to be home every night.

Being a cautious and seasoned individual, Williams wanted to know more about the new project, especially its longevity. In the maritime world, when you give up one berth for another, quite often there's no chance of going back to it if things go sour in the new berth. Ships and shipping assignments in the U.S. Merchant Marine are disappearing faster than manufacturing jobs. They have been since World War II and are extremely difficult to find. When a mariner leaves a ship, someone else is hired and instantly fills the vacated spot. Williams knew he was lucky to have a solid job as chief officer aboard the *Westpac Express*. Its military charter ensured its existence for some time to come.

Williams was assured by HMS-CATS that this Rochester project would last—at the very least—for three years. He decided he could live with that. Comfortable knowing he had three years to pursue his career by being captain of a new, high-tech fast ferry and the joy of being able to see his family every night after so many months away from them, John Williams said goodbye to his mistress the *Westpac Express* and accepted the new position. He was Rochester bound.

Shortly after arriving in Rochester in February, Williams joined Annand and Gardner in the daunting task of wading through over 1,500 resumés and interviewing candidates for the various positions.

HMS-CATS needed two additional masters and Williams was able to convince his longtime friend Danny Aycock to join him on the *Spirit*. Another young licensed master, Aycock was also serving as chief mate aboard the *Westpac Express*. He and his family lived not far from Williams in neighboring Austin, Texas.

The U.S. Coast Guard required that the ship have three crews in order to satisfy the work rule requirements. The prime purpose was to ensure that the on-duty crews received adequate rest to avoid being fatigued. To this end, a third master was hired, but this gentleman found a job closer to his out-of-state home and he departed the company a month before the ferry began operating. Without a third master, Williams and Aycock would have to cover the position.

Even before the fast ferry arrived in Rochester, the company was short marine personnel. In addition to the missing master, several other key positions in the three-crew structure were not filled, nor would they ever be.

The *Spirit of Ontario 1* was built according to a plethora of strict domestic and international rules. Found in those regulations are strict manning and training requirements. Licensed and documented marine crew personnel were needed and they were a fairly rare commodity in Rochester. I was one of the few. Finding triple crews to fill all of the positions was a difficult task. The people who answered the call came from many parts of the country. They hailed from Austin, Corpus Christi, Ithaca, N.Y., Canandaigua, New Orleans, Washington, D.C., Oswego, N.Y., Coos Bay, Ore., Davis, Calif., Houston, Long Island, N.Y., as well as Rochester and Charlotte.

Who were some of these fine people that traveled to Rochester to work on the fast ferry?

The maritime field in which I worked is a small and, yet, very important world. It is a world of huge moving objects that carry the planet's commerce and are manned, guided, and protected by small groups of people.

It is also a proud world. This is shown in many ways. We celebrate when a difficult voyage or mission is accomplished successfully. Sometimes we have to fight fires that threaten to destroy our floating home/space capsules thousands of miles from shore, or we have to deal with horrendous storms. Sometimes we have to protect our ships from pirates. Sometimes we have to help our shipmates when they become dangerously ill, when delivering an incredibly valuable cargo becomes, in a heartbeat, secondary to altering course and rendezvousing with a helicopter to affect a timely lifesaving medical evacuation. Sometimes we are called upon to rescue other mariners who have suffered a disaster, lost their ship, and are at the mercurial mercy of an unpredictable and powerful sea.

The image of the modern day merchant seaman has changed considerably since the 19th century when sailors serving in the old British Navy would come charging ashore at their first opportunity after surviving horrendously difficult voyages on relatively primitive ships. They would locate the nearest saloon and flood their bodies with alcohol until their brains and thoughts turned to a pulpy soup. Today's *Crime Scene Investigation* television shows would have a field day if they ever got a hold of one of those living, self-embalmed bodies. Long gone are the times when "mothers had to hide their daughters" whenever a ship pulled

27

into a port and sailors were uncaged and on the loose. The days of "What do you do with a drunken sailor?" have long since given way to other worthwhile occupations. "What do you do with a drunken airline pilot" or "What do you do with a drunken tax accountant or cable guy?" are more in line with the times.

Yes, things have changed a lot. In the winter of 2005, I was featured on a local television newscast as a result of my visits to area schools and my efforts to convince young people to steer clear of drugs. The broadcast began with the story of a local priest who possessed child porn on his computer and then ended with one about a sailor—me—who is doing good work with kids. It seems to me in the old days, when it came to the image of sailors and priests, wasn't it the other way around?

How times have changed!

Today's merchant mariners are hard working men *and* women with families. Most are four-year college graduates. Most commute to work by jumping on an airliner and flying to some distant and unfamiliar destination in a foreign country.

Even in death, this small camaraderie of professionals celebrate those who were once their shipmates. In the back of most maritime union magazines or newspapers, you will always find a section dedicated to those mariners who have passed on. It is in these back pages that respect is paid to the men and women who spent a large part of their lives working within the small ranks that are found in the U.S. Merchant Marine. One union calls the section "Over the Bar." In my old former union, Marine Engineers' Beneficial Association's quarterly *Marine Officer* magazine, this section is called "Finished with Engines." In each issue, it begins with

"They no longer hear the calling of the watches,
or the falling of the storm rain in the night.
Seas shall weary them no more,
for they have reached their final haven
—their further shore."

The tributes always begin with a solemn, salty introduction. "Joseph Smith sailed into the sunset on November 19th...," "Carl McNeil settled his accounts on May 31st...," "Henry Collins received his final summons on April 8th." "Edward Parmenter answered the last call...," "Jason Booth crossed over..," "Cicero Brown made the big jump..." Sailed into the next life, went to his last reward, was promoted to glory, booked his final passage, cast off toward eternity, reached the end of the line, steamed into the sunset, climbed the gangway to the great beyond, set course for calmer waters, journeyed into the wild blue yonder, crossed the final bar.

"Crossed the final bar" meant, of course, a sand bar, not a gin mill.

The obit is then followed with a brief summation of the former mariner's career and his or her age. Interestingly, most of these brave and down to earth professionals usually live to be very old. I guess there is something therapeutic about spending a large chunk of one's life working in the clean sea air.

Sometimes mariners die in their homes; sometimes they die on their ships. Sometimes they die while enroute to their ships. A former Marine Engineers' Beneficial Association engineer by the name of Jay Corcoran had just kissed his wife and kids goodbye and boarded a plane for LAX where he would join a ship bound for Thailand. Forty-nine minutes later after leaving Boston's Logan Airport his plane disappeared into the South Tower at the World Trade Center.

In this unique, little world we call "maritime," we celebrate our successes, and we quietly mourn our losses.

This is the world from where most of the *Spirit of Ontario 1's* marine crew came. Fast ferries, monstrous oil and gas tankers, container ships, tugboats, military sealift ships, freighters, Coast Guard cutters, supply boats, and Mississippi casino boats. A huge cross-section of experience was assembled and arrived in Rochester to help run our fast ferry.

Manfred "Bluto" Babcock was on vacation and at home with his fiancée in Ithaca, N.Y., when his call came. He had begun his career as an able-bodied seaman and eventually acquired enough sea time to take a USCG licensing exam. He passed his third mate's exam and then began working his way up the license ladder, finally achieving his unlimited chief mate's license. He spent time on Military Sealift Command ships. Babcock was hired to be one of the *Spirit's* three chief mates. He took a month-to-month lease on an apartment that was only five minutes from the ferry terminal.

Neil Shanahan was busy with his wife and three children in Livingston, La., when his telephone rang. He was on his day off from his job as captain of the *Casino Rouge*, a large 3-story casino boat parked in the Mississippi River. Shanahan was also hired to be one of the three chief mates. When he first arrived in Rochester, he bought a 25-foot sail boat and lived on it at the Voyager Marina along the Genesee River. Later on during the summer, he would move his entire family up from Louisiana and live in the town of Irondequoit, a short distance from the ship.

Ian Sherwood and his wife, Jennifer, were living in Washington, D.C., where the third mate was employed by the Navy as a civilian in the Naval Sea Systems Command. A 2000 graduate of the Massachusetts Maritime Academy, Sherwood had first heard about the CATS project from friends. His wife's family lived in the Rochester area and while the couple was visiting during the holidays in 2003, he was interviewed on Christmas Eve by Gardner.

In March 2004, Sherwood was interviewed again by Williams. Two days later he was hired by Annand to be one of the ship's three deck mates. His job would be to run the vehicle deck, stand navigation watches, and tend to the bridge equipment and charts.

During the ferry's startup days, the Sherwoods stayed with family until they found and bought a house in July.

Hornblower Marine found retired Coast Guard Lt. Chris Coleman near his home in Coos Bay, Ore. The former commanding officer of the *USCGC ORCAS* had taken a job as an able-bodied seaman aboard a tug.

While in the Coast Guard, Coleman had acquired tremendous experience and, like most deep-sea mariners, he had traveled to many places. He had held a cornucopia of responsible positions including: operations officer, navigator-voyage planner, navigation and seamanship training team leader, security officer, helicopter flight deck coordinator, and rescue/towing vessel operator.

His duties took him to many places close to American shores, but also as far away as the Aleutian Islands and the Bering Sea.

Coleman's post-retirement tug assignment lacked the challenge he needed and was accustomed to. He realized he needed something more in his life. When Hornblower knocked and offered him a deck mate's position on the *Spirit of Ontario 1*, he readily accepted.

The third deck mate in this first group of CATS officers was Kris Werner. Like Sherwood and Coleman, he would be responsible for running the vehicle deck. He would also stand navigation watches and take care of the bridge equipment and charts. A graduate of the New York Maritime College at Fort Schuyler, the young mariner and avid yacht sailor was originally from Queens. He had moved to Rochester three years earlier to be with his fiancée, a Rochester native.

On the engineering side of the fence, there was a young marine engineer from nearby Oswego, N.Y. Hornblower Marine located third assistant engineer John Enwright on a Military Sealift Command ammo ship docked on the West Coast just as it was about to sail to Hawaii and, possibly, the Persian Gulf. Enwright, like Werner, was a recent graduate of the New York Maritime College.

More times than not, maritime careers turn on a dime. Enwright's did on that day.

After several telephone interviews conducted over many months with HMS, the last one took place while Enwright was in port working aboard the *USNS Kiska*. The ship was busy loading 1,000 and 2,000 pound bombs at the ammunition depot at Naval Magazine Indian Island in the Puget Sound. It was scheduled to depart in an hour.

Enwright had to know *immediately* if Hornblower had a job offer for him or not. Otherwise, the *Kiska* would depart and not return for as long as eight months. He would miss out on the training in Rochester and most, if not all, of the fast ferry's inaugural season. After five minutes, Hornblower called him back with an assistant engineer's job offer. Enwright accepted and quickly resigned his post on the *Kiska*, a decision which was made easier for him due to the fact that a qualified colleague was already onboard and could relieve him.

Bryan Hald from Davis, Calif., was also hired on as assistant engineer. The bright, young 2003 California Maritime Academy graduate was working in Morgan City, La., for Seacor Marine when he received his call to join the CATS team. Seacor Marine operated AHTS vessels (anchor handling towing supply). These huge, 200-foot plus "tugboats" are equipped with winches capable of towing drilling rigs and lifting and positioning their gigantic anchors and other marine equipment.

When Hald first heard of CATS, it was at a California Maritime Academy job fair in January 2004. Hornblower Marine was present. He was interviewed in March and received the offer on April 1st.

Dan Tripp from Long Island was a graduate of the New York Maritime College. He was a third mate who had taken a QMED course while at the school. QMED stands for "qualified member of the engine department" and is an unlicensed rating. The mates' positions aboard the *Spirit of Ontario 1* were already filled and so he was hired as a QMED and would work in the engine department until a position opened in the deck department.

Tripp would be a part of the busy three-man team that would make up the *Spirit's* entire onboard engine department: a chief, an assistant, and a QMED. Any engine problem, electronic problem, hydraulic problem, shipboard services problem, plumbing problem, lighting problem, and countless other potential problems that might occur in an instant fell into their capable hands to correct.

The senior licenses on a ship—that is, the masters and the chief engineers—are always the hardest to fill. The men and women who possess these licenses are usually already situated with a permanent shipping job and are well into their child-rearing and their pension-accruing years. Rarely, are they willing to give up job stability with a company or willing to relocate. Much like the captain's position, the position of chief engineer proved to be an extremely difficult one to fill.

Two chiefs were hired by Hornblower Marine and a relief was brought in to serve as the third player, but then one of the chiefs resigned very early on.

Ante Tony Putnik came to the *Spirit* the long way from Split, Croatia, by way of Houston.

He graduated in 1979 from the Marine College in Split. Over his many years in the industry he had acquired steam turbine and diesel engine certifications. He had an extensive maritime career prior to joining the *Spirit*. His lengthy resumé included marine superintendent with Houston Ship Inc. and port engineer for Pride Cruise Line of Galveston. He had held first and chief engineering positions with Diamond Offshore Inc. of Houston. Other assignments included work with Sea Escape Cruise of Miami, Crown Cruise Line/Royal Hydrofoil of Palm Beach, Fla., Fast Line of Beirut, and Van Ommeren of Bremen, Germany.

The curse of the senior license shortage prevailed and "Chief Tony," as he came to be called, had to rotate the position with only one relief chief.

The relief chief engineer was a pleasant fellow by the name of Richard Czachur. He was from England. Due to the fact the ship was registered in the Bahamas and carried the Bahamian flag, the *Spirit* was allowed to carry multi-national officers, if needed. In this case, Czachur was allowed to fill-in while Hornblower Marine continued to search in vain for a U.S. licensed chief willing to move to Rochester and join the team.

A third chief engineer, whom I will refer to only as Chief Rhinebeck, was hired, but his time with the company was brief.

The term "unlicensed seamen" refers to the positions of able-bodied seamen (AB) and ordinary seamen (OS), and, as mentioned before, QMED. The *Spirit's* first ABs included Gary Mann, Wayne Hinkel, Rob

Minnick, Tom Hodges, Doug Buell and Yoav Ehrenhalt. The first group of OSs consisted of Lee Begy, David Bowman, Chris Briley, John Hoenig, Laura Mcgill, Chris Moore, Terry Williamson, Joyce Yaddaw, and Rick Marcellus. A late addition to the ordinary seamen roster was Erin Macallister who was originally hired on as a cabin staffer.

Most of the ABs and OSs were from the Rochester/western New York region.

I received the call on the evening of March 18th while I was attending a parents' informational meeting at the Naples High School about my daughter's upcoming class trip to Spain. By now, because I had not received any responses, I had given up on the fast ferry and assumed that Hornblower Marine was manning the *Spirit* in-house, hiring people within its own company ranks and moving them to Rochester.

To my surprise, Annand called that night and offered me one of the three chief mate's positions. I hailed from South Bristol. No, not the quaint town in the United Kingdom, but rather the small, idyllic one near Canandaigua Lake nestled in the Bristol Hills. It is located about one hour southeast of the Port of Charlotte.

It was not a great distance, but in the end I would need to take an apartment closer to the port because of the long drive which, no doubt, would be much longer in the winter. Everyone assumed that the ferry would be running during the wintertime and so most of the out-of-town marine crew had signed one-year leases with apartment landlords, leases that could not be broken.

By mid-March the majority of the marine crew had been hired. There were enough licensed and unlicensed personnel to run the fast ferry. A classroom training date was set for April 5th. All marine crew were to report on that day.

Chapter 5
The *Spirit* Sails & Training for the Uninitiated

Many highly positive events happened in the life of the *Spirit of Ontario 1* during the winter of 2004.

In mid-January, this brand-new ship set an Austal speed record, reaching a top speed of 47.2 knots (55 mph) during sea trials, making it the fastest ship the company had ever built. Later that month, the USCG traveled to the Henderson, Australia, shipyard to conduct a preliminary inspection of the *Spirit*. They found no problems. The February 6th edition of the *Democrat & Chronicle* declared, "Coast Guard team travels to Australia, praises ship's quality."

On February 16th, the ferry set sail for Rochester and headed easterly for the Panama Canal.

The original plan, as explained to me by former project chief operating officer Tony White during my first job interview in 2003, had called for the ferry to attempt the famed Blue Riband of the Atlantic. The Blue Riband, or Hales Trophy, was the coveted England to New York Atlantic speed record. In 1952, the American liner *SS United States* won the award. Her westward transit of three days, 12 hours, and 12 minutes stands unchallenged today.

There was great optimism that the *Spirit of Ontario 1* could break that record. This, of course, was entirely dependent on the North Atlantic's capricious winter weather, but if the *Spirit* were successful it would gain tremendous public relations benefits and prestige. The whole world would then know about this new fast catamaran with the half-maple leaf, half-star logo on her white hull and her new route on Lake Ontario.

To attempt the Blue Riband, the ship would have to travel west from Henderson, across the Indian Ocean, and up through the Suez Canal. From there, it would head for the starting point in England.

Unfortunately, to everyone's disappointment, with the ongoing wars in Iraq and Afghanistan and the threat to American interests in the Middle East, the vessel's insurers decided to skip the westerly route through the Suez Canal. Instead, she would take the longer, easterly route to Rochester across the Pacific Ocean, travel to Hawaii, pass through the Panama Canal and into the Caribbean, up the east coast of the United States, and, finally, past Nova Scotia and down through the St. Lawrence Seaway. This change instantly killed any pursuit of the Blue Riband.

A web site was set up so the public could track the ferry's daily route as she traveled from the other side of the world and approached from the west.

The ship and its 17-man delivery crew left Fremantle, Australia on February 16th. The crew had been assembled by Austal. Not a single CATS American employee or officer was included in the delivery crew, unlike the original White plan, which would have provided us with a much needed familiarization and shiphandling period.

Han Tiemes was captain and Asger Manoe was the chief mate. Both men were from Denmark. Though Tiemes was the skipper, he had no experience in waterjet propulsion and so Manoe drove the boat.

Tiemes had been a pilot for many years in Holland. When he retired from that line of work, he was hired by Austal to do deliveries. Prior to his assignment on the *Spirit*, he had done five or six ferry deliveries to places all over the world.

Manoe started in the fast ferry business in 1992 on a small 40-meter catamaran and then graduated to an 86-meter—the size of the *Spirit*—in 1996. In 2001, he went to Japan and had a job on the Austal-built *Westpac Express* until 2003 when it changed flags to the Stars and Stripes of the United States. It was going to be chartered to a U.S. Marine Corps expeditionary unit to carry marines and their equipment within the Orient. Manoe's next assignment was the *Spirit of Ontario 1*.

The world of fast ferries is, indeed, a small one as exemplified by the American reliefs who took over for Manoe and his colleagues. They included Captain Ken Kujala, John Williams, and Danny Aycock. Williams and Aycock would eventually replace Manoe, again, as the *Spirit's* American captains, and Kujala would eventually come to Rochester to train the crew during his time off from the *Westpac Express*.

The ferry took a route south of Australia through the Bass Strait and north of the island of Tasmania. A week later, it made its first stop in Noumea, the capital of New Caledonia. The weather was fair, but they had engine difficulties. A problem had developed with the gaskets in both starboard side engines and they had to be shut down. The two remaining port side engines propelled the ship. Just before arrival in Noumea, they were able to repair and restart one of the starboard engines.

They had all the spare parts they needed onboard and the *Spirit* stayed in the French territory for two days while repairs were being completed.

When they left New Caledonia on about February 25th, Cyclone Ivy was in the neighborhood. Ivy was a category three cyclone, with sustained winds of over 110 knots. On Thursday afternoon, February 26th, the storm passed directly over the capital city of Port Vila in Vanuatu, an independent island country approximately 350 miles to the north-northeast of New Caledonia.

Reports from Vanuata detailed damage to houses, schools, gardens, fruit trees and crops on many islands. One death had been reported.

Tiemes and Manoe were worried about the ferocity of the storm, the swells it would generate, and its effect on the *Spirit,* so they guided the ferry a bit closer toward the Fiji Islands to the east and didn't have any problems with the cyclone.

They then headed for Hawaii and found themselves bucking the northeast monsoons. It was very rough most of the way. The wind sometimes reached 40 knots and the seas were 12 feet tall. On a fast ferry with a bow ramp like the *Spirit's*, it is important to avoid head swells slamming into it. The force and weight of the sea could damage it. Sometimes they had to turn the ship around to take the sea from the stern.

The ferry would be home to the seventeen man delivery crew over the next two months. When at sea, the ferry ran 24 hours a day, except for the few times it stopped in ports. The crew worked a "watch system"—a few hours on duty followed by a few hours off. When they were not working, they slept, relaxed, and performed normal everyday chores like their laundry. There was a washing machine and dryer onboard just for the delivery voyage. It would later be removed in Rochester.

The crew slept in the main passenger cabin, wherever they could find a quiet, private place with plenty of floor area. The cabin was fully enclosed and climate-controlled so they did not have to worry about the weather outside. Manoe, for example, slept in the handicap restroom aft. Tiemes slept in the ladies room on the same deck. One crewman slept in the low-overhead Navionics room directly beneath the bridge. They had air mattresses, bed sheets, and blankets. During the rough seas, some of the crew would sleep face down with elbows out to keep from rolling.

There was a full-time, professional chef onboard. He prepared three hot meals a day and provided a variety of cuisines.

For entertainment, the crew could play one-on-one basketball on the spacious vehicle deck when the seas were calm. Some of the crew played chess and had competitive tournaments. They read books, listened to personal stereos, watched movies on their laptops, and they were also able to communicate with their families and loved ones by e-mail.

One crew member brought aboard a child's round inflatable pool to keep cool on the hot days in the tropics. When in use, the pool was set up in the middle of the observation deck. It was small enough that one could fall asleep in it and not worry about drowning. During the equator crossing party on February 28th, four crewmen staged a photo op by crowding into the little 4-foot diameter pool, beer cans in hand, and began dumping water on each other with a bucket.

The *Spirit of Ontario 1* passed over the equator at 3:19 p.m. ship's time on February 28th. By this time, she had already transited the International Date Line and had gone from the eastern hemisphere and into the western. Back home in Rochester, the equator crossing occurred at 10:19 p.m. on the same day.

Along the way, the ferry traveled to Hawaii for a promotional event and to refuel. Austal Ships wanted to show off one of its products and the *Spirit of Ontario 1* anchored off Honolulu, Oahu for a few days.

Austal had just signed a two-ferry contract with the new Hawaiian Superferry company. Their logo was an Interstate sign with the symbol "H-4," which signified the four islands the ferry would service. These new Austal super ferries would be built in their Mobile, Ala., facility and, due to the inter-island nature of the Superferries' run, they would fly the American flag. They would be designed to shuttle 900 passengers and 250 cars.

During the week, the *Spirit of Ontario 1* would visit Kauai, Maui and Hawaii, the "Big Island." At one point representatives of the H-4 project presented the ship with a plaque mounted on a wooden canoe paddle. The inscription read, "Presented To The *Spirit of Ontario 1* from Hawaiian Superferry and the Islands of Hawaii, March 2004." The *Spirit's* crew would later mount the paddle on the forward bulkhead on the port side bridge wing.

The arrival in Hawaii allowed the ship's crew to have a much-needed break while the promotional events were taking place. Due to the amount of work that had needed to be done, the crew did not have a lot of fun in New Caledonia; however, in Hawaii they had time off. They went to the bars and the beaches.

The *Spirit of Ontario 1* then continued on its journey to the Flower City, heading for the Panama Canal. From Hawaii, they had the wind and the sea coming from ENE and that posed a big problem. They had to reduce speed and go very slowly most of the way while altering courses to the southeast and then to the northeast to keep the sea and the swell on or near the beam to prevent any damage to the bow.

As Manoe would tell me later, "In rough seas it is very bad when the sea is coming in the nose. The problem is the big door (meaning, the bow ramp) and you are not able to go with even slow speed if there is a big swell. If you have the sea from the stern, it is not a problem. The steering is bad, but you are able to handle the boat."

Most of the crew suffered from seasickness at some point during the voyage, but the leg from Hawaii to Panama was the worst for everybody.

Manoe would later write, "I was seasick just after departure from Fremantle and that is the first time in my life. It lasted for a couple of days and after that I did not have any problems. But it is terrible because you are not able to do anything except stay in your bed."

While the delivery crew of the *Spirit of Ontario 1* battled the bad weather and rough seas in the Pacific Ocean enroute for the Panama Canal, back in Rochester, Captain John Williams, HR director Glenn Gardner, director of marine ops Bill Annand, and the rest of the HMS-CATS staff were deep into the process of finalizing the hiring of the *Spirit's* American crew.

They were also preparing to send a group of 100 of the new employees through a required basic safety training course, a course that all shipboard personnel are required to have in accordance with international law. It would be held at the Monroe County Public Safety Training Facility.

During the week of March 22nd, 2004, the six-day Basic Safety Training (BST) class for the crew was conducted.

Most of the marine crew that HMS-CATS had hired did not need BST. The marine crew consisted of the licensed officers and the unlicensed seamen. The deck and engine officers and the able-bodied seamen (ABs) had already demonstrated their firefighting and water safety skills at some recent point in their careers in an approved training facility and already had their BST certification. The 100 newly hired cabin staffers, pursers, and new ordinary seamen (OSs) had to be trained before they could be employed. For shoreside personnel, such as car marshals and baggage handlers, BST wasn't required; however, many were sent through the class to serve as backups just in case there was a crew shortage.

This was not your normal day job requirement, but rather that of both the international maritime community and the United States Coast Guard. Basic Safety Training ran for six days and consisted of four main elements: 16 hours of basic firefighting, 12 hours of personal survival techniques, 8 hours of elementary first aid and CPR, and 4 hours of personal safety and social responsibilities. The average shoreside restaurant or hotel employee does not have to go through such rigorous training to be eligible for their jobs.

For this meticulously handpicked group of men and women of all ages, training like they had never experienced before—*or expected*—was about to begin.

The Monroe County Public Safety Training Facility (PTSF) on Scottsville Road is located near the Rochester International Airport. Officially opened in 2002, the PSTF is a unique partnership among Monroe County, Monroe Community College, and the City of Rochester. It represents one of the best local examples in the country of intergovernmental cooperation in the public interest. This state-of-the-art facility serves as a training complex for public safety providers.

It houses the Monroe County Office of Emergency Preparedness and Emergency Operations Center. The Operation Center's command center could easily be mistaken for a NASA mission control room. Huge video screens hang from the tall ceilings. Rows of long, curved tables stretch out before the screens and are outfitted with hotlines to dozens of first-provider and regulatory agencies. It serves as a disaster-control center for the region.

The PSTF is also the home of the Northeast Fire Training Center. Its motto "As Real As It Gets" is proudly displayed on a sign in the main lobby. Below it, the other motto "See it up close and personal!" refers to live-fire training. The NFTC is highly regarded and trains firefighters from around the world. HMS-CATS hired them to train its ferry employees. BST certified marine instructors were brought in from the California Maritime Academy located in Vallejo, Calif., and worked with the NFTC instructors.

The employees were anxious to get through the training so they could be ready for the ferry. Anyone who was going to work on the ship and cross the lake needed this training.

They would meet at the PSTF every day. The 100 people were broken into four groups of 25. Each group was labeled A, B, C, and D and was cycled through the four different training modules. While two groups were going through the firefighting module, the other two groups were bused over to the Monroe Community College campus a few miles away to undergo water safety training in the school's swimming pool.

The classroom for the firefighting segment was located behind the main building. It housed a few offices, classrooms, and a garage area. The garage housed a couple of fire trucks, equipment, and gear.

Jim Orsini was one of the BST trainers brought in from the California Maritime Academy. CMA was one of the country's six maritime colleges and highly regarded in the industry.

He said to the group, "Emergencies do happen onboard. What's important is to be prepared. It's like being on an airplane. You put your faith in the crew that's flying a plane, and when you're on a passenger ship or a ferry, you're putting your faith in the crew that's operating it."

The classroom preparation for the firefighting group took two days. General safety, fire theory, fire equipment, the general arrangement of the ship, and the type of firefighting equipment that would be found onboard the ferry and how to use it were among the topics presented. The group listened to lectures and studied manuals.

The class time allowed the new crew members the opportunity to get to know one another. The bonds between them were already beginning to form after the first day.

When you step into a BST class for the first time, it doesn't take too long before you realize that shipboard work is dramatically unique and that the person sitting next to you may be the one who saves your life in an emergency out in the middle of the lake. You also realize that the enormous responsibility of saving hundreds of passengers' lives suddenly rests squarely on your shoulders and that you are part of an invaluable team that has to work together. Everyone *depends* on each other. This awesome responsibility resulted in the new recruits paying acute attention to the instructors and absorbing as much of their words, wisdom, and lessons as possible.

The employees consisted of average, everyday men and women. Their ages ranged from fresh out of high school to fresh out of retirement. All were from the region.

Tonya Allen, 33, a youthful mother of three, was from Rochester. She was hired to work in the servery, or cafeteria, to wait on and serve customers their food orders.

Carrie Cooper, 21, a young woman who had recently just become a new mom, was from nearby Hilton and would be working in the ship's duty-free shop.

Erin Macallister, the young woman from Charlotte, was crossing over from cabin crew to marine crew. Like several of the new ordinary seamen hired, this would be her first ship as a marine crew member; she never had Basic Safety Training. Macallister had recently completed two years of college and loved to play league hockey and baseball. The athletic 27-year-old already knew what teamwork meant.

Rick Marcellus was also familiar with teamwork. He had been general manager of his family's Rochester-based manufacturing business for many years before it closed its doors. In addition, he was a longtime, avid sailor who was accustomed to working with close-knit crew teams. This would be nothing new to the 50-plus-year-old and he looked forward to the training. He was hired to serve as one of the ship's ordinary seamen and hoped the ferry would provide a stepping-stone to a new deep sea career.

Software engineer Mike Masco from Irondequiot, N.Y., was slated to be one of the ship's bartenders. The engineer was between jobs and was exploring new work.

Former flight attendants Karen Marsh and Cheryl Weimer were hired to be the ship's pursers. They would be in charge of the cabin staff and direct the passengers to their abandon ship stations during an evacuation. Both women were bright, bubbly, and cheerful. Marsh had been a business and tourism management major in college and Weimer was a mother of two young children. Both women had long careers in the airlines. Prior to BST, the two had just returned from Baltimore where HMS-CATS had sent them for four days of medical training at Medical Advisory Systems Inc. in Ellings, Md. They were taught not only how to care for people, but what caused the symptoms. Both felt it had been much better than their airline training. Automated external defibrillator (AED), how to give shots, backboard, splinting were among the many subjects taught.

Energetic Chris Moore of Honeoye, N.Y., held a four-year marketing degree and had been formerly marketing director for a large energy drink company in the west-central New York region. He took an entry level position as ordinary seaman. Later in the season, he would be promoted to ship's purser.

Former Xerox tech support person Delicia Hill was hired to be one of the ship's concierges. An attractive and bright, young 30-year-old Rochesterarian, her years as a Russian and French translator/teacher and as a senior guide for Rochester's Downtown Special Services tourism organization where she assisted the public every day, made her an ideal choice to assist the passengers aboard the *Spirit*. Before the season would end, she, like Chris Moore, would be promoted to ship's purser.

Rob Centro of Sodus Point, N.Y., had been self-employed and was a member of the ski patrol at a local ski center. He would be a purser. Daren Park was another former flight attendant. Like Hill, he was hired to be a concierge.

These were just a few of the employees who found themselves at the PTSF that week to undergo Basic Safety Training. Perhaps what made them different from everyone else was their sense of adventure and a desire to try something new; to be on the ground floor of this potentially exciting, lucrative, and historic business. Thanks to the vision and energies of founders Riley and DeLucia, and many others, the *Spirit of Ontario 1,* was bringing to them an opportunity unlike any in our region.

By the end of the second day of classroom instruction, the CATS trainees were led to the gear room where they selected and fitted their fire suits, SCBAs (self-contained breathing apparatus), and helmets in preparation for the next day's live-fire exercises. Due to the requirements associated with BST, purser Rob Centro had to shave off his beard of 20 years in order to wear the SCBA, otherwise his face mask would not seal properly.

That chilly night, after that second day of classroom training on March 23rd, the *Spirit of Ontario 1* left the Pacific Ocean behind her as she entered the Miraflores Locks in the Panama Canal shortly before 11 p.m. EST.

The remaining transit through the Canal was uneventful. In less than eight hours, the ferry would find herself in the waters of the Atlantic Ocean.

The fast ferry was 284 feet long, 78 feet wide, and had a maximum draft of 10.5 feet. The Panama Canal could accommodate enormous ships with 965-foot lengths, 106-foot beams, and 39.5-foot drafts. The fast ferry easily cleared the 40-mile long canal.

After transiting the Canal, the *Spirit* docked in Cristobal. During the rough journey from Hawaii, the ship had developed leakage in the port waterjet and lost a lot of hydraulic oil. The ferry docked near the cruise ship berths and spent three days in port waiting for a gasket to arrive from Holland.

The trip from Hawaii had been tough on her crew for fast ferries do not handle well in a big sea. Arriving at the Canal, followed by a layover in Cristobal, provided them with another much needed and well-deserved respite.

In Rochester, the public interest continued to grow. The local newscasts carried stories about it. Many residents watched on their computer screens as the *Spirit* transited the locks, courtesy of the Panama Canal's webcam.

The floating vision was coming closer to becoming a reality.

On day three of BST, the live-fire, hands-on training took place. Now, it was show time. The employees arrived early and suited up.

The first group of 25 employees met in the gear room. The brightly-lit, cinder blocked room had a string of nearly two dozen SCBAs mounted on one of its walls.

The trainees kicked off their street shoes and put on a pair of bulky fire pants. They came in two colors: yellow or silver. They slipped their stocking feet into their fire boots and then donned their suspender-supported pants. They put on their Nomex fire hoods. Like a balaclava, they put the hoods over their heads and pulled them down over their necks as far as they would reach. Next came their bulky turnout coats; again, yellow or silver. The coat's turned up collars would cover the bottom of the Nomex hood and shield their necks.

Every bit of exposed skin had to be covered. They made sure that all of their turnout coats were zipped up in front, the coat's clasps were fastened, and that the coat's neck piece was Velcro-ed tight across their throats. Fire was unforgiving in its effect on delicate human skin. Everything had to be closed and buttoned-up, otherwise all of this heavy gear and the protective barrier it was designed to provide would be worthless.

They adjusted the straps on their fire helmets, but did not put them on. Their helmets and their gloves would be last items to be donned. They had to put on their SCBAs next.

Like a scuba diver's cylinder, these hefty air tank units contained 2,216 pounds per square inch of compressed air and would provide roughly 30 minutes of breathing time (a warning bell on the unit would ring when there were only five-minutes of air remaining). The cylinder and its regulator were attached to a harness-like rig. Together, the unit weighed about 50 pounds. The employees donned the SCBAs just like a backpack, one arm at a time through each of the harness's nylon straps. With the single, yellow tank resting on their backs, they then pulled their cinch-up straps tightly to secure the rig to their upper body.

After two days in a classroom, the *Spirit* crew was eager to get in there and slap down some nasty fire. Dressing as the firemen do suddenly made it real for them. Never having faced a fire before and, now, suddenly, having to do so while wearing so much bulky gear, a few people were understandably nervous. For some, it would prove difficult, and even frightening.

Before putting on the helmet and the fire gloves, the SCBA's breathing mask came next. The mask was attached to the air tank via a diver's-like regulator with a long, rubber hose.

Macallister and Cooper had some difficulty getting accustomed to the facemask. An athletic and strong, young woman in her late 20s, Macallister, the ordinary seaman, was dying to dive into the firefighting exercises. The native from Charlotte was competitive by nature. The breathing mask's window seemed tiny and completely eliminated her peripheral vision. She found she had to keep moving her head in order to see around her.

Cooper found her mask to be suffocating at first. When the young mother breathed in, there was suction and the mask compressed tightly on her face while denying her any air. It scared her. A shipmate quickly saw her problem: her tank valve was shut. The shipmate opened the valve on her tank, cool air came rushing in, and Carrie could breath.

To add to her discomfort, there was a shortage of boot sizes and the diminutive 21-year-old had to wear a size 10 boot for her size seven feet. Her feet slid around inside them like, well, like a small foot in an oversized shoe.

As he prepared to do combat with fire, former software engineer Masco wasn't too surprised by the firefighting training because he had two friends who were active firemen with the Rochester City Fire Department. The *Spirit's* new bartender already had an idea of what to expect.

Another bartender, Beverly Rouse, was nervous as she put the SCBA's breathing mask on her face. The 50-plus year-old former graphic designer stood fully dressed from head to toe in her yellow fire gear. She wasn't nervous about actually looking down the scorching throat of an inferno. She was nervous because she was claustrophobic, and had been her entire life.

Now, here she was, required to put on an air mask over her face. She put the mask on and, with great discomfort, began pulling the mask's six rubber securing straps tight around her head. Its narrow, Plexiglas window provided a constricted, tunnel vision view.

After a few moments, she "freaked out," as she would describe to me later, and quickly removed the rubber mask. She looked at instructor Jim Orsini and confessed, "I'm claustrophobic."

Orsini had seen the problem before.

"In 20 years of teaching class, I've only had a handful of claustrophobics," he told her. He then said, "Put it on and don't connect it to the air tank. Let the hose hang loose. Get used to it on your face. Walk around with it. Breathe."

Rouse followed his instructions. As difficult as it was for her, she focused on her need to do this. She was driven by the desire to get this job, a job she had been dreaming about for a long time, ever since the new ferry had been proposed back in the late 1990s. The Rochester ferry was history in the making and, like so many of the employees, she wanted to be a part of it. She decided she was not going to allow this fear to get in the way. Before long she knew she could do it. She connected the mask's rubber hose to the air tank's regulator, began breathing, and was ready to go.

Ordinary seaman Marcellus was ready, too. The longtime sailor had his gear on and eagerly awaited instructions.

Allen, the mother of three, was excited and pumped.

Purser Weimer was excited about fighting the fires, too. The former TWA flight attendant had had fire extinguisher training before with the airlines, but never had anything as extensive as this.

The group checked their gear and made sure their team members and shipmates were properly suited up.

Led by their instructors, the trainees collected the rest of their gear and headed outside for the training grounds. It was the third week of March and a cool 47 degrees. Spring was less than three days old.

The NFTC live-fire school had simulators for all types of fire training, including aircraft and fuel spill conflagrations. The charred and blackened fuselage of a 737/300 jet aircraft mock-up sat conspicuously on the corner of the asphalt training tarmac. Off to the right was a propane tank fire simulator, and further to the right beyond that was the structural fire training building where the indoor fires and confined space exercises would be conducted.

The first exercise was to extinguish a propane gas fire and then secure its cutoff valve. The group was broken into two teams of four people each and they approached the burning tank with two charged fire hoses. They had their hose nozzles set to a fogging position. This put out a protective barrier of fine water droplets which absorbed the heat and knocked down the flames as they approached the dangerous tank. The propane gas fire sounded like a small jet engine as it burned and its flames shot skyward.

While the two teams provided protection, one of the trainees reached down toward the ground where the supply shutoff valve was located and closed it. This killed the fuel supply and the fire immediately went out.

The second exercise was a ground fire. Located beneath a 20-foot square grating, it was used to simulate an oil spill or a bilge fire.

Like the propane fire before it, the purpose of the drill was for the trainees to experience protecting themselves from the heat and flames using water. This time the fire teams had three people on a hose. As the team approached this large fire, they would quickly sweep their fire nozzles back and forth at the base of the flames and push them back until they were completely extinguished.

In both exercises, for many of the trainees, this was their first encounter with the heat and noise of fire.

The afternoon exercises were entirely different and brought much more intensity. Now that the new crew had developed a degree of confidence in handling the equipment and experiencing the heat from the flames, the trainees were ready to move indoors. The interior fires would prove to be scarier.

There were three indoor exercises.

The first was in a mock kitchen with a simulated grease fire. Entering the room in pairs, the first two students saw a large grill against the walls with flames flying out of it. The weapon of choice for this drill was a heavy, carbon dioxide extinguisher that weighed 50 pounds. Each student had one. Two at a time, they entered and cautiously approached the flaming grill. The flames roared and lashed upward at the blackened ceiling. The room stunk of burned oil. Sweeping their portable extinguishers' nozzles rapidly back and forth at the fire's base, they successfully smothered the fire. They then backed out safely.

The next two students then entered and the exercise was repeated.

"Move in on it!" the instructors would yell above the noise at some of the timid students. CO2 extinguishers did not last long and could be expended in less than 30 seconds.

Entering the burning building, there was thick smoke and no visibility. The SCBAs (self-contained breathing apparatus) took on greater, life-saving importance as the students were entirely dependent on them for oxygen. The sounds in the room were muffled by their Nomex hoods and turned up collars.

Students continued to take turns and rush in two at a time.

When it was her turn to enter the hot, smoky room, Carrie Cooper thought, "Did I really want to sign up for this?? What am I getting myself into?"

A confined space with intense heat and thick smoke; the smell of burnt material and the sweat on your face; getting wet from the hose, water everywhere; loud noises from the roar of the fire mixed with the instructors' shouts. Compared with an outside fire, an inside fire allows you few places to escape. The fire is in your space and it is hot.

"Run up to it! Closer!" one of the instructors hollered.

Fighting the grease fire simulation, Tonya Allen, a servery worker who would be next to the ship's kitchen every day, knew how valuable this drill was and she aggressively raced in there with her CO2 extinguisher spewing cold, white gas ahead of her.

Down the hall in a different room, a large wood/dunnage fire was burning. For this second exercise the trainees used fire hoses charged with water at a pressure of 100 psi.

Standing outside the closed door to the room, the instructor explained to the group how to enter the space. "If you feel warmth on the door, give it a real quick shot of water."

He demonstrated this by quickly opening and closing the valve handle on the fire nozzle.

The trainees checked the door and entered the room. There was one person on the nozzle and two people on the hose. Inside, there was a blazing inferno. Huge, bright flames shot upward and rolled on the ceiling. The team advanced slowly and approached the fire in a slightly bent-over position. The nozzle man directed a stream of water at the ceiling to knock down the heat and to create a blanket of smothering steam. They then attacked the fire directly and when it was extinguished, they retreated by backing out low and slowly. They had learned never to turn their backs on a fire, even an extinguished one. You never knew when it might come roaring back to life.

They repeated this exercise several times, rotating their positions so that each person had a turn as nozzle man or hose handler.

The final exercise was a bedroom fire on the second floor.

With four people on a team, the trainees dragged the heavy, charged fire hose up two flights of stairs. They felt the heat on the door first. It wasn't bad and they entered. The room was filled with thick smoke. They couldn't even see the fire, though they could hear it burning a short distance away.

To put on 50 pounds of equipment and a heavy breathing apparatus, purser Karen Marsh found it both scary and a challenge. To go into the dark was frightening.

As she and her partners pulled and dragged their water-charged fire hose, she said through her facemask to her closest partner, servery worker Billy Belknap, "Don't leave me and I won't leave you."

The buddy system is always paramount in fire fighting. You always stick together.

Like many of the trainees wearing air tanks and masks for the first time, Marsh experienced claustrophobic feelings on occasion, especially when her facemask fogged.

To add to the intensity and the pressure of the situation, the CATS firefighters were joined in the burning room by a local news cameraman that was on hand to cover the training. A News 10NBC photographer and volunteer fireman by the name of Mike Ollendorf donned gear and went in with a small camera.

That night some of the crew would be able to see themselves on the news.

In one of the groups, the intensity was far too much for one trainee. A stressed-out bartender came out of the fire building and declared, "F_ _ _ this! I only want to bartend!"

In the end, he didn't make it through basic training and resigned.

Many of the trainees had no idea they were going to be busting into burning rooms and putting out big fires. The groups went from one fire to the next in quick succession. Some older people had difficulty carrying tanks and gear and were out of breath.

They each had a chance to face the fiery monster in a variety of situations and put them out. By the end of that day, the hands-on training had put everything together they had learned in the classroom. Most of the new employees were pleased with themselves. Amazingly, it had been only three days of training. They thought the experience had been great and that it had been a tremendous confidence booster.

They broke down the equipment, cleaned their face masks with disinfectant wipes, stowed the gear, and called it a day.

After the exercises, all of the crew members had gained an appreciation for what firefighters do.

March 2004 was a month of naming contests in the Rochester area. The day after the *Spirit of Ontario 1* transited the Panama Canal, the city's Seneca Park Zoo named its new baby orangutan "Datu."

Zoo officials said "Datu" means nobleman, or chief. The baby Bornean orangutan was born January 29. The name was selected from a contest that was sponsored by The Seneca Park Zoo Society in conjunction with local Tim Horton's doughnut restaurants. The zoo had received 2,041 entries. The winning entry earned a University of Buffalo student by the name of Jason Grubb a year's supply of doughnuts, a zoo membership, and a bicycle.

Earlier in the month, on March 4, Cindy Lucas of Ogden, N.Y. took center stage, quite literally, at the Royal Alexandra Theatre in Toronto during a performance of the hit musical *Mamma Mia!* She was introduced by CATS President Howard Thomas as the winner of a much-ballyhooed contest to find a nickname for the new ferry.

CATS had received about 30,000 entries in its "Name the Ferry" contest.

Lucas's winning nickname for the approaching catamaran earned her a free ride up to Toronto and tickets to the spectacular stage show. She also received two lifetime ferry passes, a commemorative plaque on the ferry, and a weekend for two in Toronto.

From that night on, the *Spirit of Ontario 1's* nickname would be "The Breeze."

Two days after the *Breeze* had transited the Panama Canal, purser Cheryl Wiemer woke up with blisters on her hands and knees. They were the results of dragging fire hoses and crawling out of burning buildings during the live-fire exercises. Today's switch to water safety training would help to heal her wounds.

The "Personal Survival Lecture" at the PSTF lasted the entire day. It taught the trainees about donning lifejackets and exposure suits and how to evacuate passengers using the ship's MES systems. The MES, or

49

marine evacuation system, consisted entirely of life rafts. There were no lifeboats or davits on this high-tech ship. In addition to this classroom training, the employees were required to perform actual exercises in a local swimming pool, and, eventually, they would continue their education with the drills that would take place on the ship itself. At the end of the day's lecture, the students were told to bring a change of clothing for tomorrow's exercises in the pool.

In order to pass the water safety training module in the BST course, they had to perform or fail. It would be literally sink or swim.

The next morning the group was transported to the nearby Monroe Community College campus where the exercises would be conducted in the school's swimming pool. When the students arrived, they found a large black and orange life raft floating in the still water. It was about 25 feet long and looked like an oversized child's inflatable swimming pool; the type made up of two round, inflatable tubes with one on top of the other. Covering the two round tubes was a thin, but firm, bright orange canopy which created an enclosure. It had an entrance opening at each end.

Pumped up and charged after a day of live-action fire fighting training, the confidence level of the group was soaring. They felt invincible and were ready to tackle the next series of exercises.

First, came the immersion suit exercises.

The immersion or "Gumby" suit, as they are known in the field, are neoprene life preserving suits which cover the entire body except for a small area on the face. A person dons it like a pair of coveralls, zips it up the front, and is ready to go. There is no removal of clothing, as you put it on fully dressed. The neoprene construction retains body heat, has tremendous buoyancy and can float indefinitely, and the tight seal around the face keeps water out and maintains dryness within. Only your mouth, nose and eyes are exposed to the elements. Wearing one is like being in you own spacesuit, although you do actually look like the old "Gumby" animation figure, thus its nickname. It is somewhat clumsy to walk around in and there is limited dexterity in the hands as there are only three fingers and a thumb.

There were only six suits available and so, the trainees, six at a time, had to put them on and then hurl themselves off the side of the pool. The depth at the deep end of the pool was 13 feet. Once in the water, they floated on their backs and were astounded at how effortlessly the suits kept them afloat, warm, and dry.

Following instructions, they used their arms and paddled around the pool individually. They formed a line, locked feet under arms, and maneuvered around the pool as a group. Locking arms, they then formed a circle and did a huddle exercise. It was important to stay together as a group in the event of abandoning ship.

The exercise was a piece of cake and a lot of fun. Even those trainees who were afraid of jumping in the water realized there was nothing to fear when zipped up in an immersion suit. If the remarkable suit had been around during the *Titanic* disaster, there would have been no casualties due to drowning or hypothermia.

The next exercise was the *real* test. First, the CATS employees had to put on PFDs (personal floatation devices), commonly called lifejackets.

The instructors flipped the life raft over and a man who was designated the safety diver jumped in the water. He was wearing a mask and snorkel.

The instructor then explained in detail to the group what they were required to do. In their street clothes and PFDs, they were to jump into the water, swim over to the upside down, 25-foot long life raft, single-handedly flip it over, climb into it, and deploy the life raft's sea anchor. They would then jump out of it, swim to the side of the pool, and then remove their lifejackets, and tread water for 60 seconds.

Just about everything except squawk like a chicken.

It was a test of skill and endurance. It was a test of keeping your head.

It was sink or swim. Everyone's fast ferry future hung on this one lengthy exercise.

Various trainees had mixed thoughts about this Indiana Jones-style routine.

One trainee in her late 30s was scared of being in the water. She, like several of the older women, asked, "We have to do it?"

The instructor answered, "You're *going* to do it."

The woman said, "No, I mean, you're gonna flip the raft for us, right?"

The instructor repeated, "*You're* going to do it."

Another trainee said, "What have I got myself into?"

Another added, "I can't do it!"

Servery trainee Tonya Allen said to me later, "Listening to this guy talk about flipping this big-ass, 100-person raft on top of me and getting inside it. I'm going to drown! You do know most black people can't swim?"

It was show time.

One by one, each trainee went through the exercise while everyone else sat in the bleachers and watched with great anticipation. In the water, a safety diver was on stand-by, just in case there was trouble. He was 70 years old and was in excellent shape.

Rick Marcellus jumped into the pool, swam over to the inverted raft, grabbed the righting lines that crossed the bottom of the raft, and put his weight on it. He struggled to get it over. It took him three attempts, but, then, he successfully righted it.

As directed, he climbed into the raft, tossed out the sea anchor, jumped out, swam to the side of the pool, removed his lifejacket, and then treaded water for 60 seconds. Done. Passed.

More trainees followed.

Carrie Cooper was the first woman to flip the raft. The new mother had watched the guys do it and simply thought it was a piece of cake, until it was her turn. The problem she experienced was more with the raft itself for it had developed a pinhole leak and was slowly deflating. By the time Carrie reached it, the raft was collapsing and difficult to handle.

"Pull, pull, pull with your stomach muscles!" everyone in the bleachers shouted and cheered her on.

She thought, "I have no stomach muscles. I just had a baby!"

Using the righting lines, she finally had it vertical and cleared herself out of the way expecting it fall right side up, but, instead, it fell back down on her! The safety diver was about to swim into action, but she managed to get out from under it. Again, she pulled on the righting lanyards and this time flipped it over."

Concierge trainee Delicia Hill knew she was not a good swimmer, but could do almost everything the exercise required while wearing the PFD. Treading water without the lifejacket was her only concern and she was determined not to let that inability keep her from her new job. Prior to the life raft exercise, she enlisted the aid of two other shipmates who taught her how to do it. When it was her turn to run the gauntlet, she made it. Done. Passed.

People continued to cheer each other on.

Purser Marsh completed the drill, too, despite the raft bending in two as she flipped it over. She was no stranger to flipping over rafts. As an international flight attendant, she had done this before during airline training.

Occasionally, the instructor was forced to stop the exercise and pump up the raft with compressed air.

Bartender Beverly Rouse was amazed she could do the exercise, though she did have one scary moment. As she pulled the righting ropes to flip the raft, her wedding ring became wedged between the rope and the raft.

The safety diver watched with concern.

The pressure on her finger became unbearable and Rouse thought she was going to lose her finger. She quickly cleared the line from her ring by letting the line go. The raft fell back into its upside down position and she had to begin all over again. Once she had it righted, pulling herself up into the raft was the hardest part. She realized the only way she could do it was, with the help of buoyancy, get enough momentum going to push her way up and into the raft.

Guys with big bellies had trouble getting into the life raft. They would have one leg up over the raft's edge, but then couldn't lift themselves.

In one instance, one overweight car marshal trainee, had great difficulty climbing into it.

Realizing the man might have a problem, one of the younger seaman trainees stayed in the raft to assist. When the car marshal arrived, the seaman tried to pull the man in, but it was no use. The 70-year-old safety diver then swam over and began to push.

Though it wasn't funny, it did look comical. One young man pulling, one 70-year-old man pushing. Heave-ho!

Some members of the group were concerned that the car marshal's arms might pop out of their sockets. It looked like something out of a Keystone Cops episode. The man struggled hard, but made no progress. He was stuck in the twilight zone of gravity defiance, half in the water and half out, buoyancy doing its part while the two men did theirs. The cheers of encouragement from the bleachers died after a while. People were suddenly saying impatiently to themselves, "Come on."

The instructor told him to "calm down," "slow down your breathing," "relax." Finally, he said, "Get out of the pool."

One of the trainees looked at the instructor and asked, "What constitutes passing?"

Since car marshaling was a shoreside job and the man was not going to be on the ship, it wasn't imperative that he be able to perform the task; although, now, he could not be considered for a shipboard opening should one ever occur.

The only problem ordinary seaman Macallister experienced when it was her turn was the righting rope snagged her foot and she couldn't surface. She panicked, but then quickly collected herself. She had to go underwater and clear it.

The concerned safety diver quickly swam to her and asked, "Are you okay?"

"Yes, I'm okay," she responded and then effortlessly completed the exercise.

Despite her fears, in the end, trainee Allen wasn't nervous and proved she could, indeed, swim. She did it. Done. Passed.

The employees continued to cheer each other on. Most were impressed with their achievement. Purser Wiemer praised the training, saying she thought it was comparable to her airline training.

An excited Rouse said, "This training is extensive. It's awesome. It really is!"

By the end of the day, the trainees, both men and women, who had expressed fear at the beginning, got through. Only one did not make it. Cheers echoed throughout the huge, pool room.

People had powered past their fears because of their desire to work on the *Breeze*.

On Friday, March 26, the CATS group had a surprise visitor. New York Senator Hillary Clinton came by to say hello. Clinton was in town to receive the first ever Nursing Health and Humanity Award from the University of Rochester and to talk about freeing up federal funding for homeland security in Monroe County.

She was touring the Public Safety Training Facility and made it a point to stop by and say a few words of praise and encouragement to the CATS group. She shook hands with many of the employees.

Yes, that Friday night was a big night in Rochester.

Senator Clinton was presented with an award, it was opening night for the Shrine Circus at the Blue Cross Arena, and the first group of CATS employees had successfully made it through the most difficult sections of Basic Safety Training. All that remained were first aid and CPR.

In those four, short days, the new crew members had learned things that they never knew they could do. A sense of unity and camaraderie had developed. Being the first crew, they felt a sense of ownership and, above all else, loyalty. They all looked at the approaching *Spirit of Ontario 1* as if it were their own ship.

Brimming with confidence, the crew of the *Spirit* was ready for the tasks that lay ahead.

Their ship was not far away. It was now in the Caribbean Sea, plodding northward.

Chapter 6
The *Spirit* Has Arrived

While the CATS employees were fighting fires and flipping over life rafts, sign-makers were busy installing new boarding signs inside the sparkling new Rochester ferry terminal. Award-winner Cindy Lucas's nickname for the approaching ship had now been printed onto signage. The words "The Breeze" now hung from the ceiling in the departure hall and would show all passengers in the waiting area the way to the ship.

On March 18, 2004 Director of Marine Operations Bill Annand had called me with a job offer as chief mate and I happily accepted the position. I was to report to the Charlotte terminal on April 5 to begin training.

On Wednesday, March 31, WHAM radio ran an interview I had taped the previous week with Beth Adams and Chet Walker for their popular "Beth and Chet" morning talk show. The interview was in relation to my new, young adult book *Forever Ten*. *Forever Ten* is about a young boy who runs away from his drug-infested, inner-city neighborhood and ends up in a place where children are enslaved. It carries strong anti-drug and anti-child slavery themes, and its hero is modeled after a 10-year-old boy who was actually killed in Rochester in 2001.

Also on that day, I did an author visit at Leo Bernabi Elementary School in nearby Spencerport. I was a guest reader at their 13th annual Camp Read-a-Lot.

The Rochester *Democrat & Chronicle* ran an interesting story on that day, too. *D&C* reporter Rick Armon wrote "Passengers on the maiden voyage of the *Spirit of Ontario 1* may rub elbows with some heavy-hitting celebrities and Canadian power brokers when the ship lands in Toronto. Ever hear of Renée Zellweger? Ron Howard? How about Prime Minister Paul Martin?"

The president of the Toronto Rotary Club was reportedly name-dropping in an effort to sell tickets for the "Premiere Passage" charity fundraiser that both the Rochester and Toronto Rotary Clubs had spent months organizing. To date, both sides had sold over 600 tickets at $500 each for the highly promoted April 30th event.

Returning home later that afternoon from Leo Bernabi, I received an email from my friend Paul Tracy and his wife Nina. They told me that they had heard the WHAM broadcast that morning and that I had "sounded good on the radio."

With a new job about to begin soon and the day spent promoting my literary work and reading to kids, it was an extremely good day.

That same Wednesday began differently for a local broadcast reporter.

While I was reading a book to a third grade class at Camp-Read-a-Lot, Rochester News 10NBC reporter Berkeley Brean received a telephone tip that would alter the course of his next four days. That morning CATS Technical Director Bob Mansfield called him and told him the *Spirit of Ontario 1* would be arriving in New York City tomorrow morning around 6 a.m and docking at the South Street Seaport along Pier 17. Brean and Mansfield had met in Australia when the reporter had flown down there to cover the ferry's sea trials back in January. Due to Brean's fine, positive coverage, an appreciative Mansfield decided he would be the only reporter in the region he would tip off about the ferry's arrival.

By noon, an ecstatic Brean and two of the station's news crew had jumped into the "Live" truck (satellite truck) and were speeding down the road, heading for the Big Apple. The trio had left in such a hurry that Brean had left his overnight bag in his car back in the News 10 parking lot. All he had were the clothes he was wearing and a light spring coat. Along the way, they stopped at a mall in Pennsylvania and he bought a new suit, underwear, and some toiletries.

After spending the night in a motel in the New Jersey Meadowlands, they headed for the South Street Seaport at 2 a.m. The day was April 1st.

When they arrived, it was a madhouse that morning at the South Street Seaport as hundreds of New Yorkers crowded the Fulton Fish Market. Not knowing exactly where the *Spirit* was going to dock and the ever important detail of needing to set up their satellite dish with an unobstructed signal to the southern skies, the News 10NBC crew parked their live truck on the pier just south of Pier 17. They couldn't get the truck any closer.

By 5 a.m. they were broadcasting live updates on the Rochester station's local morning show. They stood around for hours waiting for the ferry. The weather was "so damn cold," Brean would recall later. "The weather was tough. It was dark, damp, and windy on the river."

Captain Han Tiemes and Chief Mate Asger Manoe brought the ship up Ambrose Channel under the guidance of a New York harbor pilot.

Passing under the Verrazano-Narrows Bridge, they entered busy New York Harbor.

Manoe would write, "Onboard the *Spirit*, arriving in New York everybody in the crew was happy and it was quite funny on the way in. I was actually the only crewmember who had been in New York before. The rest had not. It is very special for foreigners to arrive in the Big Apple. Statue of Liberty, Manhattan, and the Brooklyn Bridge. It is very special coming by boat and seeing all the skyscrapers. Everybody was happy because a long delivery was coming to an end."

As the ship entered the East River, the crew could see the Battery and the bustling Staten Island Ferry Terminal. Ferries were coming and going.

The *Spirit of Ontario 1* finally came into reporter Berkeley Brean's view at approximately 9:40 a.m. It was leisurely heading northbound in the East River, its destination after traveling over 15,000 miles, Pier 17. Brean and his station did a "Breaking News" segment as the ferry lazily cruised behind him. It continued moving from right to left in the background as the reporter proudly announced its arrival in New York. The ferry then disappeared behind the Pier 17 Pavilion building and out of his camera's view. Brean quickly wrapped up his segment and then he and cameraman Mike Jaeger began walking around to the other side of the Pavilion to observe the boat docking.

A half-hour later at 10:15, Berkeley Brean found himself and his Rochester television station interrupting local programming, again, to bring the citizens of Rochester and the surrounding region another "Breaking News" segment.

The fast ferry was damaged. It had hit the pier and torn a hole in its hull.

Thursday afternoon on April 1st, my friend Paul Tracy called to tell me that he "had just been on the radio, too."

I knew he was referring to my own interview from the day before on the Beth & Chet Show when he said the word "too," but I had no idea what he was talking about.

I asked, "Why were you on the radio, Paul?"

He answered, "They needed a man-in-the-street comment. They wanted my thoughts on the ferry crashing in New York City."

"Ferry crashing?" I blurted. I didn't understand. "Man-in-the-street comment? What are you talking about?"

"You haven't heard??" He was astonished. "The ferry crashed into a pier in New York City and has a big hole in it!"

I was stunned! But only a moment...and then it hit me.

"Oh, I get it, Paul. It's *April Fool's* day. I almost forgot. Not a bad gag," I warmly complimented him. "You almost had me going. Ha-ha."

"Larry, I'm *not* kidding. The ferry *really* did hit a pier in New York City."

"Oh, come on, Paul. You *are* kidding. Right?"

"Turn on the TV," he said. "It's on the news."

I still had trouble absorbing the truth in his words. With some belief creeping into my head, I asked, "Well, er, how did anyone find *you* in the street to ask you to make a comment, anyway?"

Paul answered, "I called the station within moments of hearing the news because my wife and I are planning our 10th anniversary in Toronto and Montreal and we're taking the ferry. I wanted to know what was going on. The producer insisted that I speak with someone about the story and asked me if I wouldn't mind having some of my comments and concerns recorded over the phone line straight into their editing system so they could add those comments to their noon broadcast."

His story now sounded too real to be a gag. With disappointment in my voice, I asked, "You're not kidding?"

"I'm really not."

After hanging up, I stepped into the kitchen and turned on RNews. RNews is Rochester's respected, 24-hour television news channel.

It was true.

There was an image of the ferry alongside a dock, starboard side to. In the foreground was an RNews reporter by the name of Seth Vorhees. At the bottom of my tiny 15-inch screen, in huge, two-inch dramatic block letters, were the words "FERRY CRASHES." Given the size of the type—and the accompanying hype—you would have thought that the ferry had slammed into a skyscraper and killed thousands of people.

They then cut to a shot of the gash on the starboard side. It was long, jagged, and torn. Frames were bent. The damage looked considerable to me. My first thought was, thank God it had occurred above the waterline, otherwise several spaces would have been flooded.

It was no great surprise to me when, a short time later, Hornblower Marine HR Manager Sue Squires called to inform me that the April 5th starting date for training had just been postponed.

After talking to both Asger Manoe and Bob Mansfield, I learned what had happened in New York. On arrival in New York the pilot expressed concern about the peak current that was running and had asked if they wanted to go alongside right away. Captain Tiemes and Manoe said "Yes" even though the ship was down one engine. They had lost the engine two days outside of New York. In terms of shiphandling ability with only three engines, the catamaran can still be maneuvered; however, the waterjets on the side with only one engine will take about twice as long to respond and with less power.

With three engines they were confident in the ship's maneuverability despite the current.

The plan was to dock the ship on the north side of Pier 17 at the South Street Seaport. The *Spirit* cruised upcurrent of Pier 17, approached the Brooklyn Bridge, and then Manoe turned the ship to starboard. There were up to 24 knots of wind on the beam and it was blowing in the same direction as the current. Manoe's plan was to control the boat and drift slowly down onto the pier.

He tested the controls and the waterjets and found he had no problem controlling the craft in those conditions, but as the big ship drifted down the river and toward the pier, suddenly the bow was caught by an unexpected countercurrent, presumably caused by the pier itself, and the *Spirit* sheered to starboard. Manoe tried to compensate for the sudden movement by adjusting the controls to port. This maneuver required the waterjets to reconfigure themselves, which is quite normal; however, with the ship down one engine and the combined force of the wind and current acting against her, the response was slow and there was not enough power to adequately turn the ship to port and continue going astern in a timely manner.

Realizing he couldn't regain bow control, he tried to abort the docking attempt, but it was too late to escape.

All he could do was go astern.

On the dock, Bob Mansfield, stood and watched with pride as his new baby turned to starboard just before the Brooklyn Bridge. He had put many years of his life into the project and he stood proud and tall as he watched the glorious ship prepare to dock. He was on his cell phone describing the approach to both Brian Prince and Dominick DeLucia who were back at the office in Rochester.

"It's turning to starboard, just before the Brooklyn Bridge....now, it's drifting toward the pier, starboard side to....still coming...still coming...."

Suddenly the forward part of the ship seemed out of position to him and coming too fast. To his horror, Mansfield realized that Manoe had lost the bow and could not pull it away from the pier. There was nothing that could stop it.

The ship hit the corner of the pier, near its middle, as it continued backing into its berth. There was the sound of crunching and ripping metal as the thin, quarter-inch hull ground up against the pier's hard wooden piling structure.

"She's hit the pier!" Mansfield said into his cell phone.

He looked up at the bridge wing where the maneuvering console was located and could see the expression of horror on Manoe's face.

As the new ship continued to back into its berth, it crushed a group of banded wooden pilings at the end of the pier.

Mansfield would later say, "The pier was made of green hard, one of the hardest woods in the world."

Sections of hull plating were peeled back like the top of a can of Spam, frames were bent, and piping was damaged. While an ugly, jagged gash, 28-feet long was torn through her hull, the overall damage to the aluminum hull extended about 60 feet as her hull paint was scraped.

In hindsight, the pier was unsuitable for the fragile-hulled ferry. It was too low and there were no rubber fenders.

Bob Mansfield was not alone as he watched the ship grind up against the pier. The Pier 17 Pavilion was crowded that Thursday. The Fulton Fish Market was busy and, though it was winding down, there were still hundreds of people present who watched in disbelief.

One eyewitness who saw the entire incident was a fish market employee by the name of Evan Kremin. Kremin would tell reporter Brean a short time later, "It (the ferry) started pulling in backwards, started backing into the dock here. It had a little too much speed, so we (he and his fellow fish workers who were watching) kind of guessed this (a collision) was going to happen and we were just imagining all of these cars falling into the water..." —at this point, Kremin looked directly into the camera and smiled—"...into the water 'ala Staten Island' (referring to infamous Staten Island crash of October 2003), but that didn't happen, thank God. We did hear an enormous crash, a loud boom."

Of course, there were no cars onboard the *Spirit* at that time. Mr. Kremin just assumed that since it was a car ferry there were cars onboard.

Brean and cameraman Mike Jaeger walked along the south side of Pier 17 and then rounded the corner. At first, everything appeared normal. The *Spirit of Ontario 1* was still moving backwards into the berth.

"Hi Bob. How ya doing?" Brean greeted Mansfield as he walked up to him. It was the first time the two men had seen each other since the sea trials back in mid-January.

Mansfield's response was startling. "You're driving me f---ing nuts!" he barked at the newsman. He then followed this comment with, "The dock put a f---ing hole in the boat!"

Standing where he was only 10 feet away from the edge of the pier, Brean couldn't see anything out of the ordinary. He walked to the edge and looked down. At first sighting, the veteran newsman saw only a few bumps, scrapes, and then what seemed to be a six-foot long hole. Not too bad.

Mansfield then said to Brean, "You will not report this!"

Given the state of Mansfield's mind at that moment which was only seconds after the collision, and imagining the magnitude of the sheer shock and stress the man was enduring, the reporter merely responded with an "Okay." He could see that something terribly bad had just happened and that Bob Mansfield needed space.

Brean backed off.

He then updated cameraman Jaeger. "Mike, there's a huge hole in the boat."

Once the ship had come alongside the pier and tied up, Mansfield looked at the 28-foot gash and said into his cell phone, "Damage is bad."

DeLucia and Prince shouted at him to get out of there. They told him to "get on a plane and get back to Rochester right away! It's Austal's problem, not CATS's!"

That was true. It was Austal's problem since they still owned the ship and it was their delivery crew that had caused the damage to the craft.

Despite the orders being barked at him to flee the scene, Mansfield decided to stay and sort out the press. He knew and feared that the perception of this accident in the ferry news-hungry Rochester region would be blown *waayy* out of proportion, rivaling only that of the sinking of the *Titanic*, if someone knowledgeable weren't there to keep it under tight control.

Brean had been the first reporter to arrive. Mansfield quickly talked to him and offered him an exclusive interview. By then he was relaxed and calm, his old self again. Among the things he said on camera was, "It's just like crushing a tin can. There are holes in these boats all of the time. It's aluminum."

Later, as the tide came up, the true damage became horribly visible.

By the late afternoon, the rest of the Rochester news contingent had traveled to New York and descended on Pier 17. Mansfield casually told the journalists, "It's like when you bash the wing of your car. You think it's the end of the world. You take it down to the shop and your car is back like normal tomorrow."

For the organizers of Rochester's upcoming Area Foundation charity fundraiser and the Rotary "Premiere Passage" fundraiser, both of which depended on the ship's presence in The Flower City, it wasn't quite the end of the world, but there was instantly a lot of pressure to postpone and reschedule those events.

At the time, no one had any idea of when to reschedule.

As the day's updates were transmitted to Rochester, eyewitness and fish market worker Evan Kremin told reporter Brean that docking at the pier was "predictably dangerous." He explained, "You've got current going this way on that side and current coming this way on this side and because of this dock, actually, the water that comes here is churning and churning. It's a very tricky 'in'."

At the time, it was hard for the layperson looking at the television images of the damage to believe that this wasn't serious. After all, how often does one see holes, mangulated metal, and long, ugly jagged tears in the sides of ships? Some areas even looked like someone had pulled open the lid of a sardine can. It's a disconcerting sight. You rarely see them on a steel cruise ship.

As bad as it looked, Mansfield's reassuring words would be proven true and reported on weeks later as the ferry bumped its way through the St. Lawrence Seaway locks. They would also be proven true later during the winter when the docked ship was blown hard up against a frozen rubber fender and incurred several additional holes and cracks.

Aluminum ships are *not* steel ships. That's why they can go fast. They are light, but not as strong.

Later DeLucia and Prince realized that Bob Mansfield had made the correct public relations decision and they backed off.

In Rochester, the community was shocked by the news. Everyone, from the mayor to the state's U.S. senators, from the ticket agents to the waitresses, was stunned and disappointed by the bad news.

One waitress who worked at the popular LDR Char Pit restaurant, located directly across from the ferry terminal, told a reporter, "You'd have to question the competence of the driver. I mean, they had better have a backup, that's all I gotta say. A backup driver."

A cheerful New York State Senator Michael Nozzolio put a lighter spin on the event after he visited the battered *Spirit* the next day. To reporter Brean, he said, "I'm thrilled to see the ship here in New York, finally." Referring to the accident, "Yeah, it's a 'speed bump' certainly, but it's a million dollars of free publicity."

The "omenists" out there saw it as *another* sign. First, the boat wasn't christened. Now this!

Others expressed confidence that the repairs would be done quickly and soon be forgotten.

Far worse things were to happen in the life of this ferry and would eventually take the spotlight away from the Pier 17 incident.

The Austal crew had not yet delivered the boat to CATS and it was Austal's problem.

Asger Manoe would write me, "You can deliver a boat in two ways. Austal prefers to deliver the boat at the yard and let the client bring the boat to the destination with his own crew. Some clients want their boat delivered on the spot, in which case then Austal prefers to use their own crew. It is possible for the client to put a captain or a chief mate on board, but they have to pay themselves because Austal is responsible for the boat until the day of delivery."

As Manoe would later write me when I asked him about the April 1st incident, "Then we arrived in New York and I try to forget what happened up there."

He wrote this with self-deprecation. He was at the controls when the ship brushed up against the pier. Who wouldn't want to forget that? In the summer of 2005, I would have the unenviable experience of grazing the gangway in Toronto. It is not a good feeling and I could easily relate to Asger's wanting to "try to forget what happened up there."

Interestingly, in the same note, he then added, "We spent three weeks in New York for repairs, but also waiting for the ice to break up in the Seaway. Actually, we would not have been able to arrive in Rochester earlier even if we had not hit the pier. The ice was still there when we passed Nova Scotia."

Sue Squires, the HR manager at Hornblower called me again after a few days and informed me that the marine crew training was now postponed until April 12th. Later, the training would be postponed again.

After 19 days in New York, the *Spirit of Ontario 1* left New York City at 11 a.m. Monday, April 19th, and continued on the last leg of its voyage from Australia to Rochester.

As the newly repaired *Breeze* left New York bound for the St. Lawrence Seaway, the officers, the unlicensed marine crew, and the pursers began their classroom training. The classroom was on the second floor of the recently completed terminal building in Charlotte.

Throughout that first day we were introduced to various people, including Charles Guinta, head of the U.S. customs in the Rochester area, CATS founder Dominick DeLucia, Sue Squires, and type rating trainer, Captain Ken Kujala.

One of the very first things we were told was not to talk to the press. The spotlight of the news media had been on the ferry project for a very long time. On many occasions, the press had been negative. In an effort to control all news stories that were going out the door with the crew, we were instructed to politely refer all press queries to Howard Thomas, president of the company.

HR manager Sue Squires provided us with health care paperwork and then conducted a brief, but required, class in sexual harassment.

In order to work on a fast ferry, a type rating certificate was required for each crew member. The type rating certificate, much like in the airline industry, was "craft specific." It ensures a high level of competence and training in respect to a particular type and model of craft by requiring the officers to be thoroughly checked out on all of a ferry's operating systems: fire protection, life-saving, evacuation, propulsion, and navigation systems, to name only a few. The type rating you receive on one ferry would not be valid on another ferry. For the deck officers, the additional parameter of "route specific" was included in their certificates. Engine officers would additionally have engine-specific parameters.

The type rating requirements are clearly spelled out in the *International Code of Safety for High-Speed Craft*, otherwise known as the 2000 HSC Code, the bible of the fast ferry world. Fast ferry operators like Hornblower Marine provide a training curriculum which guides the newcomer through all of the systems that they are required to know.

Captain Ken Kujala, Hornblower Marine's master of the *Westpac Express,* was sent to Rochester to be our type rating instructor. As mentioned earlier, the *Westpac Express* was an Austal-built, high-speed catamaran, slightly larger than the *Spirit of Ontario 1.* Kujala had spent many years on tankers, working for American Trading & Transportation Company and Sabine Shipping. He also had worked on a Royal Caribbean cruise ship as well as research ships at Woods Hole. A rugged looking and good-natured man who kept his hair military short, this esteemed gentleman had the distinction of being the first ship's master in the entire United States to be type rated on an unlimited tonnage, high-speed vessel, becoming one of the first U.S. Coast Guard approved type rating instructors and auditors.

Over the next several weeks all of us would begin the process of becoming type rated for the *Spirit of Ontario 1*, and Captain Kujala would be our trainer and auditor.

That first evening the deck officers were sent to the PSTF on Scottsville Road and given a restraining class. A Rochester city police officer provided instruction and showed us how to control unruly passengers, and to handcuff them, if needed.

The days of classes that followed were very busy. The next day Captain Kujala discussed many subjects. The *Spirit of Ontario 1's* muster list, how to keep track of the crew members onboard, the ISM-SMS codes, firefighting, and passenger evacuation were among the day's topics.

The ISM Code (it's overly extended full name is the "International Management Code for the Safe Operation of Ships and for Pollution Prevention") addresses the responsibilities of the people who manage and operate ships and provides an international standard for the safe management and operation of ships, as well as for pollution prevention.

The Code developed as a result of a number of very serious maritime accidents, including the *Exxon Valdez* and the *Herald of Free Enterprise*, that were manifestly caused by human errors, with management faults also identified as contributing factors. In July 1998, the ISM Code became mandatory under the International Convention for the Safety of Life at Sea (SOLAS) and from that date it applied to passenger ships.

"People in the office are now just as jailable as we are," Kujala said, when talking about marine accidents and the ISM code.

"It's about time," I thought. Marine managers were constantly trying to find ways to reduce their crew numbers or burden them with paperwork and other duties that took them away from their basic watch-keeping duties or rob them of their sleep.

Kujala talked about the danger of fires on aluminum boats.

He said, "We'll only get one chance to knock out a fire. An aluminum vessel will not last long. Not like steel. It just 'disappears.' Passengers and safety first. We have only *seventeen minutes* to get everybody off the vessel."

Seventeen minutes came from the evacuation formula specified in the HSC 2000 code. According to section 4.8, "Evacuation time = SFP time minus 7, and then divided by 3." SFP stood for "structural fire protection." The material between the car deck and the passenger deck, for example, had an SFP rating of 60. This meant it would take 60 minutes to burn through the material. The number seven was for the minutes allowed for initial discovery of the fire and the subsequent attempt by the crew to extinguish it. This was then divided by 3. Thus, the *Spirit* had to be entirely evacuated of its 774 passengers and 26 crewmembers in 17 minutes.

In short, the crew was given less than seven minutes to be successful fighting a fire or else the order to abandon ship had to be given. Like so many things in the fast ferry world, the crew had to move fast.

Later, Charles Giunta, Rochester port director, U.S. Customs & Border Protection (USCBP) came in to speak to us. A short, stocky man, he wore wire-rimmed glasses, had a neatly-trimmed mustache, and thick, black wavy hair. When he marched into the classroom, he was in uniform and on his belt he wore his holstered pistol and a couple of cell phones. As he stepped in front of our class, one of his cell phones suddenly began to ring. "Hail to the chief" played loudly from the device as he took his final few steps.

This brought laughs from a few of us. You couldn't help but wonder if Mr. Giunta had told one of his men to call him at that precise moment. He was not laughing, however, so perhaps not.

Tap-tap-tap!

The head of the Rochester customs did not smile very much as he walked back and forth. He told us how bad the conditions were in Turkish prisons and that we should never think about transporting drugs for anyone because our own U.S. prisons weren't much better. He said he was more worried about us, the crew members, carrying drugs back from Canada than he was the 700+ passengers and their, for the most part, un-inspected automobiles, SUVs, RVs, boats, and trailers.

Giunta provided us with four telephone numbers in case we had to reach him at any time of the day or night for anything.

Tap-tap-tap!

He told us that the USCBP was one of only two revenue-producing agencies in the United States, the other being the Internal Revenue Service. In Rochester alone, the USCBP produced $40 million in one year, he said proudly. He told us that the USCBP was the only agency in the country that did not require probable cause or a search warrant.

Tap-tap-tap!

As he recited these impressive facts, he stood there with his thumb clipped deeply into his belt and tapped in rapid succession on the top of his holstered pistol with his first three fingers.

Tap-tap-tap!

"Nationwide, $1.2 million worth of goods are seized per day." Returning to the subject of drug smuggling, he proclaimed loudly, "Swallowers! Swallowers are smugglers who swallow condoms with dental floss tied to them. They walk bent over. When they finally go to the bathroom to produce the goods, they aren't kidding when they say to the buyer, 'Hey, this is really good shit!'"

He did not crack a smile when he said this.

Who knew that Customs 101 with Charles Giunta could be so much fun.

The customs director was later followed by a visit with U.S. Coast Guard Marine Safety Office Commander Paul Gugg from the Buffalo 9th USCG District.

I asked him if the Coast Guard had concerns about the search-and-rescue capabilities on Lake Ontario in the winter.

He acknowledged there were concerns.

The worst situation could be a sinking ferry in January with a full boat of passengers. Cold water, freezing air, hypothermic conditions, few resources to rescue everyone in a timely manner.

During the winter months on Lake Ontario, many possible rescue resources dry up. The St. Lawrence Seaway shuts down from December until March. There would be no merchant ships in the area to assist a ferry in distress. All of the private boat and yacht owners on both sides of the lake pull their boats out of the water. All that remained were a handful of tugboats, helicopters, and the 47-foot motor lifeboat at the Rochester Coast Guard station.

In the original ferry concept, one of the reasons for having two ferries was so that one could serve as rescue ship for the other. With one ferry, planning for the worst becomes difficult. There is just not enough fast auxiliary craft on Lake Ontario to be of much use in the winter.

When talking to Tony White about search-and-rescue prior to his departure, he had mentioned his talks with the USCG on the subject. He said they had focused on several things:

"Ensuring the *Breeze* had the best equipment, procedures and trained crew for such an emergency; carrying out a real time exercise on this, so as to understand actual timing; the USCG would apply for funding to obtain a fast rescue vessel that would be manned throughout the winter."

"Also, a joint agreement with the Canadians who had helicopters and other craft at their disposal in Toronto; a charter contract with a tug out of Hamilton that could be on the scene quickly and either take passengers aboard or tow the ferry to safety; and, the Rochester Fire Department wanted funding for a fast fire boat."

"It was also agreed that there would be a tabletop and actual crisis exercise in Rochester, utilizing ALL emergency services in a crisis. This would be a real test of the management plan and of who would have overall command of the situation."

Commander Gugg told the class he hoped there might be a Coast Guard cutter stationed on the lake someday.

As with the Toronto ferry terminal, it was a case of "Why invest if we don't know how long the ferry will be around?"

The days of classes went on.

On the evening of April 23rd, the Rochester Area Foundation went ahead without the *Spirit of Ontario 1* and held its "Party at the Port" in the ferry terminal building. The *Spirit* at that moment was somewhere in the vicinity of Nova Scotia preparing to enter the St. Lawrence River. The event was a fundraiser for the public art project for the terminal. The party was also for the purpose of honoring longtime Congresswoman Louise M. Slaughter for all of her years of supportive efforts to the ferry project.

Tuesday, April 27th, 2004 was one of the biggest days in years for the City of Rochester. It was a bright, sunny morning and the *Spirit of Ontario 1* was to arrive.

By 6:30 a.m. five news trucks from the local television channels were lined up in the parking lot adjacent to the unfinished terminal, their telescoping satellite dishes sprouting straight up into the air. Two radio stations were on hand, too, including popular radio talk show personality "Brother Wease." With his cast of comics, he was hosting his WCMF-FM early morning radio show from the terminal's second floor terrace.

Local dignitaries were also present on the second floor while caterers served food on tables with linen table cloths. Some were interviewed by Brother Wease.

The Rochester piers, or jetties, are very long, each measuring 2,200 feet. Four-hundred and fifty-feet separate them. The Genesee River runs between them and flows northward into Lake Ontario. Between the piers is a 200-foot wide navigation channel that is maintained to a depth of 20 feet; more than enough for the ferry with her maximum 10.5 feet draft.

Thousands of people lined both jetties to welcome the *Breeze* to her new home. Heavy traffic filled Lake Avenue. No one could remember when so many people last crowded onto the piers. It was a festive day for this proud community. It was one of those rare, once-in-a-lifetime moments that stay with you forever.

The temperature was in the low 40s and the day began with a sunny, blue sky morning, but then the clouds began to slide in. When the *Breeze* arrived at 9 a.m., it was already overcast.

The great ship approached from the northwest and entered the jetties. It blew its loud whistle several times at the waving crowds. The ferry was escorted by Chief "Bones" Mosgrober and his 47-foot Coast Guard motor lifeboat leading the way. Two other law enforcement escort boats followed.

A helicopter carrying a TV crew covered the arrival from the air, showing the *Spirit of Ontario 1* entering the long, narrow jetties for the first time. Another crew covered the arrival from a boat.

Though the ship was flying the Bahamian flag on her stern, she also flew from her midships halyards the flags of the United States and Austal Ships.

Several crew members stood on the bridge wings and waved down at the awestruck crowds. The people were astounded at the *Spirit's* huge size. They thought it was incredible, spectacular, and beautiful; its twin hulls and its five-story tall house were an awesome sight that dominated the Genesee River. People clicked cameras and looked through binoculars. Ferry fever had struck and the crowds were excited, happy, waving, gawking, and shouting out greetings to the new ship and its delivery crew.

I was in charge of the shoreside line handlers and was watching from the dock near the Link Building. I was as enthusiastic as the crowds on the jetties when I called my wife, Sue, on my cell phone. She was home watching the arrival on television. The event was being carried on all five local channels. The arrival had pre-empted network programming. Talk shows, soap operas, and whatever else they show on daytime television had been displaced.

"It's enormous!" I said to her on my cell phone. "It's coming and it's enormous!"

One ferry watcher told WHAM-TV13 (WOKR-TV at the time) news, "It's a pivotal moment in the history of Rochester!"

On the terminal's second floor terrace, Mayor Bill Johnson, CATS President Howard Thomas, and other dignitaries viewed the arrival with great pride.

CATS founder Dominick DeLucia and his partner Brian Prince were euphoric as they watched from the second floor terrace. For the youthful DeLucia, it was a dream come true; one that he had spent the last four-and-a-half years working so hard to make happen. Tears came to his eyes as he watched his great ship come in.

Tech Director Bob Mansfield would later tell me, "It was the proudest moment of my career when we sailed the *Spirit of Ontario 1* into Rochester. The feeling was absolutely amazing and right up there with the feeling I had when my kids were born."

The Rochester Yacht Club is located directly across the river from the ferry terminal and right next to the turning basin. As the ship approached, Yacht Club Vice Commodore Fred Karshick fired the Yacht Club's small 15-inch, chrome-plated cannon in celebration of the ferry's arrival. It produced a surprisingly loud BANG! Using a large rubber mallet, he hit the firing pin and gave the *Spirit of Ontario 1* a proper salute. He did this seven times.

Chief Mate Asger Manoe was controlling the *Spirit* from the port bridge wing. Standing behind the maneuvering console, working the controls, while looking out the wing's large glass windows, he brought the gleaming white ship into the turning basin in front of the Yacht Club. Captain Tiemes was close by, watching with a radio in hand, ready to issue line commands to the bow and stern mooring crews.

Rotating the console's tiny black moment knob control to the left, Manoe began his turn. The LIPS computer-driven hydraulics configured the waterjets so that the starboard side would apply full thrust aft while the port side deflector plates closed the buckets and directed the force of the

71

jets forward. With the end result being one side "pushing" and the other side "pulling," the ship's headway instantly fell off, she came to a stop, and then began swinging to port, while remaining in place.

There was very little jet wash as Manoe twirled the *Spirit* 180-degrees. The huge craft literally turned on a dime, and with only three engines. Within a minute the ship was facing the opposite direction, looking up the jetties and at the lake. Manoe released the moment knob, adjusted the joystick, and the catamaran began to go astern.

The crowds continued to watch in total amazement as the huge, football field-long ferry effortlessly and almost silently, backed into its berth.

Damage to the stern of the ship near the waterline became visible to the TV crews and some of the spectators. The tight fit through the St. Lawrence Seaway locks—the ship had only 12 inches of clearance on each side—had caused dents, dings, scrapes, and holes. They were cosmetic in nature and would be quickly repaired.

Manoe continued backing into the berth, slowly passing the terminal, and gently placing the ship against the dock adjacent to the Link Building. He brought the vessel to a stop about two feet from the ramp wharf on the stern. The *Spirit* arrived with a draft of 1.8 meters forward and 3.1 meters aft.

Shortly afterward, a motor from within the aft part of the ship whirred to life. This was followed by a sequential series of loud clunks and thuds as powerful locking lugs released the ship's stern ramp. The massive ramp then opened for the first time. The scene was reminiscent of the movies when the hatch on an alien spaceship opens immediately after landing. CATS employees and news camera crews stood around waiting to see who would appear. This high-tech ship parked in front of us was the closest thing to an alien spacecraft any of us would ever see. We half-expected an alien to appear and say "Take us to your leader."

Instead, stocky Bob Mansfield appeared wearing a dark suit. He had joined the *Spirit* in Montreal and had ridden her down the Seaway. The balding CATS tech director stepped out onto the ramp as it was coming down and exchanged a few greetings. While the ramp was still in motion, he stepped out onto its bitter end and surveyed the alignment of the partially completed shoreside ramp. Ship and shore did line up.

Customs Port Director Charles Giunta and several of his officers were the first to board the *Spirit of Ontario 1*. They had to "clear the vessel," that is, to make sure it was incompliance with U.S. Customs requirements before anything else could be done.

Shortly after the *Spirit* was tied up, the weather began to change. For the rest of the day, a series of fronts brought in unseasonably cold weather. The day had began with sun, but then quickly changed to mix of clouds, rain, and occasional ice pellets. There was a stiff breeze out of the northwest.

The Rochester and Toronto Rotary Clubs' "Premiere Passage," scheduled for April 30th, had to be postponed, as mentioned before. Ferry service was scheduled to commence on May 1st, but that, too, was postponed. To this day, people still think these postponements were entirely due to the April Fool's Day collision in New York City.

It wasn't so.

The original plan had called for the ship to be in NYC for two weeks for promotional events, anyway. At worst, the collision with Pier 17 cost only a week.

Despite all of the bad press and talk about the *Spirit* being late due to the collision in the Big Apple, not only was the ice off Nova Scotia an issue, but the Charlotte ferry terminal itself was not ready. When the ship arrived on April 27th, there was no awning-covered gangway to connect the terminal building to the ship's port side embarkation door. The automobile ramp was not assembled. The fueling station building adjacent to the stern had no walls or roof. The concrete for the sidewalks alongside the ship hadn't even been poured, nor had the in-laid brick walkway or the decorative black street lamps along the pier been installed. The terminal building wasn't entirely ready. Some of the parking lots had yet to be completed.

Training would have been another issue. The two captains and their chief mates needed to be trained in the maneuvering of the huge ship. Williams and Aycock had come to the project with fast ferry maneuvering skills and would need three days to a week to become accustomed to the *Spirit's* shiphandling. Maneuvering training for the chief mates would take weeks.

Would the April 30th event, originally scheduled for only three days away, have even been possible?

No. The event could not have happened even if the *Breeze* hadn't hit Pier 17 in New York City. There was another huge problem looming which would not be announced to the world for another 17 days. There were serious problems with the ship's MTU diesel engines.

That alone would have caused the postponements.

In the days immediately following the *Spirit of Ontario 1's* arrival, training continued—in the classroom. Unfortunately, we were not allowed on the ship.

It was very frustrating. We all were dying to get aboard, see this ship, and begin becoming familiar with it. The holdup was due to some last minute ownership wrangling between CATS and Austal. We were never told those details; however, I'm quite certain they would make a fascinating story.

Captain Ken Kujala continued doing as much as he could with the marine crew and the cabin staff without the benefit of having a ship as a learning tool. He conducted an AED (automated external defibrillator) instruction lecture, and the officers spent time going over drawings of the *Spirit's* fire and abandon ship plans.

During one of our *now* frequent coffee breaks as we waited to get onboard the *Spirit*, I heard someone say, referring to CATS, "This is the most dysfunctional and disorganized management group I've ever seen in the maritime field."

The days and weeks that followed would do much to confirm that statement.

In the classroom everyone begged for the ship's manuals. We were provided with two excellent manuals—an abridged Craft Operating Manual and a Type Rating Manual—that Hornblower Marine had developed, but after 10 days everyone was hungry for more than either offered.

Prior to the ferry's arrival, I would ask Kujala, "Where are the ship's manuals?"

"They are on the boat," he would answer.

"Why didn't Austal send copies of the manuals ahead of the boat?"

"That would have made too much sense," he replied.

Now the boat was here. After it had arrived, I asked for the manuals again.

Kujala replied, "The only manuals that arrived on the boat are for Bob Mansfield's office library."

"Where is that?"

"In the storeroom."

Finally, Kujala relented. Tired of everyone pestering him about the manuals, he led the way and the two of us marched to the storeroom. He unlocked the door and we raided the tech director's stash of vessel manuals.

Carrying out a half-dozen or so boxes into the classroom and setting them down on the tables, he announced, "Each of you...Take a manual, read it, and then teach each other."

The type rating trainer did the very best he could with the incredibly tight schedule and the materials, curriculum, and resources he was handed. He had just recently been flown in from Okinawa and had to instruct both the officers and the over one-hundred wide-eyed, never-been-on-a-ship-before cabin personnel. He was, at times, just as frustrated as the rest of us. The Rotary event and scheduled service were driving this show; safety was a close second. To his credit, he did a bang-up job and pulled it off on time.

The work he did training the cabin staff in 2004 would carry on in 2005 when some of those same employees returned for the second season.

Finally, the marine crew was able to board the ship three days later. A gangway had been set up on the stern. It was an awesome experience stepping aboard the *Spirit of Ontario 1* for the first time. The car decks were enormous. The movable centerline deck sections were huge. The passenger areas with their long rows of new, blue seats as far as the eye could see were wide and spacious. Tall, glass windows surrounded both passenger decks and allowed large amounts of light to enter. No one would be sitting in the dark on this vessel. The atrium with its grand staircase and large skylight was awe-inspiring. The other amenities like the bars, servery, kitchen, movie theaters, game room, and kids' room were clean, fresh, and welcoming. The wall colors were light and warm. One could imagine large numbers of people relaxing and enjoying themselves while skimming across Lake Ontario.

In addition to the engineering design, Bob Mansfield had been deeply involved with the *Spirit's* color selections throughout the cabin. While most of the seat covers and leather couches were either navy or light blue, there was one subtle difference in the Stern Lounge that most people did not notice. It was the only space on the ship where half of the seat covers were purple.

British Marine engineers have a purple band between the stripes which indicate their rank. This band, decreed by England's King George V, is a mark of respect for the heroic, 35-man engineering staff who were lost on the *Titanic*.

Mansfield had selected the color as a tribute to the *Titanic* engineers.

For both the deck and engine officers, stepping onto the high-tech bridge with its cockpit-style control consoles was like setting foot onto the bridge of the *Starship Enterprise*. Equipment was integrated and compacted into two main consoles. Similar to an airliner, two deck officers would sit in the forward seats, like a pilot and co-pilot, with the engine throttles between them and a myriad of controls and screens in front of them. Behind them was a wrap-around engine console where an engineer would sit and monitor every system onboard the ship.

That first walk through the *Spirit of Ontario 1* was, indeed, a truly awesome experience. It didn't matter that all of us had spent large amounts of time on ships before. Most merchant vessels have no amenities and appear as nothing more than all steel and a sparse atmosphere. *This* ship was very special. It looked like a place to have a lot of fun. None of us had ever been on anything like this before.

Long before the rest of the world knew about the problem with the MTU engines, the marine crew was notified two days after the ship docked. We were told a repair was being worked out and we continued with our training. We had no idea that another lay-off was in store for us in the near future.

Among the training included the test of the drencher system for the U.S. Coast Guard. The drencher was the heavy-duty sprinkler system that was located on both the car decks and in the engine rooms. What made it heavy-duty was it put out a great deal more water than a typical sprinkler system. It was designed to put out vehicle and liquid fuel fires.

The test took place on Monday, May 3rd. After the marine crew had worked on the car decks for several days covering electronics, sensors, cameras, and smoke detectors with tape and plastic to prevent them from incurring water damage, the Coast Guard came aboard and the pumps were started. The test was highly successful. All of the drencher heads delivered a heavy curtain of Genesee River water into the car spaces. Given the ship's down-by-the-stern trim, the water flowed aft and out through the open stern ramp door and back into the river.

When looking back at the videotapes of the *Spirit of Ontario 1's* arrival and her 180-degree turnaround in the basin just off the Rochester Yacht Club, only an educated eye would have picked it up and began to ask questions. Unlike the two waterjets on the port side, only *one* waterjet was in service on the starboard side. The starboard outboard waterjet was not in operation.

It was in class on May 10th that it was announced to us that the engine problem was major and that the crew would be laid-off immediately for the next four weeks while MTU, the engine's manufacturer, performed crucial upgrade work. The problem was described as being similar to an automobile engine blowing head gaskets. All four engines with 20 cylinders each had to have new gaskets installed.

Naturally, everyone was disappointed about the new delay and lay-off, especially since we just had a delay with the ship having to go to a Brooklyn shipyard after grinding up against the pier in New York. On Thursday May 13th, CATS called a press conference and publicly announced the engine problems and the delay to the start of ferry service.

While Howard Thomas and Dominick DeLucia were explaining the problem to the press on the north side of the new terminal, I just happened to be on the south side being interviewed by WHAM-TV13 reporter Patrice Walsh about my latest book *Forever Ten*. Sitting in a couple of folding lawn chairs beside the public boat launch, the longtime broadcast journalist and I talked about my message-oriented young adult books.

The company policy prohibited CATS employees from talking to the press and I avoided making any comments about the ferry. However, at the end of the interview, I made two, brief comments about the ferry and the operation. I thought, hey, it's my book interview and if I want to say something nice about the *Breeze* then who would take me to task over that? The ferry needed some upbeat press in the wake of today's announced engine troubles.

Being highly-positive, I glanced at the ferry and said to Walsh, "Everybody's excited, charged up, and looking forward to getting this running. It's going to be a lot of fun for everybody, including the passengers. All of us are eager to see this go."

For the owners and Hornblower Marine, my enthusiastic comments were not welcomed.

The next morning the *Spirit* left for Toronto. The selection of Toronto over Rochester as a staging area for the enormous engine overhaul was because it was easier to fly a German MTU repair crew and their spare parts into Canada and through customs than into the United States.

My book interview aired the following Tuesday, May 18th. Secrecy must have been at an all time high in the CATS offices for I was actually reprimanded for doing the interview.

I couldn't believe it.

"You were told not to talk to the press, and yet you spoke to the press," the director of marine operations complained.

I sat in his office listening to what I thought was complete nonsense. Surely, the director of marine operations for a new shipping company with a fresh off the assembly line ferry with a zillion problems had a zillion other things to do than chase after an employee who had just said a few kind words about the ferry company on local TV news.

I explained, "I've lived here for twenty-six years and I've been talking to the press on and off over the last fifteen. I speak at schools, libraries, and at Rotary Clubs. Sometimes the press writes stories about my visits."

"Any contact you have with the press, you refer it to Howard Thomas," he continued without acknowledging what I had just said.

I had actually contacted the CATS president twice about it. He seemed quite interested.

"He didn't give you permission, though, did he?" the director persisted.

What's wrong with you people? Don't you know good PR when you see it?

"Did you see the interview?" I asked.

"Well, no," he admitted.

"It was a good piece," I said. "It was a good PR story for the company, especially with the ship gone for three weeks in Toronto with engine problems."

The director of marine ops had other things to do and said, "We'll take it up again when you return for training."

That was the end of that meeting.

I didn't understand why he had taken such a hard line with me. I assumed he was being leaned on by CATS management to keep the crew from talking to the media and, possibly, embarrassing the company. My interview was about my years of writing books and not the ferry, though, it was mentioned.

Like most companies, HMS has a three-tiered discipline system. Three offenses and you're out. The *Spirit of Ontario 1* was out of town on a repair furlough and I had not even stood a single watch on her, and yet, I was being reprimanded for the first time in my entire maritime career.

I also had an errant thought that maybe I had asked too many questions about the training program, especially since I had known what the Tony White plan had been. Perhaps, they were building a paper trail in case they chose to terminate my employment at a later date. I really didn't know.

As I left the office, I did not acknowledge the order regarding the press. What I did do, instead, was simply head over to Time-Warner's RNews studio later that afternoon for a previously scheduled *Forever Ten* book interview with the lovely anchor, Amy Young.

The 60-second RNews interview entered their "news wheel" and began airing later that night. It aired every half-hour over the next 19 hours. For the next 19 hours, I was "Larry on the 5s!" My piece was on at five past the hour and, again, at five past the half-hour. It was broadcast a staggering total of 38 times! I was quite pleased with the book coverage. I had said nothing at all about the ferry in that piece.

Ironically, my place in the "news wheel" was followed by a story about an elderly CATS customer who was upset that his Brockport High School Class of '53 Reunion had to be cancelled because of the ferry's engine problems. That piece aired at least 38 times, too, at seven minutes past both the hour and the half hour. He was the "CATS Disgruntled Customer on the 7s!"

No doubt, if the man had been a CATS or HMS employee, he would have been reprimanded, too.

Weeks later, when the director of marine operations pressed me to sign a letter of warning about my interview, I took the issue straight to DeLucia. He agreed the interview was a good piece and that the hard line CATS had adopted was because he had heard some of the employees were saying unflattering things about the company. He told me not to worry about it and thanked me for stopping by.

No one at CATS or Hornblower Marine ever said another word about my book interviews.

A common question people would ask me was, "What are the Bahamians like?"

Many people seemed to think there was a Bahamian crew onboard because the ship flew the Bahamian flag. Many had no idea that the crew members were Americans who lived here and were, for the most part, from their own community.

It was clear to me during that time that CATS did not use one of the best public relations resources in its limited arsenal: their own loyal and fiercely enthusiastic employees. If CATS had done so, they could have developed a warm, inviting, and friendly persona in the media for the *Spirit*, and the community wouldn't have asked questions about those "Bahamians."

Transiting a St. Lawrence Seaway lock, April 2004
Photo courtesy of Asger Manoe, copyright 2004

One of the four MTU engines
Photo courtesy of Petr Chudoba, copyright 2005

Chapter 7
Touch and Gos: The 42.5 Million Dollar Simulator

In Toronto, the engines underwent repairs at the make-shift ferry terminal on Cherry Street.

As one of the *Spirit's* engineers would later tell me, "It was a HUGE job. All 80 cylinders (power units) were pulled out. Not a single cylinder was left in the four blocks. Each engine was stripped down as far as you could go. Each power unit had two gaskets and both gaskets were replaced. Every "O" ring, gasket, and connecting rod was replaced. Each one was rebuilt. Teams were working in both engine rooms. It was one fluid, sweeping operation completed in one-and-a-half weeks. A week was used to get set up and wait for parts to come through customs."

The problem was a material flaw in the gasket. The original gasket could not withstand the high operating temperatures and pressures which caused the premature breakdown.

"Overall, the engine is fairly sound running," the engineer continued. "They were working on the vibration issue. 1060 rpm = 85%. The original design was for 1250 rpm, absolute top speed. MTU, however, decided to derate the engines to 1100 rpm."

The *Spirit of Ontario 1* would never do the record breaking speed it had done during sea trials in Australia back in January when it reached a top speed of 47.2 knots, or nearly 55 mph.

During the first weekend in June, the *Spirit* returned to Rochester. On Monday the 7th, classroom training for all crew members was resumed.

For a couple of days the three chief mates gave familiarization lectures to the cabin staff about the firefighting and marine evacuation systems that were onboard. This was followed by fire drills for the marine crew with Captain Ken.

We simulated drills in the engine room, the galley, and on the car decks.

Captain Kujala had said, "If you can't extinguish a fire with a portable extinguisher, then 93% of the time the ship is a total loss."

It was a sobering thought and drove home the point that we had to move fast if our aluminum boat ever caught fire.

After a terribly rough two months, Captain Tiemes and most members of the *Spirit of Ontario 1* delivery crew had already left and returned to their homes all around the world. Chief Mate Asger Manoe stayed on to assume the role of training master for the new captains, John and Danny. Colm Claire from Irish Ferries was flown in to join him in this task.

Claire was captain of the *Jonathan Swift*, which was a sister ferry to the *Spirit*. Austal-built, 82-meters, nearly identical, the *Jonathan Swift* ran between Dublin, Ireland and Holyhead, England.

Tall and slim, Manoe was a soft-spoken Dane with a warm sense of humor and a casual gait. Short and slim, Claire was also of good cheer, though, he seemed to be more heavily caffeinated than Manoe. He spoke with a quick tongue and darted around the maneuvering console like a hummingbird. While John and Danny ran the show onboard the *Spirit,* Manoe and Claire would each take turns with the new masters, providing individual guidance for shiphandling when needed.

Touch and go training finally began on Thursday, June 10th. This training consisted of practice dockings and undockings. After a morning of more fire drills with the crew, the *Spirit's* powerful MTU engines thundered to life. The marine crew divided up and went to mooring stations fore and aft for the first time. All lines were let go and, with Captain Danny at the controls and trainer Manoe standing by and offering occasional guidance, the ship vectored off the dock and quietly glided away from it at a 45-degree angle. Once she was out into the river far enough, he pushed the joystick ahead and the ship began moving straight while picking up speed. He steered the ship with the small round moment knob located beside the joystick.

When the *Spirit* had passed the terminal, Danny shifted the control from the port bridge wing to the center control compartment, or the wheelhouse, from where the ship was normally steered. The black, right-hand leather seat was the conning officer's chair. The steering joystick was affixed to the end of its right armrest.

It was such a busy period that I cannot honestly say who had the first turn sitting in the conning seat when driving the *Spirit* outbound through the jetties; either one of my fellow chief mates, Bluto Babcock or Neil Shanahan, or I had the first opportunity to handle the steering joystick. All three of us took turns and by the end of the day, we each had done it.

Once the ship had cleared the jetties, we turned the *Spirit* around and reentered the river.

During my first experience steering the *Breeze*, I drove her out under Manoe's tutelage, but after turning the ship around and making the approach to the jetties, I gave it back to him because I didn't have the feel. As the afternoon went on, I would quickly get the hang of it as the touch and gos continued.

To be fully type rated as masters, John and Danny had to demonstrate their ability to handle the ship. They were required to do six daylight dockings and undockings in both Rochester and Toronto. They were also required to do six nighttime dockings and undockings in both ports. Training masters Manoe and Claire stood by the young captains' sides as they each took shifts and practiced.

As the ship slowly approached the Rochester terminal for the first touch and go, I looked out the bridge windows high above the Genesee River. From that vantage point, it did not appear that there was a whole lot of room in the turning basin off the Rochester Yacht Club in which to maneuver. I asked Claire, the Irish training master, what he really thought about it.

His eyes quickly swept the basin and he instantly replied, "There's so much room to turn around, it's f---ing unreal."

The rest of the day was devoted to touch and gos with Captain Danny.

On June 11th, the *Spirit* departed Rochester shortly after 7 a.m. for touch and gos in Toronto. Traveling at a reduced speed to conserve fuel (and, I suppose, to be nice to the newly repaired engines), we arrived around 1:30 p.m.

The terminal in Toronto was a big disappointment. We were all well aware of its temporary structures and white tents as shown on the news, however, seeing it in person made it appear worse. It consisted of a series of four or five modular buildings slammed together. Adjacent to it were the tented areas. The buildings could hold only a couple of hundred people. The pier where the remainder of the 774 passengers were to wait was open to the elements. There were no awnings. Being located bumper-to-bumper with the container port next door didn't help with the terminal's meager appearance either. Travelers heading for the *Spirit* would find themselves driving through mini-canyons for the road to the ferry terminal was lined with stacks of 40-foot containers.

The fendering along the pier where the *Spirit* berthed was a disappointment, too. Unlike the cylindrical rubber type which were chained to and lined the pier in Rochester, Toronto's pier boasted an odd assortment of old tractor tires secured to the sea wall. The only true maritime-looking fender was the huge "Yokohama" that Bob Mansfield had brought up from Australia with the ship. This large, inflatable fender measured eight feet in diameter and 12 feet long, and had been installed near the bow when the *Spirit* was previously in Toronto for engine repairs. Its purpose was to keep the ship parallel alongside the pier.

Touch and gos lasted the remainder of the day and late into the night with each captain and trainer taking a shift while the other two men rested.

The small cruise ship *LeVant* was docked just aft of the ferry for a while and provided a little more of a seamanship challenge to the new shiphandlers as they had less room to maneuver into their berth. Both captains handled it superbly.

As the training went on into the night and into the wee hours of the morning, the off-duty and on-duty crews rotated and took turns staying at the downtown Westin Hotel.

It was fairly routine. The touch and gos went on. Day became night.

Night presented a different picture as navigation lights automatically turned on and as other visible landmarks disappeared in the dark. The young captains brought the ship alongside, put her in position, and then took her off the dock. From there, they would twirl her around in the channel, head out a ways, turn around, and repeat the entire docking sequence. The only time lines were put out and the ship tied up was for the Westin Hotel crew change.

There was only one scary moment that night. It occurred at around 2 or 3 in the morning. Captain John, Manoe, and I were on-duty. The captain was at the controls on the starboard bridge wing in the middle of a touch and go, approaching the dock. Ordinary seaman Rick Marcellus and deck mate Chris Coleman were standing by in the starboard side mooring station.

Suddenly, out of nowhere, appeared a 25-foot sailboat with its sails up. It came from under the *Spirit's* bow and was so close that both men in the mooring station had to look nearly straight down to see it. It cut in toward the pier while the *Breeze* was only about 50 yards off and closing. Its sidelights were dim. Coleman called the bridge to make everyone aware of it. Talk about shock! By then, we were all well aware of the boat's presence. Captain John slowed the approach to the pier and we all watched as this Friday night sailor took his boat down the *Spirit's* starboard side and cleared our stern.

It was early morning around 4 a.m. on June 12th when the last Toronto touch and go was completed. Under the guidance of both Manoe and Claire, both Captains John and Danny had mastered the LIPS stick.

After the last touch and go had been completed, I asked both the trainer and Captain John, "Are the chief mates next?"

One of the two gentlemen responded, "We've got to get back to Rochester for the christening event."

"What christening event?" I asked. No one had been told.

"It's tomorrow."

No time had been allotted for training the chief mates on the LIPS stick.

A comment made by the waitress at the popular LDR Char Pit restaurant directly across from the ferry came to mind. She had said, "I mean, they had better have a backup, that's all I gotta say. A backup driver."

I couldn't have agreed with her more, but I adopted a wait-and-see attitude. CATS was placing tremendous pressure on HMS to meet the June 17th Rotary inaugural cruise, only five days away.

Disappointed with the lack of LIPS training, and, yet, hopeful it was to come, I, along with the rest of the crew of the *Spirit,* headed back to Rochester. We arrived at 6:30 a.m.

The bible of the fast ferry world is what is known as the 2000 HSC Code, or the International Code of Safety for High-Speed Craft, 2000. Every fast ferry in the world must adhere to the rules and guidelines laid down within its text. Former CATS COO Tony White was among its authors. Its rules are quite specific, especially in regard to training. For example, section 18.3.1 states,

> "The level of competence and the training considered
> necessary in respect of the master and each crew member
> shall be laid down and demonstrated in the light of the
> following guidelines to the satisfaction of the company in
> respect of the particular type and model of craft concerned
> and the service intended. More than one crewmember
> shall be trained to perform all essential operational tasks in
> both normal and emergency situations."

The chief mates of the *Spirit of Ontario 1* were never given any LIPS maneuvering training prior to carrying the first passenger on the June

87

13th christening event. We never had our hands on the controls or backup systems. For that matter, we didn't receive any LIPS training throughout the remainder of the month of June and well into July. There was no redundancy of skilled officers who could dock the vessel.

Recalling Bob Mansfield's email to me of November 2003, he had said, "The problems we (CATS) will encounter is training officers as yourself to be confident in the use of the vessel."

At that time, he never imagined that the kind of problem we would face would be a lack of funds on the part of CATS management to provide us with the opportunity for this all-important required training.

I felt particularly bad for Hornblower Marine. It seemed to me that they found themselves stuck in the middle between a mad race to get this ship up and running in time for the Rotary event, followed by daily service, and making sure that all of the regulatory requirements were in order.

Given the limited time and resources they had to work with, all of which had to be done on the heels of both the New York City pier collision and the MTU engine delays, Hornblower Marine did an admirable job in preparing the crew in all other ways. They did the best they could to please their extremely demanding client.

Tony White's initial plans called for three masters and two chief mates to spend four weeks on a high speed craft in the United Kingdom on their way to Austal in Australia. He had agreements with both Condor and Sea Containers for this. Our crew would do the sea trials and the delivery voyage entirely with an Austal type rated master and chief engineer to further train and type rate our people on the delivery voyage. He had planned to do crew changes along the way and have one crew fly home from Panama to have a few days off before the ship arrived in Rochester. He had an agreement with LIPS to have a specialist available in Austal and onboard during the delivery voyage to train ALL officers (including the engineers) on the LIPS system.

"No European operator would allow his HSC into service without masters and mates all being type rated on the water jet system," he would tell me.

After hearing this, I had thought it was just the kind of program I would need and I felt comfortable with it. Having been through many union training programs, complete with modules, training manuals, simulators, and knowledgeable instructors, I thought—and expected—no less here when it concerned a vessel carrying passengers. The preparation

88

for the liquefied natural gas fleet in which I was previously involved, for example, offered six weeks of class. I was well prepared when I finally set foot aboard an LNG ship.

Obviously, Captains Danny and John could not provide the maneuvering training because they themselves had just learned and had not yet developed the skill or confidence to train others.

Even the Charlotte-Cobourg ferry had an incident in which redundancy saved the day. Back in 1925, the captain of the *Ontario No. 2* suffered a stroke and died in his stateroom as his ship approached Charlotte.

More recently, the lesson that should have been learned from the Staten Island ferry collision of October 2003 was that it occurred because there had been no redundancy in the wheelhouse. There was only one officer in the wheelhouse and he suffered a blackout.

You would think that this horrible accident, where 11 people died and dozens of others were injured and lost limbs, would have made the "powers that be" *insist* that LIPS training for the chief mates assume an even greater magnitude and urgent priority.

This is especially true in the wake of the *Spirit's* own collision with the pier in New York City which demonstrated the fragility of the ferry's thin, aluminum hull. This was all the more reason to ensure there were *two* qualified men capable of docking on the bridge at all times.

On the *Ontario No. 2*, the second in command had taken over and docked the ship without incident.

There must be redundancy. Not only is it required under the HSC code, but it is good seamanship and just plain common sense.

I guess times were tough. Money *had* to be the issue. It was only the 12th of June and we had not even started service yet.

Due to all of her delays, the *Spirit of Ontario 1* could not claim the title of being the first fast ferry to begin operating on the Great Lakes. Instead, the smaller, Austal-built, passenger-vehicle ferry *Lake Express* took the title. It began service on Lake Michigan between Milwaukee, Wis., and Muskegon, Mich., on June 1st.

Hornblower Marine, however, could still claim they were the first company to operate a fast ferry on the Great Lakes. They were managing both the *Spirit of Ontario 1* and the *Lake Express* operations.

Chapter 8
Christening Event, Injury No. 01-04,
and the Rotary Premiere Passage

Besides lack of maneuvering training for the chief mates, something else was missing: a group photo of the crew. After months of anticipation, training, lay-offs, drills, and uniform fittings, a group photo of this hard-working crew would have been appropriate for both historical and future promotional purposes. A group photo also reinforces a crew's sense of pride and teamwork.

The only group photo of any of the crew that exists is of the cabin staff. They are seen standing on the stairs of the atrium in their attractive uniforms. It was taken by a crew member on the day of the christening event. It is included in this book.

The christening event took place on Sunday, June 13th. It was an invitation-only, blessing ceremony for the ferry. Finally, the *Spirit* would receive her proper send-off. There were approximately 300 guests that included members of the press, politicians, dignitaries, community leaders, and friends of the founders.

A long, red ribbon was led from the *Spirit's* bow down to the pier. A bottle of champagne was suspended from it and close to the bow. An 11-year-old girl by the name of Alissa Amalfi was selected by DeLucia and Prince to cut the red ribbon. Standing on the pier under a light rain, Alissa was given scissors and, with the assistance of her father, she cut the ribbon.

The bottle didn't break.

In the maritime world, *that* is a sign of bad luck.

First, no gloating owners welcomed the new ship in Australia; second, a hard landing in New York; and now, this.

The "omenists" continued to roll their eyes.

After several more failed attempts to break the bottle, Chief Engineer Richard Czachur climbed out onto the bow, hauled up the bottle which dangled in the breeze, and smashed it on the bow by hand. The crowd on the dock erupted in cheers!

The boarding of the guests then began.

The *Spirit* may have been upset because no one had greeted her in Australia nine months ago, but she acted like a lady when called upon to perform. When it was show time, her lines were let go and, with Coast Guard escorts, she slipped quietly and proudly out through the Rochester jetties with her cargo of dignitaries.

For the brief 30-minute ride there were wines and hors d'oeuvres set up at various locations onboard. Rochester's Riverside Convention Center provided the catering. Drinks for the guests were complimentary.

Most of the cabin staff's duties during the trip were, seemingly, to mingle, circulate, and answer questions. The crew's real purpose and focus was on safety, for even during a short hop as this one was, you never knew when an emergency would erupt.

Captain Danny Aycock had the joy of commanding the *Spirit* on this special occasion. The gregarious Texan got on the public address system and welcomed everyone aboard. He then announced he was going to do a speed run. As he throttled up the engines, the *Spirit* outraced the escort contingent of Coast Guard, sheriff, and pleasure boats that were paralleling the ship and left them in its magnificent twin wakes. It hit a breathtaking speed of 44 knots, or 50 miles per hour. Even Chief Bones Mosgrober's fast, high-powered 47-foot, USCG rescue boat fell behind and out of sight.

Captain Danny announced to his riders he was going to do a crash stop.

He pulled all four airline-style throttles back and the ship's speed instantly melted away. Though everyone onboard was hanging on—clutching—expecting to be catapulted forward with horrendous force, no one felt a thing. Not a single, unattended glass of wine or champagne slid off a table. Folding tables full of unsecured Constellation Brands wine bottles did not budge.

The audience woo-ed!

He then announced he was going to do a 360-degree spin and turn the ship around on a dime. Holding the ship's spring-loaded moment knob with his five fingers, he turned it gently as far as it would go to starboard. The four huge waterjets reconfigured themselves and within seconds, the big ship began to twirl. Everyone watched in amazement as the shoreline, the distant city skyline, and the Rochester piers swept rapidly across all of the large windows. They seemed to fly by. One moment there was the shoreline; the next just a watery Lake Ontario horizon.

The audience wow-ed!

The *Spirit of Ontario 1* was enjoying showing off to her well-wishers and naysayers.

Captain Danny then guided the ship back into the river. He twirled it in the turning basin just off the Rochester Yacht Club and expertly backed it into its berth.

Everyone was impressed.

The gangway was set and the guests then departed.

I was helping people off the ship when I heard a call on my radio for a first aid kit to be brought to the observation deck. I was near the concierge desk where one was kept. I grabbed it and hurried upstairs.

When I arrived, I found purser Rob Centro treating a passenger. The passenger, an older gentleman, was seated in one of the outside deck chairs and was surrounded by several family members. As I worked my way through them, I noted the man was bleeding from cuts and scrapes on his leg, hand, and head. The purser had a first aid kit already on the scene and was busy tearing open a bandage to apply to one of the cuts. I jumped in to assist.

To my surprise, the older gentleman, turned out to be Rochester Mayor Bill Johnson.

As I treated the fast ferry's biggest supporter, I learned that he had tripped over the raised door threshold that leads to the port side bridge deck where the life rafts are stowed. Door thresholds are typically raised on ships in order to contain water. His foot had caught the threshold and he had fallen forward. The *Spirit's* outside decks are coated with what is called "non-skid." Non-skid is basically sand thrown into paint and then is applied to the decking. This prevents people from slipping when the decks are wet. Johnson scraped his knee and hand on the deck as he fell and hit his head on one of the horizontal railings.

Accident reports on vessels typically follow a chronological number-date format. On christening day, the mayor's fall became the *Spirit's* first accident report and was written up as "Injury No. 01-04."

When people say that Mayor Bill Johnson had put a lot of his own blood and sweat into this project, they really did not know how true that was. He was the first person to literally spill blood over the ferry.

As we treated him, I kept talking to him to make sure he was alright, cohesive, not getting dizzy or suffering any other bad effects from the fall. He was fine. I wiped the blood from his hand while the purser patched up his scraped forehead with a bandage.

After he was treated, Mayor Johnson requested a hat to cover his head wound so the press wouldn't go ga-ga when they saw him. He was embarrassed enough. Cabin staffer Beverly Rouse went to Danny and the jovial captain handed her a baseball hat with the CATS half-star, half-maple leaf logo.

Mayor Johnson placed the hat on his head, covered his wound, and thanked us. I then escorted him and his family down the atrium stairs and to the gangway.

The quick trip had been very successful. Pessimistic people were turned in favor of the ferry. Many commented how great it was as they were departing.

The last few days leading up to the service startup were intense.

Between 8 and 10 the next morning, the *Spirit* and crew left the dock once again and Captains John and Danny completed the last of their required touch and gos alongside the Rochester terminal.

A 10 o'clock a "hoistable decks and ramps" instruction class was conducted on the car decks for the officers. We were instructed on the operation of the centerline hoistable decks and its ramps. This machinery allowed us to reconfigure our car decks. The hoistable deck when raised all the way to the overhead would allow us to take buses and other tall vehicles onboard. The hoistable ramps when lowered would be used to load the second car deck with small vehicles.

In the afternoon, Captain Kujala held a "vehicle parking" class in which he provided us with traffic directing practice. Crew members used their own vehicles and lined them up in the parking lot near the customs gates. The remaining crew members used bright orange signal flags and directed the vehicles into one of the three gates. The gates were used to represent the three sections of the car deck—port, center, and starboard. Each of us would practice funneling vehicles in through each gate.

Later that afternoon, I found Kujala on the dock with a chainsaw. Beside him were several eight-foot lengths of six-by-six pressure-treated lumber. He was cutting up the lumber into eight-inch lengths with one side cut at a 45-degree angle.

"What are those for?" I asked.

"Wheel chocks," he responded.

Wheel chocks, or blocks, are wedged between a vehicle tire and the deck. Their purpose is to prevent the wheels from turning and keep the vehicle in place, especially in rough weather.

Even though CATS had ordered a $42 million dollar ship capable of carrying 220 vehicles over a year ago, they had not bothered ordering proper wheel blocks to secure vehicles on the car deck. Instead, here was the master of the U.S. Marine transport catamaran *Westpac Express*, and the only high-speed craft type rating examiner approved by the USCG in the United States of America, being required to utilize his valuable skills, time, and expertise to improvise and carve makeshift wheel chocks with a chainsaw for a company that could not afford any.

None of us had any idea how financially tight things really were.

Tuesday the 15th, was MES (marine evacuation system) day. As mentioned before, the MES is the inflatable slide-raft arrangement which is used to evacuate the passengers from the ferry. We had to demonstrate to the Coast Guard that a unit worked and that the crew knew how to use it.

The day before, the door to MES unit #4 had been removed with a crane. To the layman, these doors are easily seen from the side of the ship. They are big and square, and there are two on each side of the *Spirit*; one forward and one aft. MES #4 was located on the port side, aft.

The *Spirit* was then turned around and docked starboard side to the pier. MES #4 was now facing the river. An abandon ship drill was conducted. The crew mustered with lifejackets and the MES was activated. As advertised, the slide and raft inflated in less than 90 seconds. Crew members began going down the slide.

It made big news on local television that night. The drill was successful and the Coast Guard was satisfied.

Wednesday the 16th, was dress rehearsal to Toronto day. The crew was onboard at 9 a.m. We did a Rochester-Toronto-Rochester shakedown run to test everything. The engines, the bridge and engine procedures, the crew, the catering staff and their equipment. Everything worked fine.

We departed Rochester at 1 p.m. and arrived in Toronto at 3:15. The time to travel the 88 miles took two hours and 15 minutes, just like the schedule said in the promotional literature. Later on we would learn that 2:15 worked great...when the ship was empty and carried no cars.

While docked in Toronto, a couple of large trucks carrying furniture and supplies for tomorrow night's inaugural Rotary "Premiere Passage" drove aboard.

We left Toronto that evening at 8 p.m. and arrived in Rochester shortly after 10 p.m. Most of the crew worked until eleven. It had been a long day.

During the entire night, workers and volunteers for the "Premiere Passage" set up for the big event.

When all was said and done, despite all of the technical problems, cancellations, the race to train the 150 employees and crew, and delays with both hull and engine repairs to the grand new ship, concurrent with the completion of the new Rochester terminal, the proud Rotary Clubs of both Rochester and Toronto finally held their long awaited "Premiere Passage" on Thursday, June 17th. The new date had been set and they had stuck to it as if it had been carved in stone.

The affair was a Rotary fundraiser for charity. Tickets cost $500 per person. The proceeds would benefit three worthwhile initiatives close to Rotary's heart: the Rochester Rotary Sunshine Campus (a facility for people with disabilities and city youth), the School 8 Scholarship Program benefiting the students at Rochester's Roberto Clemente School, and Rotary International's PolioPlus initiative.

Ninety-five years earlier a passage was held on June 18th, 1909. Though with far less grandeur and actually quite common, the "Grand Excursion by the Palatial Steamer *Ontario No. 1*" was scheduled to leave Cobourg at 7:45 a.m. and then leave the Genesee Dock at 5:30 p.m.

By that time in 1909, there had been daily excursions on the Cobourg ferries for nearly a year since the introduction of passenger service. The Rotary Premiere Passage, this inaugural Rochester-to-Toronto voyage of the *Spirit of Ontario 1*, represented the beginning of what was hoped to be a common occurrence aboard this grand ship. There was no reason that organizations and companies from both sides of the lake could not use the *Spirit* for their own company gala events, outings, and benefits.

History continued to nip at the *Spirit's* heels.

There were no movie stars back in 1909 when the *Ontario No. 1* held her Grand Excursions, and, as it would turn out, there were no movie stars onboard the *Spirit of Ontario 1* for the Premiere Passage in 2004. Even though Renée Zellweger, Ron Howard, and Prime Minister Paul Martin did not attend as had been originally rumored, the Rotary event was truly an incredible gala event beyond compare, never needing any assistance from anyone in entertainment or politics. The Premiere Passage would turn out to be biggest event the *Spirit of Ontario 1* would ever play host to in her brief, two-season existence.

Over 500 people paid to ride the ship on that inaugural evening.

Everyone was dressed in evening wear. Valet parking took care of the guests' automobiles. The afternoon began with a power shortage which resulted in a minor one hour delay. Some couples who arrived early for the 1 p.m. boarding went over to the Char Pit Restaurant across the street while they waited. Ladies in fabulous gowns were seen seated on low, swiveling counter stools.

"Where are you folks going?" a curious waitress asked.
"To that swanky event across the street," one lady answered.

For many of the Premiere Passage guests, the first memory of the *Spirit of Ontario 1* was of the brass and glass in the atrium as they entered through the port side embarkation doors. The boarding was festive.

Passengers were greeted with a glass of champagne, caterers served duck and salmon, and they were entertained by the Rochester Philharmonic Jazz Quartet. At the base of the atrium stairs was a harpist.

Across the atrium was a chair massage therapist with a line of people waiting for a turn. Coats were removed and shoulders were rubbed, possibly to relate to the boat's relaxing experience.

People were stunned by our ship.

Rochester's WHAM-TV13 news anchor and longtime Rotarian Don Alhart and his wife Mary were the event's Honorary Chairpersons. The Alharts helped greet people at the gangway as they came aboard. At one point, Mr. Alhart made a few announcements in the atrium about the evening's events and thanked everyone for coming.

It would be a working night for him. With his co-anchor Ginny Ryan, Alhart would be doing live reports via satellite phone during the voyage, as well as doing the 5 and 6 p.m. newscasts live from the Port of Toronto.

There were people out on the smoking/observation deck. A light rain earlier had left puddles in the aluminum deck dimples.

Hundreds of people ashore were waving or watching.

A buffet was served on the car deck. There was an ATM and a coat/bag check provided on this special passage.

There were tickets available for premium services and special foods on the Upper or Bridge Deck.

During the night the two car decks had been miraculously transformed from an empty, aluminum parking garage into one giant party house. On the main car deck, huge rolls of carpet had been laid out and living room settings consisting of leather couches and coffee tables had been placed on them. Catering areas and a variety of casino games for the amusement of the guests had been set up, along with bars both fore and aft.

The main attraction, however, was toward the after end of the ship. A huge stage with a lightshow support grid had been installed. A curtain on the back side of the stage served as a screen for a projection system. In front of the stage, a dance floor was laid down. It created a smooth area to dance by covering the dozen or so securing "D" rings that were part of the ship's deck and used to tie down automobiles. Off to the side were a rock band's audio mixer and light show controller. A monster sound system with amplification equipment and speakers surrounded the stage, and electrical cables snaked everywhere on the car deck. Austal Ships electrician Adam Bennett had worked 30 hours straight preparing the ship's electrical system for the car deck stage, band, and "disco."

Upon arriving that morning, Captain John, Chief Mate Babcock, and the crew were busy checking the fire stations and emergency exits on the car decks to make sure they were unobstructed. Several fire stations had been blocked and equipment had to be removed. The crew checked to make sure the stage hands had not damaged the vessel.

The weather was good and the temperatures warm for the afternoon journey. The skies were overcast gray and an early morning rain shower had ceased. Once the *Spirit* was up to full speed, the rain puddles on the observation deck soon evaporated due to the relative wind blowing across her deck. The trip across the lake was smooth and uneventful. The guests continued to be astonished by the *Spirit*. Her speed, her amenities, how she glided across the lake. Like many of the crew, most had never seen a ship like her before.

Different international food stations had been set up in the Panorama Lounge and in other areas of the passenger cabin.

The cabin looked amazing with white linens and flowers. The food presentations were beautiful. In a few areas in the cabin there was even a Japanese theme thanks to the efforts of the Toronto Japanese Tourism Board.

The *Spirit* arrived in Toronto to a great fanfare. The crew put out her mooring lines and the bow ramp went down. A grand reception was sponsored by the City of Toronto, which included a bagpipe troupe that played as they marched up the ramp and into the vehicle deck. A fire boat stood by a short distance away with its fire monitors shooting water and mist high into the air in several directions. It looked like a floating water fountain in the channel.

The Toronto event was called "Ice Breaker 2004." It was a grand evening onboard the *Spirit* with our Canadian neighbors, featuring a gourmet dinner, musical entertainment, casino gambling, and a charity auction.

Grandly dressed ladies. Hundreds of men outfitted in tuxedoes. Regalia and pageantry blended in one's mind.

During that wonderful night in Toronto at the Cherry Street pier when the two cities came together, over 1,500 visitors had been aboard. It was probably one of the best meetings the two cities had ever known or remembered.

The party between the two cities ended sometime after 11 p.m. when it was time for the *Spirit* to leave.

As the ferry left Toronto, many of the guests went outside onto the observation deck. For some, it was a magical time as they watched the incredibly beautiful, brightly-lit city skyline recede into the windy dark as the *Spirit* raced at full speed back to Rochester.

It had been a long day of reveling for many and the trip back was relatively subdued. A late-night buffet featured desserts, coffees, cocktails, and quiet entertainment.

Some people were playing cards in the aft lounge while others slept. Ladies removed their shoes to give their feet a much needed break. They had been in those shoes for more than 12 hours.

During the Toronto visit, the crew members of the *Spirit* had been stationed around the vessel to assist passengers, to answer questions, and, like silent, omnipresent guardians, to simply be there just in case a shipboard emergency erupted.

The weather continued to be pleasant.

One of the few inconveniences that occurred on the return trip was we ran completely out of fresh water and the toilets could not be flushed. The ship's fresh water tanks did not contain enough capacity to accommodate the huge number of people who had visited the ship that night. The Toronto terminal had no fresh water connection for us to replenish our supply before departing. Perhaps, in future voyages with large groups of people such as this, a water cart should be brought aboard to supplement the ship's supply. Thoughts for the future.

The *Spirit* returned to her home port. The weary passengers began disembarking just before 2 a.m. It was now Friday.

While passengers waited in line at customs, they presented parking valets with claim checks and their cars were awaiting them in front of the terminal after they were cleared.

It had been a magnificent evening and one heck of a kick-off party for the new fast ferry service.

The *Spirit of Ontario 1*'s first arrival Rochester on April 27, 2004.
Photo courtesy of T.C. Pellett, copyright 2004.

Part II
Around the Lake
in 80 Days

Chapter 9
Now, Down to Business

(Friday, June 18, 2004) — The gates to the terminal of the Spirit of Ontario ferry opened at 7 a.m. this morning, and the first customers went to pick up tickets for a weekend trip to Toronto. Many tickets were still available this morning. And at 7 a.m. there was no throng of passengers waiting at the gates for the rescheduled 9 a.m. departure.

The last boarding call was at 8:30; the ferry left the port at 9:13.

A power outage yesterday delayed ticketing and departure of the ferry; it's unclear whether all related problems were solved this morning. The automatic doors of the terminal were not functioning, and were propped open.

- Reporters Jeffrey Blackwell and Lara Becker Liu, *Rochester Democrat & Chronicle*

There was only one round trip to Toronto on that first day of CATS ferry service.

With less than 100 passengers onboard and a small number of vehicles, the *Spirit of Ontario 1* began Voyage #1. It was a "media day" and roughly a quarter of those passengers were actually members of the local press. It was reported later that only 67 were actual fare-paying passengers. On the first return from Toronto, there were 171 passengers. The bumpy start to the service had its effect.

The CATS Canadian staff was extremely excited about the *Spirit's* first trip to Toronto. As the ship was leaving, the smartly uniformed group lined up on the pier and all hands began waving goodbye to the passengers. In a pure act of spontaneity, and with perfect precision, this hearty sendoff evolved from hand waving to the whole group doing a human wave. "Seeing the ship off," the staff called it. A tradition had been born at that moment. For the entire season, the Toronto staff would continue doing "the wave" with every departing voyage.

At the end of our first day, U.S. Customs denied access to our country to five Canadian citizens. With no Customs space dedicated for this purpose, these "guests" became the first Canadians to spend the night aboard the *Spirit*.

Captain Williams, the other officers, and I did not like the idea of detainees being forced to stay on the ship. We felt there was a potential danger that some of these people might be angry—they usually *were* angry when they were detained—drunk, drugged up, or all three, and then run

103

around the ship, down to the engine room or up to the bridge, and inflict serious damage to the equipment. Granted, a security guard was assigned to keep an eye on them during the night, thus freeing us crew members to continue with our own work. However, if an irate detainee decided to bolt for the bridge and destroy a radar or radio, the security guard would most likely not be able to stop him in time. The whole ferry operation was so fragile and had so few replacement parts that it would not have taken any detainee much effort to cause a cancellation.

Why were these folks refused entry into our country? We never knew. The form that Customs would give us with each individual usually said one of two things: "Criminality" or "Not admissible." Sometimes a crew member would ask a detainee why they were turned around. One pleasant lady answered that she didn't know, but then added, "I did bounce a check once about 10 years ago."

So, after our first night of service we had five detainees onboard. There would be many more as the season went on.

Welcome to the Hotel Breeze.

On Saturday, June 19th, the *Spirit* began making two trips a day. My first week went by fast.

Returning to my apartment in downtown Rochester, I found an email query from my hometown newspaper. Messenger Post reporter Allison Cooper asked me how it was going.

I wrote, "One of the most fun things about my job is I drive the ship into and out of the two ports, almost right up to the terminals. It's very cool. The captain does the job of twisting the ship around and the docking/undocking. The other fun thing about the job is I get to see the happy faces of the passengers and hear their compliments about the fine service they had just experienced aboard the fast ferry. It is all very satisfying."

It was an exciting time.

Saturday, June 26th was my day off and I attended my daughter's high school graduation. While I prepared to sit in a folding chair on the grassy grounds beneath the large oak trees that graced the well-manicured front lawn of the Naples High School watching my daughter receive her diploma, the *Spirit of Ontario 1* was making an unexpected visit to Toronto Harbour. One of the worst days of Captain Danny Aycock's and Chief Engineer Tony Putnik's time aboard the *Spirit* was about to occur. It was the day the ferry almost hit the dock in Toronto.

Captain Danny was conning the ship north up the Eastern Gap entrance toward the dock. Just before turning left onto the second and final leg to the ferry terminal, the after engine (ME#4) in the port hull suddenly shut down due to a "high temperature on main bearing sensor #4." Chief Putnik felt it was a false alarm and that the engine was still safe. The engine needed to be restarted, but there was no time to take any action since the ship was approaching the dock. Captain Danny could still maneuver the ship into its berth with three engines. Putnik decided he would restart it after docking.

The *Spirit* was only 150 yards off the dock when *another* alarm suddenly occurred on the forward port engine (ME#2). The engine console's Marinelink monitor indicated that a "low level alarm for the cooling water expansion tank" had occurred. Chief Putnik tried to check the port engine room for cooling water leakage and water loss using the ship's closed-circuit television system, but the camera in that engine room wasn't working at that moment. Sometimes vibration would knock out the cameras. If the camera had been working, he would have seen green steam from a leaking engine water jacket on his monitor.

Putnik sent Andy, the QMED, down to check for leakage on the engine.

Assistant engineer Bryan Hald had already gone down to the port engine room to check on the high temps that were being reported by the #4 bearing sensor.

As engineer Hald would later recall, "ME#4 was shutting down on a faulty high bearing temp alarm, and I was in the engine room with a heat gun looking at bearing temperatures. I was crouching between the number four engine and the inboard bulkhead when I heard a sort of 'popping' sound. I looked over to my left at ME#2 and there was water flowing out between the head and the spacer on one of the cylinders. I wouldn't say it was shooting across the room, but it was flowing pretty fast! My first thought after we got the engine shut down was that the three-week overhaul in Toronto did not fix the problem. And that was exactly what Andy thought too; that we were going to see this happening just like it did on the delivery voyage."

Andy called Chief Putnik on the radio. "There's a very high leak on #2. Water is shooting out of the engine."

Andy tried to compensate for the water loss by diverting more into the engine, but it could not keep up with it.

A gasket in ME #2 had blown. This was the first power unit to blow since the major overhaul in May. The only thing Chief Putnik and his assistants could do was to shut it down immediately before it overheated and caused irreparable damage.

Captain Danny was already out on the starboard bridge wing behind the LIPS console maneuvering the ship toward the dock. Putnik yelled out to him, "I need to shut down #2!"

"No! Not now!" the captain hollered back as he maneuvered his ship toward the berth.

Chief Putnik repeated himself, shouting out to the bridge wing. "I have to shut down the engine. I have a heavy water leak."

The two men had to shout at each other because the distance between the engine console, located in the wheelhouse and the bridge wing's maneuvering console where Captain Danny stood was over thirty feet apart.

Andy the QMED continued to describe the bad happenings in the engine room to Chief Putnik.

Putnik repeated to Danny, "I have to shut down the engine."

With the loss of both engines in the *same* hull, the catamaran could not perform docking maneuvers. Docking maneuvers required the ability to vector sideways at various angles and speeds and that required at least three engines. With engines only available in one hull, the *Spirit* could go only ahead with an *extremely* limited amount of steering and control.

Captain Danny immediately decided to abort the approach and to proceed directly into Toronto Harbour. With three engines still online, he altered course to port and steered the ship clear of the ferry terminal's protruding ramp wharf. Putnik then shut down the engine.

Entering the Toronto Harbour was another *Spirit of Ontario 1* fast ferry first, although, not the type of "first" one would find in the brochure. When things settled down, Captain Danny made a proper announcement to the near sell-out crowd of passengers and informed them of the delay.

With the ship out of danger, Chief Putnik called Andy to come back to the bridge to relieve him. When Andy arrived, the chief then went down to the port engine room to see for himself. Putnik quickly assessed the situation and realized there was nothing he or his department could do while the ship was in Toronto. It had been a big leak and there was nothing that could be done about it for the remainder of the trip. The ship would have to sail back to Rochester on only three engines.

He then checked over the ME #4 with a heat sensor gun to check for hot spots. He was certain the engine had shut down due to a bad sensor and was, in reality, not overheating. He returned to the bridge and informed Captain Danny that he had confidence in ME #4.

Five minutes had elapsed from the time that Captain Danny had cleared the berth and proceeded into the harbour to the time Chief Putnik restarted ME #4. For a half hour, Putnik and engineer Hald worked on the 49-ton engine, monitoring and testing it. Putnik checked the sensor and cleaned it. They then checked the engine over with a heat gun once more to make sure.

Down in the Panorama Lounge, passengers were busy taking pictures of the harbour. As ordinary seaman Erin Macallister made her rounds about the cabin, a couple of people approached her and wanted to know "Why does the Toronto skyline keep circling?"

Once the chief had decided ME#4 was good to go, he told Captain Danny. The ship could perform docking maneuvers on three engines. The *Spirit's* captain then turned the ship around and the ferry headed outbound, back toward the Toronto terminal. Once abeam of the terminal, Aycock twirled the ship around again and docked it.

Overall, the delay had been 45 to 60 minutes.

The ship had to return to Rochester on only three engines. It was scheduled to arrive at 1:00 p.m., but did not return until 4:15 p.m.

Due to the long, three-plus hour delay, the afternoon trip was cancelled. Buses were provided for the over 300 people who were traveling from Toronto to Rochester and refunds were given. Not unlike seagoing traditions dating back to the *Titanic* when there were few lifeboats and too many passengers, as passengers waited to board buses at the Port of Toronto, women, children, and disabled people were boarded first. Some male passengers had to wait an additional hour before beginning the bus trip back to the United States.

The *Democrat & Chronicle* would quote passengers the next day. On June 27th, it reported,

> Hope Hopkins of Rochester was one of about 300 people who needed a ride back to Rochester late Saturday afternoon. "They let us know about the engine problems when we came over this morning, so I guess there is nothing else they can do but reimburse us." She called the ferry "a wonderful experience" but said she'd wait a while before trying it again.

Some people, such as Anna Arcoleo of Webster,
tried looking at the bright side. "It isn't anyone's fault that
it broke down, and I think they are being fair about the
whole situation."

That evening, the MTU technicians changed out the power pack
with the blown gasket. The ship was ready to go with all four engines the
next morning.

It was just a little more than a week into the operation when this
first gasket blew after the long three-week gasket overhaul in Toronto in
May. Why the gasket failed, no one truly knew at that point. Water
jackets, high pressure, too much vibration, and extreme heat were said to
have played a part in its failure. Later, it was determined there had been a
manufacturing flaw and the material the gasket was made of was not up to
the job.

After the incident, a grateful Captain Danny began calling Putnik
"Chief Tony, the Croatian Sensation" for his phenomenal performance
under pressure.

The next day, Sunday, June 27th, the *Spirit* returned to service.
This was supposed to be the day that a three-trip per day schedule was to
go into effect, however, due to the potential for more engineering
problems during this obviously needed "systems break-in period," as well
as ridership concerns, it was decided to run the ferry only two trips a day
indefinitely.

Between the two trips that day 1,312 passengers were carried.

On Tuesday, June 29th, CATS finally took ownership of their
$42.5 million classy chassis catamaran from Austal Ships. As would be
reported in the press (*Democrat & Chronicle,* July 7, 2004), "The final
financing package involved money from CATS, New York State, City of
Rochester, Dutch bank ABN AMRO, the Export Finance and Insurance
Corp. of Australia (EFIC), and Daimler Chrysler/MTU (the engine
manufacturer)."

That night the ferry was delayed due to another engine issue. In
addition, Captain John was having difficulty with the steering system. The
hydraulics problems seemed to be getting worse. The ship arrived in
Rochester sometime after 11 p.m.

The day after CATS took ownership of the *Spirit*, a routine test of
the steering gear before the morning sailing resulted in a trip cancellation.
As passengers were boarding, the steering test revealed that the waterjets's

buckets were slow in responding and the hydraulic pressure would drop while attempting any type of action. When control was taken on port bridge wing console, there was no response at all.

Somehow, the system's electric pump had picked up some metal shavings and had pushed them through the entire hydraulic system. One of the LIPS hydraulic pressure relief valves was bad and needed to be replaced. The engineers began the process of filtering out the filings and replacing the hydraulic oil, and checking each valve in the system to see if they were working and clean.

As the engineers labored on the problem, passengers were losing their patience and becoming angry. Finally, at 9:45 a.m. it was decided to scrub the 7:30 a.m. trip and let them go. As work progressed, Bob Mansfield was optimistic that the 4 p.m. run was doable.

Upon returning to work that afternoon, I learned that the morning voyage had been cancelled. I went to the bridge for an update and found Captain John with radio in hand. Shoreside was calling and wanted to know whether the trip was a go or not.

The work on the maneuvering system hydraulics was proceeding slowly with no end in sight. After consulting with the engineers and with time running out before the 4:00 p.m. sailing, Captain John decided to cancel the trip. He called the car marshals and duty officer ashore on his radio and told them the trip was off.

Within minutes, Dominick DeLucia rushed up to the bridge. He was visibly upset.

"Who gave you the authority to cancel a trip??" DeLucia asked, chewing out Captain John.

If he had read his company's own "*Spirit of Ontario 1* Type Rating Manual," it clearly stated, "The ultimate authority to cancel or delay voyages rests with the master."

Captain John had spoken to Mansfield only minutes ago and had been informed that they still had not yet diagnosed their problem. He calmly informed the young ship owner, "They haven't sorted out the problems down there yet."

"The engineers may have a solution in 10 minutes," DeLucia replied.

Passions and emotions were running high during those last few days in June. CATS had just taken ownership of the *Spirit* the day before. This hydraulic system problem was about to cost it one-and-a-half days of revenue and hand CATS another round of unwanted bad press. This was a tough moment to try to explain to Mr. DeLucia that there was a big difference between *knowing* what a problem was and then *repairing* it. He didn't seem to understand that finding a solution and making a repair were two different things.

Rather than vent any steam at his boss, Captain John just walked away from him.

As the young captain walked around the engine console and passed me, I said to him, "You did the right thing."

Naturally, no one, including Mr. DeLucia, wanted to see the ship sail if it you couldn't steer it and it was unsafe.

Despite all of the frustrations and problems experienced by everybody that day, one good thing did occur. Auditor Lou Ludwig of Germanisher Lloyd was aboard to do a security audit.

Germanisher Lloyd, or GL, was the *Spirit's* classification society. A classification society is a company that ensures a vessel is built to strict international standards, that a vessel is seaworthy, and that its managers and crew are operating it in compliance with international rules. It is dedicated to safe ships and clean seas. GL is one of the world's 10 largest class societies. More than 90% of the world's cargo carrying tonnage is covered by the class societies.

Classification rules are developed to assess the structural strength and integrity of essential parts of the ship's hull and its appendages, and the reliability and the function of the propulsion and steering systems, power generation, and auxiliary systems which have been built into the ship in order to maintain essential services on board.

GL was present every step of the way when the *Spirit* was being built. On the after bulkhead of the Panorama Lounge is a large, brass plaque which proudly says "Hull No. 251, P/V 'SPIRIT OF ONTARIO 1,' Proudly built by AUSTAL SHIPS in February 2004, supervised and certified by Germanisher Lloyd."

A "class society," as they are commonly referred, essentially puts their "stamp of approval" on a ship and its operation so that regulators and insurers know the ship is in complete compliance. Their word is gold.

Ludwig completed his security audit and when he was finished at the end of the day, he presented the ship with its ISSC, or International Ship Security Certificate.

A critical part for the steering hydraulics had to be sent to Toronto for repair since there was no shop locally that could do the job. It would be returned via cab later on that night for installation.

With the ship down for the day, I had the crew spend the afternoon painting. Being chief mate, my duties included ship's maintenance. The bulkheads behind both port and starboard engine stacks up on the observation deck had been painted white at Austal. By now, after months of running the four diesel engines, those bulkheads were black, covered with soot. With scrub brushes and cleaner, the crew washed them down as best as they could and then painted them with black paint.

Money was so tight at this early point that I had to get after Bob Mansfield to send our ship supplier out to buy rollers, trays, extenders and cheap, one-use painter's coveralls. The only supplies we had on hand were a couple of two-inch throw-away brushes.

The soot buildup problem on the sun deck and bulkheads required constant attention and became a standard item in our weekly maintenance of the ship.

Later that night, the crucial part for the steering hydraulics returned from Toronto, the lone passenger in a taxicab. The engineers installed it and by the next morning, the steering system and the ferry were back in service.

Chapter 10
The Typical Days of July

Purser Cheryl Wiemer began rubbing tech director Bob Mansfield's bald head for luck early on in the operation. Every morning the short and stocky Englishman would board the ship and inspect the Lady Spirit to ensure that she was fine and to learn of any problems that she might have developed. A tall and vivacious woman, Wiemer would greet and joke with him when he crossed the gangway. Towering over Mansfield, one day she began rubbing his head like Moe rubbing Curly's. She said it was for good luck.

Though it did not work initially, it seemed to work on July 1st. After the month of June ended so poorly with problems and cancellations, the first day of July went exceedingly well.

It was Canadian Independence Day and with it brought to date the largest number of passengers coming back from Toronto. Six-hundred and thirty people and nearly 180 cars rode the *Spirit of Ontario 1* to Rochester. It was an encouraging day.

One thing that I observed about the fast ferry that was vastly different when compared to conventional ships was there was rarely a normal day. A normal day was one where you load the ship in Rochester, cross the lake to Toronto, and unload the ship. And then, you do the same thing for the return trip to Rochester. A normal day is an uneventful one where everything goes according to plan; where the mechanical stuff works and the passengers present no problems.

The months of July and August would present endless challenges to the crew and would keep Purser Wiemer busy rubbing Bob Mansfield's bald head.

The *Spirit* was still short a captain and the burden of the daily ferry runs continued to rest entirely on the shoulders of Captains John and Danny. The two captains never had a day off and, as the days wore on, they were getting tired. Williams had been working, nonstop, since February.

Hornblower Marine found a candidate for the missing captain's spot. They hired a master who I will refer to only as Captain B. He was an older gentleman who lived in New England and who had spent nearly three decades traveling the globe aboard a variety of huge cargo ships. He was good-natured and was very eager to learn this new, airliner-styled ship called a fast ferry.

A Danish training master in his late 30s who I will refer to only as Hädh was brought in for the month of July to train Captain B. The plan was to get Captain B up to speed and have him slide into the third captain's rotation. At the same time, training master Hädh would temporarily cover the open master's position and provide Captains John and Danny with a chance to have some much deserved quality time off. Danny was going to use one of his weeks off to move his family up from Austin, Texas.

The ship continued to have troubles with minor technical failures.

Shortly after the touch and go training in June, the ship's whistle stopped working. The nights of the touch and gos apparently had overtaxed its abilities. Training master Colm Claire had blown it every time the ship left the dock and, as a result, a defect in the unit came to light sooner rather than later. It had lost its ear-deafening blast and was reduced to sounding like to a gasping cow. A half-dozen, hand-held compressed air whistles—the kind that small boaters commonly use—were purchased from the nearby West Marine store and placed in both forward mooring stations for use until the parts for the half-dead whistle arrived from the other side of the world.

Sometime during the first week of operation, the ship's only elevator died and it, too, was awaiting parts from Australia. The elevator was designed to be used only for individuals requiring special needs. However, a supplier had overloaded it with bottled water one day and, due to a mismatch between the voltage needs of the motor and the circuit breaker which fed it, it caught on fire and cooked the whole motor controller.

It was covered under warranty and would be replaced at Austal's expense, but without the elevator the marine crew had to carry numerous handicapped individuals in their wheelchairs up the two flights of stairs from the car deck to the passenger areas. This would take time and manpower away from the loading operation. One individual in a wheelchair weighed roughly 300 pounds and it took five of us to carry the person up the two flights of stairs. While four crewmen carried, one crewman spotted our footwork. When the couple appeared for the return trip to Rochester, we had the good sense to ask them to drive their car up to the mezzanine deck, thus eliminating one grueling flight of stairs.

The *Spirit's* wake was a source of complaints for some residents along the lakefront. The ferry's high-speed through the water created a shock wave and was causing some damage on the Rochester side of the lake. Director of Marine Ops Bill Annand found himself making numerous trips to various residences to check out the effects and to assuage angry property owners.

In early July, I decided to take a short trip to nearby Braddock Bay to the west of the port and observe the effect for myself. There is a pleasant small beach and cove at Braddock Bay. Several people were lying on towels and sunbathing. A few children poked their toes into the edge of the flat, calm water. Then, the *Spirit* appeared. It was two and a half miles offshore. It quietly crossed the horizon and then disappeared beyond the point. The fast ferry had been out of sight for nearly eight minutes when the first waves began rolling in. Surprisingly, the waves grew to be two to three feet in height and lashed the shoreline for about 10 minutes. Adults who were sunning had to quickly gather their things and move inshore about fifteen feet. The children thought it was fun. They grabbed their air mattresses and dashed into the water to ride the incoming surf. One lady who had lived there for most of her life told me she had never seen anything like that before.

Surf's up that day at Braddock Bay.

In an effort to minimize the effect of the wakes, the three captains (Williams, Aycock, and Hädh) experimented with different approaches, trying to find the right one that would cause the least problems ashore. These included a combination of taking the *Breeze* further offshore, slowing her down earlier when approaching Rochester, and/or pointing her in different directions when slowing down. In the end, there was no one solution that would resolve the problem and appease all of the residents.

The ship was creating two types of wakes. The side wake, created as the ship passed by, was minimized to a degree by keeping her further offshore. The bow or energy wake, was created by the fast-moving, 1,500 ton ship pushing water ahead. It could not be minimized when the ferry traveled at full speed and was a matter of pointing the ship in the direction of where you wanted the wake to go. Naturally, the goal is to send the wake in a direction where it would do the least amount of damage.

"Dumping the energy wake," as it was called, would happen when the speed was dropped drastically from the high-speed of 40 knots down to a maneuvering speed of about 10 to 12 knots. Immediately after the speed reduction, the bow wave would continue on its way in the direction the ship was pointed. As an indicator that the energy wave had passed and we were no longer generating it, we would wait for almost a minute to watch the stern of the ship go up and the bow go down as the wave passed.

As we approached from the west, we tried dumping the wake in Irondequoit to the east of the jetties, and then, on another occasion, we tried dumping it further to the east in Webster. One day we dumped it a little too close to the Ontario Beach Park and water broke over the jetties, causing people to flee and get wet.

We even tried dumping it on the Rochester U.S. Coast Guard station and Captain B's apartment building, both of which sat side by side next to the east jetty.

This, oddly enough, turned out to be the best solution.

The energy wake traveled down the east side of the jetty where it was completely absorbed by the heavy, rocky breakwater in front of the apartment complex and the Coast Guard station.

This was the best we could do with the *Spirit's* wakes. In 2005, we would adopt this east breakwater approach idea for the entire season.

The U.S. Coast Guard in Rochester, under the direction of the indefatigable Chief Boatswain's Mate William J. "Bones" Mosgrober, continued to meet and escort us into the Rochester jetties throughout the season. Sometimes he'd have as many as three boats out there waiting for us. As we approached at high-speed, Bones and his crews would circle the *Spirit* and then crisscross in front of us like jet fighters doing "fly bys" over a control tower. In this post 9/11 world, on the stern of his large 47-foot motor lifeboat stood one of his men armed to the teeth with an M16 rifle, raised and ready for use, if needed.

We thought they were much too close to us at times. Sometimes their boats would disappear beneath the *Spirit's* bows. We wondered, when they were so close to the bows or the side, whom are they trying to protect, anyway? When you're too close you can't see the bigger picture. Plus, if they had an engine failure directly in front of us and they were out of our view, it would be disastrous.

"Bones" and his teams would clear the area in the vicinity of our arrival outside the jetties and then lead us in while clearing the channel of boaters that sometimes would congregate for the purposes of photo-ops or to simply gawk at the ferry.

In order to have time to prepare his boats and crews for our arrivals, Bones requested that we notify his station via VHF radio upon passing the 078 degree west longitude line. Within a short time, we affectionately began calling 078 west the "Bone line," named after the chief. We even programmed a red navigation line into both of the ship's radars to appear on the screen as a reminder to call in whenever we approached the "Bone line."

The morning of the Fourth of July brought an unexpected surge of automobiles as we were loading for Toronto. Only 60 were booked, but then, completely out of the blue, 60 more showed up. Fortunately, the deck mate on duty had packed the cars tight and was prepared for it. Sometimes with a light load, you allow more space between cars so the passengers can have an easier time getting in and out of them.

The afternoon run to Toronto provided those passengers with a powerful, Independence Day display of nature's fireworks. The *Spirit* encountered thunderstorms, brief moments of heavy rain, bolts of lightning darting across the sky and hitting the water, and a half-dozen waterspouts along a squall line descended like narrow fingers from the dark clouds and touched down on the lake. The passengers in the Panorama Lounge had the best seats in the world. They were entertained by and were in awe of the violent acts of nature that played out before them on the other side of the *Spirit's* protective safety glass. No amount of ticket money could have ever purchased a voyage like this.

As we approached Toronto, the storms and waterspouts were replaced by low lying, thick fog. We could clearly see the skyscrapers of Toronto, but not the entrance buoys or the lighthouse. They finally did appear, but not until the ship was almost upon them.

For the most part, despite the mechanical problems and occasional delays, the passengers loved the *Spirit of Ontario 1*. They enjoyed its features, its comfort, its service, and its crew. They enjoyed not having to drive the QEW and over the crowded bridges into and out of Canada. One of my duties was to be at the gangway and assist the passengers during disembarkation. I had the great pleasure of hearing all of the wonderful comments and receiving all of the compliments on behalf of the crew. The passengers and their children would pass through the side port doors and leave the ship delighted, full of smiles and, no doubt, with many fond memories.

On July 6th, as the *Spirit of Ontario 1* glided across the lake to Toronto, it was announced in a late afternoon press release that CATS CEO DeLucia and CATS President Howard Thomas were stepping down. Thomas would be replaced by Cornel Martin who had joined the company in May.

In an RNews interview soon after his promotion, Martin said, "The future of the passenger vessel industry in North America is looking to this project to set the stage. If this project works—and I'm confident it will—there will be many more fast ferries across the lakes, on the east coast, gulf coast, and west coast."

It was a reassuring statement and was exciting to think that the *Spirit of Ontario 1* might be spearheading a fast ferry movement in our country.

Among the 200 passengers we carried to Rochester that evening was the Canadian Minister of Tourism, the Honourable Jim Bradley. Bradley was traveling to Rochester with a bus full of cast members from the Toronto hit musicals *Mamma Mia!* and *Hairspray* for a Rochester promotion visit.

Arriving in Rochester, the press was gathered at the terminal as the *Spirit* entered the jetties, twirled, and docked. They were interested in covering the tourism minister and cast's visit, but they also wanted ferry crew reaction to the management changes. Crew members leaving the terminal were asked for opinions about the "shakeup," but few of us had seen the news as we had been "on the road" traveling to Toronto.

Most crew members simply answered as they had been trained to answer: "Ask Howard Thomas" some politely replied without knowing the man was no longer with the company.

While the press was asking about management, the cast of *Mamma Mia!* and *Hairspray* along with the tourism minister cleared U.S. Customs, boarded their bus, and departed the terminal bound for downtown.

After the passengers had departed the vessel, it was going to be another night of performing inspections for my crew and me. As I had mentioned previously in this story, HMS-CATS employed the three-crew system. While the first crew did the morning run and had an eight-hour day, the second crew did the afternoon run, had a 12-hour day, and was responsible for the vessel's inspections. The third crew was on their weeklong respite.

I sent my crew to clean the car decks. I then changed into my work clothes and headed off to the void spaces for the weekly aluminum crack inspections. Along the way, I received a call on my radio from U.S. Customs. They wanted me to come to the atrium and sign for another detainee.

I had lost count how many overnight visitors the *Spirit* had played host to by this point. After three weeks, it was becoming *routine*.

117

Arriving in the atrium, I found an attractive young woman sitting next to the concierge desk. She was crying, upset, and couldn't believe that she had been denied access to our country.

I was curious why Customs had turned her around. It never really is appropriate to ask any detainee, nor do you really know if you are going to get an honest answer.

I signed the paperwork and led the young woman up to the business class section where there were comfortable leather couches on which to stretch out for the long night. I retrieved from the nearby bridge bar a beer and a bag of chips and gave them to her. We normally don't serve our overnight "guests" at the Hotel Breeze, however, she was very upset and I thought a drink might make her feel better. I think I gave her a remote control for the 24-channel television monitor in the overhead in front of her. I usually provided a remote control to all of our detainees.

The young woman told me that she was traveling with the tourism minister and that she was the lead player in the musical *Mamma Mia!* She also told me she had several interviews with the local media scheduled and now she would be unable to meet with them.

I asked her why she thought they had detained here. She said she was having her visa application venue changed from Toronto to Montreal. For some peculiar reason, her information was not showing up on our Customs' computers and they weren't prepared to take the time to locate it on the computer or to take the time to listen.

She began to relax and thanked me for my kindness. I resumed the business of doing the void space inspections.

The next morning, the young woman returned to Toronto on the *Breeze*.

After the fast ferry departed, posters of the Toronto production of *Mamma Mia!* were hung in several of the large, lighted advertisement boxes that were mounted inside the terminal. The poster displayed a picture of the musical's lead character.

The security personnel who had spent the night onboard said the woman in the poster was the woman they had guarded. Though, it was an artist's rendering, it did bare a striking resemblance to our guest in the Hotel Breeze.

That night, a very tired, but determined actress by the name of Kim Huffman went onstage at the Royal Alexandra Theatre in Toronto for her nightly performance starring as *Mamma Mia!'s* Donna Sheridan, the feisty, independent mother whose life is about to change with the imminent marriage of her daughter.

The two-time Gemini Award winner (the Canadian equivalent for a television Emmy) had been accidentally misplaced in the Immigration and Naturalization Service system. As a result of her unexpected evening aboard the *Breeze*, she would eventually resolve the issue.

Master's training was going well for Captain B. In only eight days, his type rating check-off list was close to being complete. He was up to speed on most of the ship's systems and operations. The biggest challenge that remained for him was the shiphandling requirement and mastering the LIPS stick. Under the instruction of training master Hädh, he was making progress.

During the early evening docking in Toronto on July 8th, Captain B was at the starboard side controls attempting to bring the ship alongside. Hädh was standing close by. The sky was partly cloudy and visibility was excellent, however, the wind speed was about 18 knots and blowing the ship almost directly onto the dock.

As he pulled the ship into the berth, Captain B began having trouble laying the *Spirit* on the large, eight-foot diameter Yokohama fender that was chained to the pier near the bow. The ship began pivoting on it and then developed a slight angle to the pier. Captain B tried to counter it to straighten the ship. While using the LIPS stick to walk the ship sideways toward the pier, he turned the moment knob to adjust the ship's heading.

It was a hard lesson learned.

When attempting to vector the ship sideways while adjusting the moment knob, the computer reconfigures the waterjets to deliver what you want, *but* in the process it causes the ship to suddenly surge forward.

We all felt the bang when the ship slammed the port bow tip into the ramp wharf.

The *Spirit* groaned with pain.

Training master Hädh quickly took over and completed the docking.

Fortunately, the jolt wasn't too great and there were no crew or passenger complaints or injuries.

Once the ship was docked, the officers went down to the forepeak and the forward void spaces to look for leaks and damage. They were dry and no internal damage could be found, though external denting could be seen on the port bow tip.

It was decided that it would be safe to proceed to Rochester and a diver was ordered for a hull inspection upon arrival that night.

119

While the Danish training master and Captain B ran the ship, Captain John Williams took a much deserved break. One day in July, he actually appeared onboard the *Spirit* as a passenger with his wife and daughter. He was taking the family for the first time to see the sights in Toronto.

One night during one of my days off, I took my wife to the world-famous Dryden Theater in Rochester for a movie, and then up to Charlotte to show her the *Breeze*. The ship had just come in for the night. I introduced her to several of the officers and, once the ship was put to bed for the night, the group adjourned to a nearby riverside bar.

Sitting outside on the bar's massive deck, my wife met training master Hädh, Chief Richard Czachur, Captain B, Dave Killion, and a few other crew members. She enjoys hearing stories from sailors. We were there until almost 1 a.m.

As the happy-go-lucky Danish master spun some yarn about yacht owners, Richard said to me, "Laddy..."

Chief Richard from England rolled his R's like the actor Sean Connery when he spoke. "Larry" became "Laddy."

"Laddy, there's a th-rat dancing on the next table." He rolled his R when he said rat.

"What, Richard?" I asked.

Richard looked beyond me and repeated, "There's a th-rat *dancing* on the next table."

I turned around. Sure enough, there was a river rat on top of the next table. The river rats of the Genesee come out late at night. I never knew they existed. In the future, I would make sure I ate indoors.

My wife found the evening entertaining. Later she would say to me, "Mariners live in an entirely different world than most people and they bring that other world home through their stories and tales; they bring the excitement, the exotic, and the mystique of the sea. They can leave their families for months on end and that takes a lot of courage and strength. The same applies to the wives who are left behind."

There are good days and there are bad days. While most of our days on the *Spirit* that first season were good, sometimes the juxtaposition of events, machinery flaws, and people can line up like the tumblers in a lock and conspire to produce one BIG BAD day.

Such an untypical day for the crew occurred on Friday, July 16th. The day began for me at 2:30 a.m. when I relieved Chief Mate

Babcock. As usual, I would have my two ABs clean up the car deck while the deck mate and I performed the safety inspections. Fire stations, rescue boat inventory, and the weekly hull crack inspections were on this morning's docket.

By 5:30 the cabin staff had arrived and were preparing the bars and stocking the catering areas. Purser Karen Marsh arrived and began doing her daily checks and preparing the crew list.

At 6:15 the deck mate and I completed our chores and changed into our uniforms. Emerging from the locker room, fire alarms suddenly sounded on the engine console on the bridge. They turned out to be false alarms. One was in the galley. The galley was small and the heat detector was located in the ceiling only five feet from the hot ovens. Over the weeks, it had become a nuisance alarm, but we always checked it out since you never knew when it was the real deal. The other alarm was in the starboard engine room and that turned out to be a faulty detector.

By now the remainder of the crew had arrived and we began boarding passengers at 6:30 a.m.

We departed Rochester on time at 7:30 a.m. with 182 passengers. The ride to Toronto was uneventful. It was a nice, clear summer day. The *Spirit* proudly flew over the calm sea and the passengers enjoyed the views, the rides, the movies, and the experience of sailing on a high-class ferry.

Shortly after docking in Toronto, the tumblers in the lock began to line up.

While the passengers disembarked, Chief Rhinebeck sent his assistant engineer and QMED down to the jet room to change out a lube oil filter on the #2 engine gear box. The jet room was located immediately aft of the engine room. The job would take a good fifteen minutes.

Prior to going down, the chief and his two engineers agreed to stay in radio communication so that there were no engine startups until the men called and reported they were out of and clear of the jet room. A startup with a man working on the gear box could easily cause a fatal injury since the shaft from one of the powerful diesels was directly connected to it. As a precaution, they would lock out the #2 engine to avoid any accidental startup.

With the focus being on the #2 engine, the #4 engine was not considered during the preparatory talks. The shafts from both #2 and #4 engines are only several feet apart. The engineer and the QMED locked out the #2 engine, but did not lock out #4.

The jet room has a low overhead. The two men had to walk half-stooped over to move around in the space. On that day, the decks were slippery due to hydraulic oil that had leaked from a recent repair. The area by the gear box was so slippery that the men had to brace themselves between a frame and the shaft flanges. At one point, the engineer was leaning against the other engine's bolted shaft.

The pair worked fast changing out the filter, but the job took a little longer than expected. The two engineers were still working as the Rochester-bound passengers and autos were being loaded. Before long, the loading was almost done and departure time was fast approaching.

On the bridge, the chief was becoming anxious. He kept glancing at his watch. It was time to start the engines and let them warm up.

The chief called down on his radio and asked, "Can we start it up?"

The assistant engineer replied, "No."

More minutes passed. The chief looked at his watch, again, and thought that his two engineers must have completed the job by now. He attempted to contact them on his radio, but this time they did not answer. He then assumed that the radios were not working, even though he had just spoken to the men several minutes earlier.

Without hearing anything from his two engineers, Rhinebeck assumed they were out of the space and clear. He pressed the start buttons. Engine #2 was still locked out and nothing happened, but #4 wasn't.

Down in the jet room, the two engineers were startled and shocked by the scream of the compressed air engine starter unit above them as it revved up, and then by the deafening noise of the #4 diesel engine thundering to life. Only moments before, one of the men had braced himself on the flange assembly of that engine shaft. The huge shaft and flange assembly instantly began turning and, in no time, was spinning at 450 rpm. There was no protective shroud over it. Had he been bracing himself on it at the time of the start-up, the rotating assembly with its circle of 20 bolts would have chewed him up like a food processor.

Both men were angry beyond description at their chief for his failure to ensure they were clear of the jet room. The young engineer was shaking as he climbed out of the jet room. At the end of the shift, the incident was taken up to the captain and written up as a near-miss.

Rhinebeck's career on the *Spirit* was quite brief. He was quickly shown the gangway.

The *Spirit* left Toronto with 369 passengers and over 150 cars. Another near-miss occurred during the docking in Rochester.

The tumblers continued to line up.

Captain Danny was backing the ship into her berth when the #4 engine unexpectedly shut down. He lost LIPS hydraulics and with it control of the ship. With the ship moving rapidly astern at five knots and parallel to the pier, he dashed up to the center console, switched control to the bridge, and pushed the center console throttles ahead to stop the ship. The ship immediately came to a halt. He then pressed the emergency hydraulics override button and switched the control back out onto the starboard wing. He had control of the *Spirit* once again.

One of the results of this incident was the installation of emergency hydraulic override buttons on the engineer's console. The chief engineer is always at his console during docking and he can press the button if needed, thus eliminating the captain having to make a mad dash to the center console.

The suspected cause of the engine shutdown was a faulty reading of the main engine bearing sensor and was similar to what had shut the engine down during the Toronto docking in late June.

Mechanical problems had not finished with us yet that day.

Shortly after docking, deck mate Ian Sherwood had a bad day down on the car deck during the discharge.

The forward hoistable ramp inside the car deck is used to discharge small cars from the mezzanine deck when returning from Toronto. When it was being lowered, one of its securing flippers did not clear and the ramp partially lowered and tilted. While the engineers attempted to correct the problem, Sherwood quickly decided to use the *after* hoistable ramp instead and have all of the cars in the mezz deck back up and then drive down that ramp. At the foot of that ramp, the drivers then had to turn around and head off the ship. Crew members were on hand to direct them.

"Sorry," the ABs on the car deck told everyone as they directed the drivers to back out. With efficiency, the sailors fed the cars one at a time from each side of the ship into the ramp. Overall, people understood and were good about it. They knew the ship's crew was working on the problem. With the cooperation and patience of the drivers, the delay was only 20 minutes.

The second shift arrived and everyone was grateful to be relieved.

My day was done and as I left the *Spirit,* I ran into Captain B. A bad day was about to begin for him, too. If only I could have seen into the future.

We spoke briefly about the finesse needed when handling the ship's maneuvering system. Captain B was pumped. He said to me, "This is it. I do it tonight or that's it. It's about time."

He had given himself a deadline and was psyching himself up for mastering the ship's LIPS maneuvering system. I gave him a few words of encouragement to give him a boost.

Unfortunately, the words did not help.

Three hours later, Captain B drove the port bow hard into the pier in Toronto again while attempting to dock. He had inadvertently done the LIPS sideways-moment knob combo again. This time the 349 passengers and 26 crew members felt a big jolt, more so this time than the last. Many had to grab hold of a seat to maintain their balance. A motorcycle reportedly fell over on the car deck, but none of the 79 vehicles were damaged. Many looked out the large windows and assumed the ship had just bumped hard against the rubber fenders.

The *Spirit* herself groaned again in pain. Her port bow tip was now fully bent over 180-degrees.

Once again, the officers raced down from the bridge and inspected the void spaces, looking for any leaks. As before, none were found. The damage was added to the 2005 shipyard repair list.

Despite the accident, no one was injured, the passengers loved the trip, and when the *Spirit* sailed, the CATS Canadian staff did their human wave.

With her newly "reshaped" port bow and the added resistance as she sliced through the water at full speed, we clearly noticed a new noise in the Panorama Lounge. It was a continuous, low-pitched groaning and vibration. For all I knew, the *Spirit* might have been in pain, as though she had stubbed her big toe.

July 16th was still not over. It had one more incident up its nasty sleeve to test the crew's mettle. It would also turn out to be Purser Marsh's worst day of the entire 2004 season.

Arriving in Rochester at night with 248 passengers, there was one passenger who refused to leave the ship.

A crew member would later tell me, "The passenger was a male about 35 years old, white, and casually dressed. He had a clean-cut haircut. There was nothing odd about him other than his behavior and the peculiar fact that he was wearing sunglasses at night. He wasn't someone who you would suspect had a mental or emotional disorder because he didn't show any external signs. He was carrying a black leather duffel with a change of clothes and toiletries, including a couple of prescriptions, one for depression."

Chief Mate Shanahan and Marsh tried questioning the passenger, but his only response was, "I'm fine, I'm fine, I told you I'm fine." He would then turn his head toward the window and look away from them. Over the next two hours the crew tried, but could just not get through to this man and he continued to repeat himself.

At one point, Marsh offered him a cup of juice and the man slapped her hand. The cup was not full and did not spill.

During the two hours this drama played out, U.S. Customs and the Monroe County sheriff became involved. Customs thought the man's behavior might be a big act in order to gain entry into the country. Eventually, someone decided the man needed medical attention and an ambulance was called.

When the ambulance arrived, it was time for the man to leave. His ticket and everyone's patience had long since expired.

The chief mate and three of the crew lifted him out of his seat. He had been sitting on an inside seat. One crew member got behind him, lifted him under his arms, and pulled him toward the aisle. The other crew members got hold of him as he was moved into the aisle. The fellows "cocooned" the man so that he was unable to flail his arms or kick his feet. He grunted and groaned loudly as he tried to wiggle and made noises all the way down to the main car deck.

The *Spirit's* crew handled it like a SWAT team; very synchronized and well done with no injury to the disturbed passenger or anyone else.

As he continued to resist, they carried him off the ship and placed him on a waiting stretcher. He was then taken to a nearby hospital.

For Purser Marsh, a seasoned veteran of many years with the airlines, she wasn't scared, however, she felt concern for the man. She was fearful that the man might become comatose or stop breathing. He never had communicated with them. She had never seen this kind of behavior before during her airline profession. She had seen a lot of things in the air like heart attacks and a man dying, however, she had never experienced a situation where there was no communication with a passenger. It was disturbing to her.

To her dismay, the next morning the man would be back on the boat returning to Toronto. Fortunately, for the purser and the *Spirit's* crew, the man would have in his company a couple of "friends" along for the ride: two security guards. The ship had requested them.

It had been quite a day for the crew of the good ship. A twisted car ramp, a couple of engineers nearly turned into hamburger, a loss of control during a docking, Captain B stubbing the ship's toe, and the chief mate and purser dealing with a passenger from the cooler side of hell who wanted more from his ticket than he paid for.

All in a day's work.

There were no detainees onboard that night. Except for the night watch, everybody was off the ship.

The *Spirit* could rest again. She, too, had had a long day.

By comparison, the next day was back to normal. Well, as normal as it gets.

I arrived at 2:30 a.m., sent my ABs Wayne and Gary to wash down the smoking deck bulkheads in the vicinity of stack, and proceeded to perform inspections with the deck mate. Captain Danny and the rest of the crew and cabin staff came in early for the once-a-week 5 a.m. fire and abandon ship drills. The drills usually required members of the marine crew to suit up in fire coats, pants, and SCBAs. As chief mate, it was my job to select the drill and today I had the crew do a simulated car fire using dry chemical as the extinguishing agent. This was followed by a debriefing.

Following the drills, at 5:45, I did my daily, pre-departure visual check of the four waterjets. This check was done every time prior to the vessel's departure. The problem of logs flowing up the Genesee River, some from as far away as Pennsylvania, was widely known. While at the downtown CATS office back in April, I had seen several huge logs going over the edge of the 100-foot tall High Falls. The northward flowing river would frequently deposit logs of various sizes into our south-facing waterjets.

The port side jets were clear, but then I discovered a thick, four-foot log wedged between the two starboard side jets. I gathered my ABs and OSs and prepared to lower the starboard rescue boat. Macallister the new ordinary seaman wanted to go. The adventurous female and I climbed into the boat and the crew lowered away. Once in the water, we started the 35 horsepower outboard motor and released the fall. We then zipped aft to the waterjets and, using a boathook, she and I removed the log and sent it on its way in the river.

126

That morning we had 507 passengers aboard. It was a Saturday and a lot of people were traveling to Toronto for the night.

A problem developed immediately with one of the engines and the chief was forced to shut it down. We crossed the lake on three engines. Our speed was only 33 knots and resulted in a late arrival.

In Toronto, at the request of CATS, a police boat with a "stick-cam" arrived. They inspected the damage to the bent-over port bow and shot video by plunging a waterproof video camera on the end of a long stick into the water.

In addition to arriving late, we experienced a delay when we left due to Canadian Customs. It was becoming a common occurrence that Customs would not let us leave until every one of our departing passengers had been cleared or rejected. They wanted the rejected travelers to be on the trip back to Rochester. Our delays were proportional to how many passengers we carried. Today's trip with 507 people being processed resulted in a 22-minute delay. It was an issue that needed to be resolved.

We left Toronto, finally, with 347 passengers bound for Rochester.

Occasionally, passenger tours of the bridge were allowed by our two captains if someone in the crew knew the visitors. On our way back to Rochester, a young lady and her boyfriend visited briefly. The young lady turned out to be from my hometown of Canandaigua. She was very impressed with everything and everybody. Like most people who received the VIP tour, the pair loved it. As they left, she was so delighted that she went around and kissed everyone on the bridge.

A short time later, we crossed the "Bone line" and called the Rochester USCG.

After my shift I visited with Captain B at his apartment. He had resigned that morning. He was in the final stages of packing a trailer and preparing to head back to New England. We then had dinner at Silk O'Laughlin's, a restaurant which is situated beside the river and next door to the Coast Guard station. Across the river from where we were sitting, a watchful *Spirit of Ontario 1* kept an eye out over the port.

As we ate, Captain B was relaxed. At one point, he said, "I am relieved that it's over."

He then headed home to New England with trailer in tow.

The transition from a conventional ship to a high-speed craft is not always easy, as I had been finding out. It can be very intense for the newcomer coming from the big, slow ships to an HSC.

Tony White had told me back in May 2003 that some guys just love HSC (high-speed craft), while others hate it. He had said, "We found that for every 10 master/mates from conventional ships that came to us, nine hated HSC and could not get off quick enough as they were so different from anything they understood; but the tenth guy loved it and thought he was in heaven."

Part of this is the difference between the physical watch-standing on the two types of craft. In one, you're free to wander around a large space with a wide expanse of windows stretched out before you, while in the other you are confined to the limited area of the cockpit. The really big difference, however, is that the deck officer is expected to be able to dock the HSC entirely by himself and has direct, hands-on maneuvering control, versus the traditional ship which uses the assistance of pilots and tugs to dock.

In a case like Captain B's, the mastery of the controls had proven to be too formidable an obstacle. He had the courage, however, to admit to himself that he was not going to get it.

Later in the week, Toronto Terminal Manager Will Bennett brought his laptop onboard and showed us the DVD of the port bow damage. The tip was, indeed, bent over 180-degrees. Fortunately, the damage was not serious. Nothing had been ruptured. The clever techie who had burned this copy of the DVD had a sense of humor about the minor event. He had sound-tracked the video with the James Horner score to the movie *Titanic*.

With the departure of Captain B, training master Hädh still had one more week on his contract with Hornblower. He shifted his attention to teaching the mysteries of the LIPS maneuvering system to the mates. Both the chief mate and the deck mate on his watch were given opportunities to dock and undock the ship. Hädh also influenced Captains John and Danny when it came to the training of the mates for they occasionally took one of us aside and allowed us to undock the ship, though, rarely did they allow us to dock her. By now, they were becoming confident enough in their own skills where they could begin to assume the role of training masters.

To this day, when asked what was their best moment on the *Spirit*, most of the deck officers answer, "When the captains allowed me to dock or undock the ship."

That's how much of a thrill it was.

I was reminded of a New York Times article that appeared on November 1, 2003 following the Staten Island Ferry disaster. The subject was about how much human error played a part in many of *that* carriers' accidents over the last 25 years. Journalist Mike McIntire had written,

"Investigating the hard landing of a ferry five years ago, Coast Guard officials found that managers had increased the risk to passengers by allowing a captain in training to practice his mooring skills by docking the fully loaded ferry."

"New vessel operators should be given the opportunity to practice docking ferry vessels without passengers aboard," investigators said. "Passengers should not be subject to the additional hazards of practicing captains."

Training with the fast ferry itself was common practice in this industry. Here we were, practicing with our fragile, 1/4" thick, aluminum-hulled boat. It did surprise me that more training wasn't done first on simulators. These fast ferries grow bigger and more expensive with every new generation of ship produced, and they are just as fragile as the *Spirit*.

On the morning of July 21st, the Danish training master made the history books. He cleared the Toronto Eastern Gap entrance buoys outbound at a record-breaking 44 knots! It had never been done before with a vessel this large.

Yippee-kai-yea!

According to the *Canadian Sailing Directions* the speed in the Inner Harbour is 10 knots while speed in the entrances to the port is 5.4 knots.

No one filed a complaint against the ship on *that* day.

Two hundred and twenty-six passengers were riding the *Breeze* that morning, but little did they know they had just taken part in a record-setting "event."

At the end of the day, I would have my crew clean up the car decks. Before we could wash down, we had to wipe up brake fluid and oil drippings and pick up car parts. Clamps, screws, rivets, and buttons were the common items.

Sometimes passengers seemed to think the two car decks existed for the purpose of dumping trash. During clean-up, we would find chewing gum, lollipop sticks, candy wrappers, crackers, McDonald's wrappers, food, combs, pennies, cigarette butts, crushed pens, Q-tips, Kleenexes, baby diapers, and occasionally dog droppings.

Using two putty knives, I had members of my crew go around the car decks and scrape up the chewing gum and globs of grease. When they had completed that job, I had them hide those putty knives in secret locations. Those were the only two putty knives CATS owned and I did not wish to lose them.

Here we were, more than a month into the operation, and I was still waiting for our requisition for a blanket for the first aid room, Rain X for the bridge windows, D-cells for our flashlights, yellow paint for the car decks, and additional putty knives.

Sometimes I had the crew wash down the atrium's huge skylight. One time I noticed the skylight was filthy and saw out in the distance over the lake there was an approaching thunderstorm. I had the crew go to the skylight deck with a bunch of cleaning tools and scrub it down quickly before the deluge arrived.

A short time later, nature's rinse down took place and we had a clean window.

The limited maneuvering training for the chief mates came to an abrupt end during that third week in July. It was on the 23rd when one my colleagues informed me.

He said, "One of the founders doesn't want 'the rookies' to dock the ship anymore because we're taking too long and slowing up the schedule." He was referring to the three chief mates.

Apparently, the founders were either unaware or they didn't care that they were still not in compliance with the HSC code which required redundancy on the ship's maneuvering controls.

In the world of dealing with the public, there will always be incidents of some odd nature. The *Spirit of Ontario 1* was no different in this regard, especially when it involved the public *in combination* with their vehicles. Sometimes, fender-benders occurred on the good ship's car decks.

While offloading in Rochester, a large white pickup truck pulled out before being instructed by the crew and sideswiped a support column, leaving a large dent in the right side of the truck and damage to its flared wheel well. The driver departed the ship and no additional information was available. There was no damage to the ship.

A brand-new Mini Cooper was damaged when the baggage cart tractor towing two carts drove past and the driver opened his door at just the wrong moment. One of the baggage carts caught the driver's side door and bent it forward resulting in damage to the door panel, back edge of the door, and the hinge system. The baggage cart was undamaged.

Upon driving onto the vessel from the Rochester Terminal, another motorist was directed by the crew up to the mezzanine deck. As he turned onto the center section of the mezz deck, he struck the starboard side wire rope falls with his right side mirror. Upon inspection it was noted there were several light scratches and broken plastic on the outer edge of the mirror housing. There was no damage to the ship's wire rope or support structures.

Sometimes a passenger would look for a free repair to a previously damaged car. One such passenger approached our crew in Toronto after driving onboard and angrily claimed that his vehicle had been damaged as he drove across the bow ramp. He said he "heard a loud bang" as his car "bottomed out."

The auto was an average Buick and not anything special like a "low-rider." Dozens of other average cars had already come aboard before him without any problems. "Bottoming out" seemed extremely remote in this case.

The irate passenger continued with his complaint, saying that after parking his car, he noticed an increase in the vehicle's exhaust noise.

The deck officer examined the car with the passenger and noted that the forward exhaust pipe had, indeed, separated from the muffler. However, upon looking closer, the deck officer then noticed there were no clamps on either end of the pipe. It appeared that the two sections had simply separated. Undeterred by this discovery, the passenger further stated that his vehicle had just been serviced that morning and the mechanic did not mention any exhaust problem. Despite the missing clamps, the man continued to blame the ship and company.

In all fairness, it must be said that the ship's ramps could be hard on a vehicle, but *only* when the drivers were not paying attention and not following the crew's directions to slow down. A car racing up or down the ramps at high speeds *will* slam hard when it hits the ramp. Every day we'd find a handful of "plastic buttons" and/or small screws that had popped off of cars that had hit the ramps too fast and too hard and banged their front or back ends on them.

In early July when the Packard Car Club came aboard for the trip to Toronto with 12 beautiful classics, it was discovered at the end of the voyage that one driver had not engaged his first gear as instructed and the car had rolled forward against the bow ramp. Usually, the cars are parked 8-10 inches apart. We did not know how many times the vehicle rolled back and forth during the trip, but we assumed very few, if any, since there had been a calm sea that day and there was no damage to the car or the classic behind it.

The worst car crash occurred in late July 2004. It was a light car load day and all of the vehicles were stowed in the forward half of the main deck. The vehicle deck on the *Spirit* is 235 feet long. With the number of cars loaded that day, there were 118 feet of space aft of the last car. Motorists are always instructed to ensure that their car is in gear and their parking brake is set. One woman failed to do both.

The cars were usually parked with about eight inches between them and, if her car had been lodged between two other cars, there would have been no story to tell. Unfortunately, her car just happened to be the last one at the end of one of the nine lines.

After clearing the Rochester jetties, Captain John and I pushed the throttles to full speed ahead, as was normal. The ship swiftly accelerated from 14 knots to 41.6 knots in a minute.

Down on the car deck, in accordance with Newton's theory, as the *Spirit* shot forward to cruising speed, the vehicle shot aft down the center section of the main deck a distance of 118 feet. Crew members were astounded to see a driverless, blue Volkswagon racing backwards! If ever there was a slogan in advertising that had more relevance, then "Drivers Wanted" in the Volkswagon commercials was it.

Witnesses said the car was traveling at about 20-plus mph when it smashed into the stern ramp. The stern ramp was up, in the closed position, and served as the back end of the main car deck.

The damage to the car was substantial; a true fender bender. Crumpled rear fenders and trunk lid, broken tail lights, and a shattered rear window. Pieces of glass and plastic were all over the deck. It took the crew an hour to clean it up. The owner was distraught and cried when alerted of the mishap, but by the time we arrived in Toronto she was composed and related her story. The poor woman was on her way to visit a relative who was in a Toronto hospital. Fortunately, her car was still drivable.

It was lucky that no one was hit by the car. The ship had not been damaged.

At the meeting that followed the voyage, an angry director of marine operations came aboard and demanded to know what had happened. This brought up the subject of the deteriorating wheel blocks. The pressure-treated six-by-sixs fabricated back in June were taking a brutal, in-service beating. The pieces that remained didn't stay in place long when set or they simply vibrated loose.

New ones had been supposedly ordered. The other two chief mates and myself requested them constantly. When I asked the marine ops director where the new blocks were, he said he'd look into it.

In the end, they would never arrive.

Tuesday, July 27th was the most unusual day.

The day began with a problem detainee. Arriving on the *Spirit* that morning, I found three men had spent the night. There was a father and his son, and one other man. The other man, who was slight in build, was the problem child.

One of the terminal security guards is a fellow who I will refer to as Van Damme. He had spent the night onboard with these folks and said, "The man was drunk, didn't sleep, and spoke, crazy, threatening things."

Van Damme was a large and powerful-looking body builder; not one to be messed with if you're half his size. He recommended to me that security personnel should ride the ship to keep an eye on him.

I wasted no time in requesting a guard to ride to Toronto with us. After all, if our Herculean night security guard is spooked over this diminutive detainee, then why risk trouble?

My request was followed shortly thereafter by a fire alarm in the terminal. It was around 6:30 a.m. The building was quickly evacuated of passengers and personnel. A short time later, the fire trucks from the Lake Avenue firehouse roared up in front of the terminal. After some investigating, it was determined to be a false alarm. The terminal building's new fire system, still new like the ferry's, had suffered a glitch.

A small delay in passenger processing in the terminal would mean a small delay to our departure time. As soon as we could, we began boarding.

As I assisted passengers coming across the *Spirit's* gangway, I was pleased to discover that my friends Elaine and David were among them. They were from the Finger Lakes. They were making their first trip on the ferry and were very excited. They had business class tickets and I directed them to their seats.

Captain Hädh was onboard for the morning trip. Today was his last day on duty. The *Spirit* departed 10 minutes late at 7:40 with 587 passengers and 59 vehicles.

It was a windy day leaving Charlotte. The winds were easterly at 15-25 knots. The swells were running at about two to three feet when we began our journey.

Elaine and David came up to the bridge briefly for a tour. They were thoroughly amazed with the "Starship" layout and impressed by the technology. The bridge was larger than they had imagined.

As the trip went on, the rain intensified and visibility was reduced to two miles or less. Never one to like sitting in the cockpit seats during poor weather, I stood to watch the radar and alternately look out the window. With the weather deteriorating, I politely asked my friends to leave.

Elaine would later tell me it was remarkable how reliant we were on our own eyes, and that there were people actually out there on the lake that we could run over; especially on a foul weather day as this.

By the time we arrived in Toronto, there was a solid six-foot westerly swell running. I was concerned about this because I knew that once we made our course change into the channel, we would have these swells directly on our beam. Given the fact that catamaran platforms have a tremendous amount of stability, I expected her to roll to some degree; perhaps, even snap-roll like a conventional ship.

I looked at Hädh and asked, "Do you think we should begin angling in a bit towards the buoys and avoid putting the swell on the beam?"

The captain quickly surveyed the lake's surface and answered, "Ah, it's not much of a swell." He said he had seen far worse in the English Channel.

Not entirely convinced, I suggested, "Maybe we should warn the passengers."

"Nah, we don't need to warn them," he said bluntly.

Passing the lighthouse, both of us pulled the throttles back to idle and the ship's speed melted away. Once the bow wave had passed, I pushed the steering joystick to starboard and swung the ship to north to line up with the Eastern Gap channel. With the six-foot swell on the beam, the ship immediately began to roll heavily. It was the worst rolling I had experienced aboard this ship so far.

Beer bottles flew out of bar refrigerators and dishes broke in the servery and galley. In an instant, the bar's decks became awash in a slurry of beer, liquor, coffee grinds, and shattered glass. Just about anything that was not secured by a bolt was on the deck.

Purser Marsh hurried to the PA system and made announcements. The passengers were shocked, but listened. She was stern and serious on the PA, telling everyone to sit down immediately and take the first chair that they came upon.

The passenger decks were unusually quiet except for the sounds of items falling and breaking.

Her first thought was "I hope everyone is fine and we will not continue to roll."

All of the business class seats were full that day.

My friends Elaine and David were sitting in that section in one of the comfortable, large, blue leather couches. In this section of the Bridge Deck, there are eight pairs of leather couches. Each couch in a pair faces the other and a coffee table separates them.

Across the coffee table from my friends were a father and his 10-year-old son from Naples, New York. The little boy was a baseball player.

The three adults were drinking coffee from cups and saucers.

When the ship rolled violently the first time, David's coffee slid off the table and the little boy quickly moved and caught it in mid-air.

"He made a good catch," Elaine would tell me later.

She continued, telling me, "The waitstaff person, a man in his early 40s, was carrying a tray with food. As the ship rolled, he began walking left and right, and then stuff fell off his tray. The stuff falling off his tray was the first thing to hit the floor. And then came the CRASH of bottles in the Bridge Bar. He eventually fell into a seat and waited it out."

Elaine remembered the noise of the breaking bottles in the bar and watching the horizon line going up and down in the window. The noise of the breakage was so loud it drowned out most other sounds.

Being an athlete and an adventuress, she thought it was fun and exciting.

She would tell me, "The most remarkable thing was the doors to the beer cooler in the Bridge Deck bar opened up and everything flew out. It took two rolls to empty the cooler and, as a result, there were two loud waves of crashing."

She felt a helpless desire to stand up and render assistance, but decided to stay in her seat. She didn't want to add to the chaos.

The passenger cabin became eerily quiet when the ship began rolling. There was a low hum of voices and some light gasping as people reacted to the roll.

"Wow, that was wild," someone said.

People who were walking when the rolling started found themselves staggering. They quickly grabbed hold of whatever they could just to hang on.

Ordinary seaman Erin Macallister was making her rounds of the ladies' rooms when the rolling began. She said that she "saw passengers falling all over the place. Some were ill. It was early in the morning and they had empty stomachs. People weren't used to the motion. Trays of food flew off the tables." Macallister said she heard light, little screams.

At one point, she glanced up and looked out the windows. She saw water on one side and sky on the other.

Duty Free staffer Carrie Cooper was in the crew area on break when the rolling occurred. She could hear through the closed crew area door the glass break in the Bridge Deck bar. Heading aft to help, she had great difficulty walking and was tossed from side to side. She had never expected it.

Cooper searched for a mop and broom to help clean up. They were hard to find because there were so few onboard. She located a couple of plastic crates in the galley and used them to throw away broken pieces of glass. She found she couldn't walk in the bar areas because of the spillage, and the upstairs was worse. Liquor bottles smashed; coolers opened and emptied.

One of the oddities about the ferry was that the doors on the coolers were not designed for ships. Magnets, not latches, held them shut. In addition, racks (like you'd find in a kitchen oven) were used inside the coolers for shelves, and not full, solid shelves. Most of the bottles were supported by two thin, round metal rods.

Down on the main car deck AB Wayne Hinkel was busy checking the automobiles. They remained secured and unaffected.

Once the ship was safely in the channel and protected from the swell, Captain Hädh said loudly, "This is nothing compared to the North Sea. This will teach them that they are on a ship. They need to be *taught* that they are on a ship!"

Yippee-kai-yea!

I asked him, "Who are we teaching? The passengers or the crew?"

While he considered the merits of the question, just then the purser called on her radio. "Purser Karen to the bridge."

"Go ahead, Karen," I answered.

In a matter-of-fact voice, she reported, "I just wanted to let you know that I've done a sweep of the cabin and no one was injured."

For her, it wasn't the mess or the broken glass strewn across the decks that she was worried about. It was making sure the passengers were all safe.

That was, indeed, good news. I thought if Purser Karen Marsh had a license she would have made a great captain.

I thanked her for calling.

Other than a barrel full of broken bottles and the smell of stale beer permeating the air, the ship had survived the rolling and no one had been injured. None of the 59 vehicles were damaged.

After returning to Rochester, I, along with the other officers, said goodbye to Captain Hädh from Denmark.

No one would ever forget his last day.

Chapter 11
August: the Half-Price Busy Days

The first day of August began with an unsettling event for Captain John Williams after returning from the morning trip to Toronto. At 1:38 p.m. the vessel arrived in Rochester and by 2 p.m. had commenced offloading passengers and vehicles. Ten minutes later, Captain John was notified by a crew member that a passenger had found a note on the deck in the aft lounge.

It said "Bomb on boat."

The note was given to one of the Customs officers. By now, all walk-on passengers were ashore; however, approximately 16 vehicles were still aboard. The crew was notified to immediately commence a security search of the vessel and to expedite the offload of the remaining vehicles.

All of the law enforcement agencies were notified. USCG Rochester, USCG Marine Safety Office Buffalo, and the Monroe County sheriff.

Purser Karen Marsh organized the entire cabin staff for the search. She kept a running log of the spaces cleared by crew members and kept Captain John informed. Meanwhile, the officers and marine crew searched the bridge, the vehicle decks, and the machinery and hull spaces. The search took a half-hour. By 2:45 p.m., the sweep of the vessel was completed and nothing suspicious was found in any space.

Even so, the vessel would not be cleared until a Monroe County K-9 unit had inspected the vessel. The K-9 units arrived and the sweep with the dogs was completed by 5 p.m. The vessel was then cleared by the USCG and U.S. Customs officials. The threat had been a hoax. The afternoon trip had been delayed one-and-a-half hours.

The crew response had been efficient and professional. Captain John even recognized Purser Marsh for her fine handling of the situation.

Sometime during that first week in August, CATS announced a half-price fare promotion for Mondays, Tuesdays, and Wednesdays. Due to a small miscommunication, the call center was unaware of it until customers began calling in and wanted to take advantage of it.

It seemed a little strange that they'd run a promotion in the middle of the peak summer season when there were plenty of travelers to begin with. I would have thought that waiting until *after* Labor Day to reduce rates made more sense, but, to its creators' credit, it did generate bigger numbers for the month. As was proving true, the more people that traveled on the boat, the greater the word of mouth advertisements.

August 3rd, 2004 was a solemn day for me. I had just read in *Marine Officer* magazine in the "Finished with Engines" section that one of my former captains had passed on.

"Capt. John J. Donahue sails into a safe haven," read the obit section.

Finished with engines. Over the bar.

My warm memories of Captain Donahue, or "Happy" as the crew would refer to him, came to mind. He was a large, good-natured Irishman. He had more Christmas spirit during the holidays than the sum of the crew onboard. He would break out the wine from the bonded stores locker and allow the steward's department to serve it to the off-duty crew during lunch and dinner. He was probably the most relaxed captain I have ever sailed with. Nothing ever bothered him, no matter how bad a situation might be. Whether it be an oil spill, a wretched typhoon and monstrous swells, or during a rescue of Vietnamese refugees or crews from sinking ships in the South China Sea, Donahue always maintained a calm demeanor, and usually with a smile; thus, the origin of his shipboard nickname "Happy."

Unlike other captains who I have heard travel with notorious reputations for distrusting their crew, he did not "sneak up to the bridge and spy through the windows on the mate and helmsman on watch." He wore wooden clogs on his big feet. When the door to the bridge opened and he began trudging up the 20-foot long steel stairs to the wheelhouse—*clunk...clunk*—there was absolutely no doubt in anyone's mind that he wasn't trying to hide his arrival on the bridge. Even if anyone was idiotic enough to be *sleeping* on watch, the clogs would have long since awakened even the deadest of Sominex users.

Captain Donahue said a lot of humorous things and had a lot of funny stories. Stories about his time on ships as well as his time as a Naval aviator flying off and landing on aircraft carriers (he referred to those landings as "controlled crashes"). There was a story about the time he was chief mate aboard a freighter anchored near jungle banks in the Orinoco River in Venezuela. When it came time to shift the vessel from the anchorage to the berth, the crew discovered they could not raise the anchor because a 30-foot long anaconda had wrapped itself around the anchor windlass and had gone to sleep. The chief engineer was summoned with the ship's revolver and shot it. The crew then unwrapped the snake, tossed it over the side, and heaved anchor. There was a story that took place aboard another freighter in which the ship had a rare hit-and-run with a roadside parked van somewhere along the Columbia River. The ship had unexpectedly sheared toward the shoreline and the engines were thrown into full reverse. Before the astern bell could kick in, the ship's bow had driven into a soft bank. On the bank was a road running along it, and the parked van. The bow slammed into the van just as the stern bell kicked in and pulled the ship back out into the river. Regaining control, the freighter continued on to port.

The stunned driver returned to find his van lying inexplicably on its side.

There are far too many tales to tell in this book, however, there is one thing that Captain Donahue used to say that I have always remembered.

Every night at the end of the day and before he went to bed, he would come up to the bridge and write out the night orders for the watches, just like every other captain on every other ship throughout the world. "Night orders" were instructions to the watch officers that included things such as course changes, radio comms, wake up orders, etc. After he'd write the night orders, Captain Donahue would head to the steel ladderwell and wish everybody a good night. As he headed down—*clunk...clunk*—he would always add, "Don't dent the boat."

Don't dent the boat.

No words were ever truer than on a thin-hulled, aluminum fast ferry whose hull was only a quarter-inch thick and could easily be cut with a seven-inch circular saw.

Wednesday, August 4th was one of the few normal days we experienced. It was another nice day with light winds from the northeast.

Despite the word to keep "the rookies" off the stick, Captain John and Danny had begun to buck the order from the founders. Now that they had become comfortable with their own skills, they realized that the chief mates needed training. On this particular day, Captain Danny provided me with a little experience on the LIPS stick by allowing me to take the ferry off the dock leaving Rochester. We had 468 passengers, 52 vehicles, and one bus onboard for the morning run.

After clearing the jetties, we pushed the throttles down and off we went.

As we zipped across the lake at 40+ mph, Captain Danny picked up the telephone and ordered breakfast from the galley. Danny was a cheerful man, brimming with colorful anecdotes. The act of ordering breakfast reminded him of food service during his days on merchant ships. Putting down the phone, the young captain launched into a short vignette about a cook he had once sailed with, nicknamed "Nine-fingered Rosie." I don't recall how the cook lost a finger, but I do remember she was the cook who dripped sweat on the grill.

"*ss...ss...ss*," Captain Danny said, recalling the sound he heard as he waited in the chow line for his eggs. He also mentioned one of Rosie's galley assistants was a terribly gross man who iced a cake with his dirty bare hands.

Anyone who has gone to sea for any length of time, especially on deep sea ships, has had the good cook, bad cook experience. All of us on the bridge that morning could relate to the captain's tale and were thankful that we didn't have service like that onboard this ship.

The *Spirit's* caterer Kurt Ritchie and his Horseshoe Hospitality Company did not employ anyone remotely resembling nine-fingered Rosie and her assistant. Horseshoe was one of two FDA approved commissaries in the Monroe County area. His staff consisted of over 100 people. Most had gone through the Basic Safety Training in March. While a team of his nicely uniformed employees worked on the ship cooking food and serving passengers, many others worked at his catering facility on nearby Ling Road. It was there that the food for each trip was prepared. Ritchie had set up the 8,000-square-foot facility specifically for the fast ferry.

The trick with food preparation for the *Spirit* was knowing how much was just the right amount so that you wouldn't run out or prepare too much which would later be trashed. Ritchie would stay in close touch with ticketing to get an idea of the number of passengers expected.

Once prepared, food items were packed into insulated wheeled carts and then trucked over and delivered to the ship. Once onboard, the final preparations took place, such as cooking, placing in coolers, or putting items on display shelves.

Despite the large number of passengers the *Spirit* could accommodate, the ship's galley was incredibly small. It was tight, very hot, and poorly ventilated. It set off the fire alarm daily. It was so hot sometimes that it was a miracle there weren't any nine-fingered Rosies dripping sweat all over the Turbo Chefs.

Though he had several other business interests in the area, Kurt Ritchie loved the ferry and enjoyed being a part of it.

Aside from not making our schedule, as usual, it was a good day. An 18-minute delay due to turnbacks being processed through Canadian

Customs was the only abnormality. We left Toronto with 389 passengers, 92 vehicles, and one truck.

We arrived at 1:40 p.m., 40 minutes late.

When the bean counters decided that the ship could achieve a port to port run in two hours and 15 minutes, they failed to take into account two important factors: a ship with a load of cars is heavier and travels slower than one with no cars; and they also did not consider the time it takes to slow down, enter the port, and to dock.

We rarely made the posted schedule and were usually 15 to 30 minutes late.

Running from Rochester, New York to Cobourg, Canada, the Ontario Car Ferry Company (OCFCo) and its two vessels had established a lucrative sideline in "Excursion Charters" to groups and businesses on both sides of Lake Ontario over its many years of operation between 1907 and 1950. The added revenue helped to offset the cost of their operation. In 1946, for example, a sampling of their charters as listed in *Coal to Canada* by Ted Rafuse includes:

> The Kinsmen Club of Cobourg, Warden of
> Northumberland & Durham County, Goodyear Tire &
> Rubber Company, Kodak Park Athletic Association,
> United Auto Workers, Cobourg Branch Canadian Legion,
> Rochester Telephone Employees, Canadian Locomotive
> Club, Damascus Shrine, General Motors War Veterans,
> Independent Order of Odd Fellows, Delco Local 509,
> Knights of Columbus, Real Estate Board of Rochester,
> Canadian Corps, Kiwanis Club of Cobourg, Hot Stove
> Club of Belleville, Hawkeye Athletic Association, Kodak
> Camera Club, Post 143 Regular Army, Rochester
> Independent Workers, Camera Workers Recreation Club,
> and News Carriers Peterboro Examiner.

"The OCFCo's primary purpose was to transport coal to Canada. Passenger service, while important, never assumed the same stature within the company. Yet it is the excursion service that is remembered most by people with regard to the ferry service between Cobourg and Genesee Dock," wrote author Ted Rafuse.

With CATS and the *Spirit of Ontario 1,* passenger service was the number one priority. In the summer of 2004, while the good crew and their grand, high-tech ship were busy shuttling delighted and amazed passengers back and forth across the lake every day, staff members ashore were busy doing their part providing customer service, selling tickets, and making reservations.

Call Center supervisor Mary Howard-Lawrence and her eight-person staff and eight computers were busy working from 6 a.m. to 9 p.m. handling the reservations. President Cornel Martin came in and expanded the reservation center. At one point, there were 19 full- and part-time people. An 800 call center in Florida was added and helped to reduce their load. Some of the problems with the reservations were finally beginning to smooth out.

In addition to the dedicated, frontline staff dealing with the public every day, there was one other person who was very busy, though, few in the public ever saw her.

Jenny Lorenz was the CATS special events coordinator. A young and energetic lady with a quick wit, she loved the whole endeavor with the ferry and, like everyone else in the company, was driven to do her part to help make it succeed.

A busy mother of five who was born and raised in the Rochester area, she had been hired in June. As special events coordinator, it was her job to promote and work with groups, businesses, and organizations and to orchestrate excursions for them, both on the *Spirit of Ontario 1* and in the Rochester terminal.

She brought a lot of experience to her new, one-woman department. She had been a congressional aide for Louise Slaughter and had been involved in numerous fundraising functions. A string of assignments and jobs including working at Rochester's Riverside Convention Center, Frontier Field (Rochester's baseball stadium), and Fabulous Foods (a private catering firm), all of which she was involved in food and beverage management, provided her with additional background.

It was the result of a contact with one of her old Riverside Convention Center managers, a Rochester Institute of Technology graduate by the name of Dave Killion, that Lorenz was hired by CATS. Killion had moved on from the Convention Center and was now CATS's on-board and terminal services manager. He had been talking to her since February and, finally, brought her aboard in June.

During the 2004 season, Lorenz was responsible for putting together dozens of special events for private parties. The tools of her trade were a desk, telephone, phone books, a calendar, and a laptop. An office was optional as she would soon discover.

First, she was set up in a cubicle in the CATS office upstairs in the main terminal building. Sometimes she would work out of her home. With all of the activity going on in the office, she kept herself portable. As the CATS office space evolved during the early summer, Lorenz found herself moved into the distant Link building. The Link Building was the part of the terminal closest to the *Spirit* and used to board the passengers, thus the name "Link." A tall and narrow, glassy structure, it housed the ship's spare parts on the ground level, office space on the second level, and the third level was the corridor by which the public used to board the ship.

Working in the Link Building was not like being banished to the dark corners of the universe. To the contrary, it was a busy place as it was the operations center for Hornblower Marine and contained the offices of Marine Ops Director Annand and Technical Director Mansfield. It also housed Killion and his small staff of two. He was involved with food and beverage and the hiring of staff. Logistically, it made sense to have the on-board services department close to the ship.

Passing through the Link Building to report to work, crew members would frequently see her working the phone, pen in hand, scribbling down details, talking to organizers, caterers, florists, making phone and contact lists. She was a walking Rolodex of information and was always busy making arrangements and cultivating new ones.

Lorenz proudly shared with me some of her notes one day from the many events and parties that had taken place during CATS's brief run. Among the dozens of events that she either had a hand in or coordinated entirely on her own included the following: The Rotary Premiere Passage gala event, Miller Brick Company of Rochester, the Irish Children's Fresh Air Kids, Greater Rochester Enterprise, USA Realty, United Way Gala, Dox Electronics of Rochester, Royal LePage Realty, a speed dating event, several anniversary and family parties, numerous bus tours, and the Zielinski's 50th anniversary party.

It was a terrific list for the first year of the fast ferry.

The Premiere Passage was the biggest event held to date aboard the *Spirit of Ontario 1*. "The Rotary gala was a fabulous black tie, huge VIP and media event; catered by Riverside Convention Center and enjoyed by all," she would tell me months later with enthusiasm.

During the first week of the ferry's operation, the Miller Brick Company of Rochester was aboard for a 150-passenger day trip. The event was complete with breakfast buffet, screen and PowerPoint projector in the business class section of the ship, with boxed lunches to go. She had provided some assistance with the land transportation in Toronto, dinner arrangements, and drink chips being given for the southbound trip.

"They were a rowdy bunch, a riot, and had a GREAT time. A great thank you letter was given. They had a ball!" she said.

"There were also many, many bus tours booked through Mary Howard-Lawrence, Kim Truebger, or myself directly before operations were up. They were complete with small and large food events such as buffets, trays of 'family style' meals, and tons of boxed lunches and suppers to go."

"The Irish Children's Fresh Air Kids kick-off event. It was held on the Rochester terminal second floor terrace. Two-hundred people came, including the kids, sponsor families, organization staff, and media. Dry snacks, pop, and cookies were provided. CATS founder Dominick DeLucia's wife had suggested the successful event."

The Greater Rochester Enterprise small motor coach day trip for 25 convention site planners took place on June 26th. "This one would turn out to be the trip from hell as the engine-crippled *Breeze* had to limp home on like half an engine and everyone's life was a nightmare for days!"

The United Way Gala was one of the events Lorenz was most proud. It was held in the departure hall and then followed by a tour of the *Spirit* when the ship returned at about 10 p.m.

"It was a totally gorgeous event with beer, wine, soda, absolutely right-on perfect food (hors d'oeuvres, pasta stations, exceptional desserts, European cheeses and fresh fruit); flow, service, decorations all a dream. Chief Mate Neil assisted with the tours and made everyone's night. We got tons of leads and bookings from that party, including a solidified relationship with Wegmans Food Markets."

Another event that she was extremely proud of was the Zielinski 50th Anniversary Party.

"The Zielinski 50th Anniversary Party was, of course, a smashing success. There was added excitement to the event when the hostess snuck off the ship just before departure to gather roses she had left at home. She was nearly left behind! There were 120 very happy family members there. Canadian Customs even came aboard to clear them all on the ship."

And so it went. Many events, many people, many photographs, many happy faces, many fond and priceless memories.

In early August, Lorenz's focus was already zeroed in on the future; a future that was eight months away. She had begun booking events for spring 2005.

Some of those events included: eight weeks of Friday evening Finger Lakes wine sampling in the *Spirit of Ontario 1's* spacious Stern Lounge; the staging of "Joey & Maria's Wedding" and a "Murder-at-Sea" mystery, both to be performed by community theatre; many family and corporate events; two weddings; and several events were in the works with the Wegmans.

For March 2005, she had organized an event in the terminal for the Alternatives for Battered Women (ABW) annual silent auction fundraiser. Four hundred to five hundred people would be attending the event.

For April 2005, she had lobbied for and scheduled the Golisano Children's Hospital Gala fundraiser. The entire ship would have been booked. In the past, this fundraiser had raised over $75,000.

The Ford Friendship Express annual giveaway—a promotion that was usually hosted by Mayor Johnson and Congresswoman Louise Slaughter and held at the City Hall—would be held at the ferry terminal. Three new vans were to be displayed in front of the terminal and given away in a big media splash with the beautiful *Spirit of Ontario 1* docking in the background.

With so many events taking shape, with so many things to organize, Jenny Lorenz needed permission from her immediate supervisor Dave Killion to continue with the mounting details, both for the ferry's and the customer's plans.

For some inexplicable reason, the on-board and terminal services manager kept telling her, "Hold off on that for now."

It drove her nuts!

"Hold off on that for now."

Arriving for duty at 5 a.m. on Friday, August 6th, the crew began the day with a security sweep drill in the wake of last weekend's bomb threat. Captain John, vessel security officer/deck mate Chris Coleman, and myself were pleased with the crew response.

Later, I turned the vessel around leaving Toronto. Maneuvering the ferry was a kick for all of us, but, more than that, it was an opportunity to get the training we hadn't received back in June or July. Even so, there was still no training routine established and what we did do was infrequent.

The next morning, I arrived early for work to find that I could not get into the terminal. The front door was locked.

I had noticed a Hess fuel oil truck in the parking lot making a delivery to the in-ground tanks. With the front door locked, I figured that it was a "tanker truck-detainee" combo night when the security was stretched thin. One guard was with the detainee onboard the ship; the other with the tanker truck. I had the AP security number on my cell phone and I called it to request entry. To my annoyance, there was no answer.

Eventually, the security guard arrived to open the door. He had seen me drive in.

I asked, "What's wrong with your cell phone?"

He answered, "It no longer works. CATS didn't pay its bill."

Red flag.

CATS being unable to pay the cell phone bill for the security company was the first bit of news for the day. However, that was quickly displaced by Chief Engineer Richard Czachur of England announcing that he was leaving on August 17th. The big question was who will be the next chief? No one knew.

For that matter, who would be the next captain? Captains Danny and John were eager for the third master to show up and give them a break from their incessant, daily schedule. Chief Mate Babcock announced he was scheduling his master's exam very soon. He had his sea time in and thought this would be the perfect opportunity to take the exam and then grab the open ferry captain's job.

Though, I already had my master's license, I did not feel comfortable about throwing my hat into that ring yet. I had virtually no maneuvering training and I was still learning about my job as chief mate on this new type of vessel. All mariners work hard to acquire their licenses and I was not willing to risk mine at that point.

Good things happened during the week.

While deck mate Chris Coleman was making a round of the passenger cabin, a shy, little boy stopped him. He held in his hand a small green and yellow Staten Island ferry boat.

The first-grader asked, "Could you take this to the captain?"

Coleman smiled and said, "I think I could do you one better. Would you like to give it to the captain yourself?"

It made the little boy's day.

147

Coleman brought the young boy and his father to the bridge so that he could present Captain John with the plastic toy ferry boat. The boy's name was Nicholas (we never knew his last name) and he handed it to the captain while saying not one word. Captain John took it and thanked him. He then placed it in the small space between the engine throttles. The toy ferry remained in that place of honor throughout the remainder of the season.

Concierge Delicia Hill received word that she had been approved by Cornel Martin to be promoted to purser, however, the office seemed to be dragging its heels about her official promotion date because they didn't want to pay the purser's salary.

The Rochester School for the Deaf brought a group of kids aboard for a quick tour of the ferry between trips. The group was led by a delightful teacher by the name of Kim. I was their guide and showed them the passenger decks and the bridge. They were amazed and grateful for the opportunity to see the *Breeze*.

During one trip that week, I medically treated a 7-year-old boy by the name of Jacob. Jacob had scraped his left knee while running around and falling on the observation deck. He was sad and weeping as I placed a Band-Aid on his injury, but he cheered right up when I offered to take him and his dad to the space-age bridge for a tour. After his tour, little Jacob had forgotten all about his knee.

Director of Marine Ops Bill Annand was onboard for that trip. After arriving in Toronto, it was learned that the return voyage was a sell-out. The absolute maximum capacity of the *Spirit* was 774 passengers and 26 crew members, or a total of 800 people onboard. That day, due to the heavy load, we had 32 crew members onboard. With 768 passengers waiting on the hot dock and 32 crew members onboard, Captain Danny pointed out to Annand that he would be number 801.

Captain Danny said, "I cannot sail with over 800 people."

The Director of Marine Ops suddenly realized what the young captain was saying to him. "So, I guess I should get off," he deduced.

"Thanks, Bill," Captain Danny replied.

Just before the ship was to sail from Toronto, I noticed that Annand had left his cell phone on the bridge. I picked it up and ran it down to him on the dock where he stood all alone.

Returning onboard, I said to deck mate Chris Coleman, "Sometimes it pays to have a license on this ship."

The last image any of us had of Mr. Annand that day after the 768 passengers walked by him, was him standing alone on the dock talking on his cell phone, most likely booking a hotel for the night.

A first-grader's gift to Captain Williams, August 9, 2004. Photo courtesy of Larry Dickens, copyright 2004.

Chapter 12
Red Flags and Hurricane Warnings

For deck mate Ian Sherwood, the first red flag was the day we couldn't order a single gallon of Simple Green bio-degradable detergent for cleaning the ship's massive deck because the Grainger catalog account was temporarily shut down until CATS paid its bill.

For me, the first red flag could have been any one of several things: 1) the chief mates not being trained to maneuver the ship using the LIPS system; 2) type rating instructor Captain Ken Kujala being tapped to use his impressive skills to carve makeshift wheel chocks back in June with a chainsaw and pressure-treated six-by-sixs; 3) my request for one blanket for the ship's first aid room taking six weeks to fill; or even 4) CATS's inability to pay the cell phone bill for its security company.

But noooo!

The RED FLAG of ALL MOTHER RED FLAGS occurred on Friday the 13th of August.

Walking down the dock to work that day, I saw the marine ops director, Captain John, and Captain Danny conferring in a small circle. Huddled together, they were quietly talking, their expressions grim. Something bad had happened.

At 7:30 a.m., with passengers and vehicles aboard, Captain Danny, usually outgoing and gregarious, loud and laughing, stood at the maneuvering console on the port side, preparing to take the ship off the dock. As he waited for the shoreside personnel to take the gangway off, he was sullen and quiet. Not a word.

I asked him what was wrong.

He shook his head and muttered, "Later."

He was holding something back as he looked out the bridge wing window. I could tell he was simmering.

A short time later, after the ship was away from the dock, we jumped into the bridge seats and began piloting the ship outbound. Captain Danny finally broke his silence. It was as though somebody had just pulled opened a floodgate lever.

"There's no room in the budget for coffee for the crew! They're taking the coffee away!"

Chief Tony Putnik, our seaway pilot Richard Tetzlaff, second mate Chris Coleman, and this chief mate were stunned.

"What do you mean?" one of us asked.

Captain Danny continued in a loud and animated way. "I don't even talk to my *wife* until I've had my first cup of Joe!" He shook his head, in part disbelief, part anger, and repeated, "There's no room in the budget for coffee for the crew!"

As important as coffee is to the average office setting ashore, coffee is *extremely* important to the well-being and life onboard a ship. Most professional mariners will tell you in less than a heartbeat that coffee for a ship's crew is more important to a vessel's operation than fuel oil is for the engines.

CATS was removing the Bunn Pour-o-Matic coffee machines from the boat and the office. David's Gourmet Coffee of Rochester had been awarded a contract to supply both. No one knew why Kurt Ritchie's Horsehoe Hospitality catering operation, just one aluminum deck below, wasn't contracted to do this simple job. At the time, no one knew, nor cared. Now, all we knew was that CATS was cutting out the coffee for the crew.

As a friend would later say to me, "It's the small things that really affect how people perform on a team or on their jobs in a corporation."

How true. Morale and company loyalty took a big dive on that day.

Customer service, however, did not falter.

Looking out the port bridge window at the second floor of the terminal building where the CATS management offices were located as the *Spirit* cruised passed, Captain Danny shook an empty, upside down coffee mug menacingly at it.

"'Why are we running late??'" he said, mimicking both DeLucia and Prince who were constantly asking that question. "'Cause I didn't get my coffee, DUDE!!'"

Pilot Tetzlaff snickered and added wryly, "A quarter of a million dollars is spent on a lobbyist group in D.C. for reflagging or video lottery terminals, but no coffee for the crew." He, too, just shook his head in disbelief.

Later that afternoon, Captain Danny would write in his turnover notes to Captain John, "*Viva la Café! Viva la Revolution! Viva la Café!* You know, they took the coffee away from the colonists back in 1776. That's what actually started everything... & we kicked Britain's ass then, too.....*Viva la Café!*"

I nearly called a reporter friend to tell her, "Things are so tight here that they're taking away our coffee machine!"

But, I didn't. I was trying *very* hard to be a team player.

It was a bright, sunny day and there were lots of sailboats in the river as we left Rochester. It was such a sharp contrast to the darkness that was beginning to seep into the morale of the crew.

Two days later, we ran out of coffee.

The Bunn Pour-o-Matic still remained onboard awaiting someone to come and pick it up. Towering over unused coffee cups and sugar packets on the serving shelf, it stood tall, empty, and quiet; a small and insignificant symbol of failure. Caterer Kurt Ritchie lent us a few bags of coffee and the machine sprang back to life. I never understood why he wasn't given the contract in the first place. After all, he had coffee supplies just one deck below the crew area. When I asked him, he didn't understand it either.

Incidents on the car deck didn't change much in August. There were a few more drivers who didn't follow crew directions and left samples of their car's paint on the *Spirit's* support columns, along with pieces of their side view mirrors.

In Toronto one afternoon, there was one couple who left their keys in their car. Canadian Customs would not clear the ship and allow us to load until the vehicle was off the car deck. A locksmith was called. There were 750 people standing on the dock waiting in the scorching sun while the locksmith tried in vain to jimmy open the vehicle. Duty officer Kent Ehler attempted to convince Canadian Customs to clear the car on the ship so we could begin loading and get the people out of the hot sun, but they would not budge.

When the locksmith failed, this chief mate sent ordinary seaman Chris Briley to fetch an axe. When the axe arrived, engineer John Enwright broke in through a small, rear side window. The owners were okay with it. They were embarrassed that they were delaying hundreds of people. Reaching in through the hole in the glass, the door was unlocked. A minute later the car was gone, the ship was cleared, and the 750 passengers began coming aboard.

On August 19th, the director of marine ops called me at home with surprising news. He told me that Hornblower Marine and CATS were having a parting of the ways.

Later, I received an email from one of my colleagues onboard. He wrote, "We will be getting new offer letters from CATS soon. The captains have suggested that we not sign anything until we have all talked.

153

Almost everyone on board is in favor of that."

The concerns that were raised so far were the uncertainty of the job during the upcoming winter, would there be a change to the working hours and original terms, and who would replace marine ops director Bill Annand. The employees' last day with Hornblower Marine was August 20th.

Sometimes the events pendulum would swing. We'd have a great success one moment and then a failure the next.

On Monday, August 23rd, after the ship arrived in Rochester, the U.S. Coast Guard came aboard and requested to see the crew do both a fire drill and an abandon ship drill. These drills were conducted during the brief layover the *Spirit* had between trips. Captain John sounded the signals, the crew went through their paces, and performed perfectly. The USCG was very impressed and, afterward in the atrium, they would tell the crew "Well done!" The drills caused no delay for the passengers.

Immediately after the shift change and just when passengers were beginning to board for the afternoon trip, the ship's air-conditioning stopped working. The cabin temperature rose and felt like it was 100+ degrees. People were sweating and were very uncomfortable.

Purser Wiemer had to get T-shirts for the cabin staff from the duty-free shop because everyone's uniforms were soaked with sweat. Colby Amidon, the CATS financial officer, was onboard and he approved her using shirts from the shop. Wiemer then walked around the cabin serving complimentary sodas and water on trays.

Once again, Chief Tony came to the rescue. "The Croatian Sensation" diagnosed the problem and had the system back online within an hour.

CATS had just given Hormblower Marine the door and wanted the crew to sign up with them. CATS President Cornel Martin met with the ship's officers at 2 p.m. on Tuesday, August 24th and presented all of us with new job offer letters. Martin's office was packed.

The new job offers were identical to the old ones. The wages, vacation days, and the benefits were the same. The only difference being the letterhead read "CATS" instead of "Hornblower Marine."

Deck mate Chris Coleman was the first to ask the question that was foremost on everyone's mind. "Is it CATS's intention to run the ship through the winter?"

Coleman had yet to move his family from Coos Bay, Ore. They were waiting word from him when to move.

Martin replied, "Yes. CATS has no intention of shutting down."

He said that they had trucking contracts and assured us that a shutdown would not happen. He added, "Our numbers look good for the winter months. The business model had taken into account the low passenger numbers."

Hornblower Marine and CATS were non-union companies. There was no union representation. Both had "at-will" contracts. "At-will" contracts basically meant that no crew member had any long-term obligation. The contract allowed an employer to drop an employee without reason at any time.

By the same token, it also allowed an employee to quit at any time. Technically, a captain could take the ship over to Toronto in the morning and then quit on the spot and catch a plane to a higher paying job, leaving behind the ship, her crew, and passengers to be stranded until the company supplied a relief to bring the ship back. When a disreputable company uses this form of contract, promotion of backstabbing can be a tendency and employees have few, if any, rights.

Since Hornblower Marine had no other openings available in their other vessel operations and since the terms of employment had not changed, everyone signed their new job offers with CATS, including the two captains.

155

Chapter 13
"Second boat, dude"

For Pursers Karen Marsh and Cheryl Wiemer disgruntled passengers and hearing complaints were a part of their territory when dealing with the public. They had learned this during their long careers as flight attendants. Though the two women fielded the complaints of passengers throughout the summer, the complaints were few and none of them were memorable. Most of the people onboard were always very happy.

Wiemer tells a funny story from her airline years. It could just as easily have happened on the *Spirit of Ontario 1*.

One time she was working in first class, serving wine. Two of the passengers were an Asian couple who did not speak English. They were in their 60s. The couple indicated to her they needed cotton because their ears were hurting from the cabin pressure. Using hand motions as well as words, Wiemer told them there was Kleenex in the bathrooms. The next time she saw them they were sitting in their seats with tampons and strings hanging out of their ears. They were happy and full of thank you's.

"Happy and full of thank you's" was the description of the *Spirit of Ontario 1* passengers.

During the brief run of the *Spirit,* romance had found its way to the great ship, too. Each purser became a player in wedding proposals.

During one particularly good day for Marsh, a beautiful couple was riding to Rochester. The gentleman spoke to her about where on the ship would be the best place to propose marriage. The bubbly purser knew immediately and made a suggestion.

With the sun sinking below the horizon in the background, the gentleman proposed to his surprised girlfriend in the ship's Stern Lounge.

The purser then made an announcement. "Ladies and Gentlemen, we have our first engaged couple on the *Breeze*," and then she announced their names.

The cabin erupted into loud applause.

One day when Wiemer was on-duty, a fellow approached and asked her to be part of a "skit," and that it was to be a wedding proposal. The couple was in their mid-30s.

She agreed and a short time later made an announcement over the PA, paging them both to the concierge desk. The purser had already blocked off traffic up and down the atrium's grand staircase. As the couple walked down the stairs from business class, the young man suddenly dropped to his knees, pulled out an engagement ring, and proposed marriage to his unsuspecting girlfriend on the atrium stairway's mid-landing. She was extremely surprised. Caught off-guard, she began to cry. With tears in her eyes, she happily accepted.

Wiemer brought the couple two glasses of champagne to help them celebrate. She then announced over the PA, "On behalf of myself and the crew of the *Spirit of Ontario,* we'd like to congratulate the (blank's) on their engagement."

As before, the cabin erupted into loud applause.

There is something magical and romantic when a girl is proposed marriage by a gentleman on a ship at sea.

Not enough can be said about the role of the purser on the fast ferry. They are the first person the public sees when they board and the last one they see when they leave. They greet them and then bid them a good night. They help the special needs passengers, as well as the young mothers with strollers.

They are there to answer passenger questions. They render assistance and provide passenger reassurance when it is in doubt. They help everyone and make sure everything flows smoothly in the cabin.

One time a young autistic boy scratched his dad. The father was worried his son might bite other passengers. To accommodate them, the purser moved the family to the privacy of the first aid room. When a passenger forgets their medicine and leaves it in their automobile, the purser arranges for an escort to take them down to the car decks.

A purser is usually the first person on the scene when there is a medical emergency during the voyage. Many such emergencies occurred during the summer. One man thought he was having a heart attack. One woman experienced the constriction of her throat and had trouble breathing. Seasickness, brush burns, scrapes, and cuts. In all cases, either Marsh or Wiemer were on hand to start the treatment or get further assistance from the officers. They would alert the captain to call ahead for an ambulance, or send someone to the first aid room to retrieve an oxygen bottle. In an "abandon ship" emergency, they were there to evacuate the passengers.

By law, a foreign flag vessel transiting any of the Great Lakes or the St. Lawrence Seaway is required to have a pilot onboard. Lake and Seaway pilots are licensed mariners whose expertise is knowledge of the local waters, ports, and regulations. Their expertise is invaluable to those foreign mariners who are not familiar with an area. The pilots typically conn a vessel and serve as navigation advisor to a ship's captain. They also perform the dockings and undockings.

The *Spirit of Ontario 1* was registered in the Bahamas, flew the Bahamian flag, and was, therefore, a foreign flag vessel, despite the fact that her crew was entirely American. With Lake Ontario bordered by two countries, there are both American and Canadian pilots. With the *Spirit* running between the countries, the American and Canadian pilots evenly split the workload. One American pilot and one Canadian pilot would each take a turn and make one round-trip daily. The American pilots traveled from the Cape Vincent area (on the far eastern side of lake) in limousines while the Canadian pilots traveled from the St. Catherines area (on the far western side of the lake) and drove themselves.

Their duties on the *Spirit* were limited since the fast ferry's captains were the only ones skilled to perform the dockings and undockings with the LIPS system. The 88-mile route between Rochester and Toronto was straightforward and the two-man navigation team which occupied the cockpit seats needed no advisor to assist them. The only duties that remained for these highly trained individuals was to handle the few radio communications with traffic and port control, to advise us on any unusual traffic movements, and to assist with lookout.

The pilots were costing CATS approximately $1,500 (Canadian) per crossing, or $6,000 a day.

Sometime during August, word came down from the office that a U.S. Coast Guard pilotage exam was now scheduled for the *Breeze's* deck officers on September 3rd. Also, the long-awaited reflagging was now only a week or two away.

CATS had gone to great lengths to arrange the exam. A route-specific pilot's endorsement was unusual on the Great Lakes, though not unprecedented. A specialized exam just for Lake Ontario with the focus being on the ports of Rochester and Toronto had to be written. With the reflagging to the U.S. imminent, the deck officers required a pilotage endorsement on their licenses in order to replace the pilots.

Even with the U.S. flag, if we didn't have the endorsement, the pilots would still be required. It was important that we all pass the exam. Study materials were obtained and passed around. All of us began reading and going over the charts.

It should be mentioned here that in addition to the immediate and substantial savings that the elimination of the Lakes/Seaway pilots would yield, there are other important benefits to bringing the *Spirit of Ontario 1* under the U.S. flag. The ferry company could apply for various grants and subsidies; funding sources which she is ineligible while registered in the Bahamas. A U.S. flag would provide employment for tax-paying Americans. In most cases, foreign seamen working on the *Spirit* pay no U.S. income taxes. Reflagging the ship would open up the doors to a steady supply of manpower, and American crews provide an additional frontline layer to the nation's security due to the vetting process that American mariners undergo.

During the last week in August, the *Spirit* played host to sell-out trips as the ship carried baseball fans to Toronto for the New York Yankees-Toronto Blue Jays games. The games lasted for several days. CATS altered the afternoon schedule on Thursday and Friday so that the Toronto-bound fans could make the evening games on time. Instead of sailing at 4 p.m., the ship left at 2 p.m. The crew worked incredibly hard and fast to make these quick turnarounds happen. Discharging passengers and vehicles, removing the garbage, restocking the bonded stores and Horseshoe food supplies, cleaning up the cabin, and then loading hundreds of passengers and vehicles. They did all of these in less than 42 minutes on both days! This included a crew change-out as well. The crew performed admirably. The thrill of the ball games and the excited passengers was contagious.

Every now and then local television celebrities would ride the ship during their time off. During the week of baseball games, one popular meteorologist was aboard with his family and given a tour of the bridge. He was thrilled to be invited up and to see the heart of the *Spirit's* command and navigation center, and very delighted to meet Captain John Williams.

What made working on the *Spirit of Ontario 1* interesting for many of us was how nearly opposite were our two captains' personalities. Both men were caring, helpful, and honest with the crew, and, as a result, they were both well-liked by the crew. While Captain Williams was reserved and quiet—members of the local press and the crew thought he was "shy"—Captain Aycock was loud and boisterous. Not a man to contain his thoughts, you always knew what was on Captain Danny's mind.

For example, I discovered the next day that Captain Danny was very opinionated when it came to TV weathermen. I mentioned in passing about our visitor touring the bridge.

Captain Danny blurted out, "If I had been here I would have *never* let him on the bridge. I hate TV weathermen! Hell, I can predict the weather better than those guys. *You* can predict the weather better than those guys. They use bones in a cup or tarot cards to guess the weather!"

Triple Doppler radar be damned when you have chicken bones.

The full loads kept our crew busy, especially during those baseball days.

The job of the ordinary seamen during the voyage was to empty the cabin trash and to ensure the bathrooms were clean. Several wheeled plastic dumpsters were kept on the main car deck for the trash. At the end of each trip in Rochester, the marine crew would wheel these small dumpsters ashore and empty them in the big city compactor that was parked in the corner of the car lot. The three ordinaries were in constant motion.

As seaman Erin Macallister made her rounds, she noticed a long line of women standing in the corridor outside one of the restrooms. She entered the restroom for a sanitary check and noticed that no one was in any of the five stalls. She went back out and told the women they could go in. The first woman in the line looked at her and pointed to the red light above the door.

Macallister looked up at the light and politely said, "No, that's the ventilation shutdown light."

Even though it was labeled as such, the lady thought it meant the restroom was occupied.

The next day, Friday, was the day my daughter went to college. I wasn't there to help her move, so my wife did it alone, as she has done for the family on so many occasions before during my absences while at sea. Such is the life of a merchant mariner's wife, even if the mariner is only one hour away.

The day ended when my wife called to let me know how the move went. All was well. She had returned home from relocating the daughter and was very sad because she was gone. Such is the life of a merchant mariner. It doesn't matter whether you are 8,000 miles from home or 80 miles.

On Saturday, August 28th, as I greeted people coming up the gangway, Dominick DeLucia and his family came aboard. They were on their way to the baseball game. I greeted him and asked if we could have a word later on.

I had been reading in the newspapers over the last couple of years about CATS co-founder Brian Prince's philanthropic activities since he had returned to his Rochester hometown.

In November 2002, Prince and his Prince Family Open Society Fund had provided the University of Rochester with an initial gift of $1-million dollars, with a pledge for an additional $1-million dollars in the future. On January 2, 2004, the *Democrat & Chronicle* had reported that Prince had donated $85,000 to the Flower City Habitat for Humanity to build a new home in the city's Susan B. Anthony neighborhood. He was also founder and president of Renaissance Finance, a group which invests in low-income areas of Rochester.

Having written about a struggling Rochester neighborhood and the drug problem in my novel *Forever Ten*, I thought DeLucia could help me meet with Prince and attempt to interest him in helping the decaying Jay-Orchard street section of the City's west side.

Later, DeLucia appeared to the bridge.

In greeting him, I asked, "What have you been doing since stepping down as CEO?"

He replied, "Working on the second boat, dude."

The *Spirit of Ontario 2* was still on his mind.

It didn't entirely surprise me. Former CATS COO Tony White had originally planned for a two-ferry system. Also, I had read in *Marine Log* a few months earlier in May 2004 that CATS was looking for bidders to build a second ship.

This bolstered my spirits about the grand future of this company and left me feeling pretty good.

DeLucia then asked me when I was going to get my master's license.

"I already have it," I reminded him, and added, "I like the chief mate's position because it's a good position in which to gain experience before going captain."

He nodded, seeming to think it was wise plan for career progression. We then moved onto the subject of the Jay-Orchard street area which was the reason why I had asked to speak with him in the first place. After a few minutes, we agreed to talk more about this at a later time, and he left to return to his family.

The second ship idea did dance around in my mind. The two-fast ferry concept had been around for years ever since it was first proposed by Mr. Wilkinson and Mr. Smith back in the mid-1990's. I was quite encouraged and thought after spending a season of breaking into the workings of a fast ferry on the *Spirit of Ontario 1* as chief mate, I'd be ready to assume command of the *Spirit of Ontario 2*.

161

Chapter 14
Goodbye Bunn, and Good Luck

The Ultimate Red Flag occurred on Tuesday, August 31st.

I went to work early to study for Thursday's pilotage exam. At boarding time, I assisted passengers at the gangway. Just then I saw Eric Mueller, the assistant onboard and terminal services manager, coming down the atrium stairs. In his arms was the Bunn Pour-o-Matic from the crew area. He had been instructed to take the coffee machine away.

It finally happened.

First, the bagged ground coffee stopped. We had been saved when Caterer Kurt Ritchie stepped up to the plate and began providing—at his own cost—coffee for us to use in the crew area. Now, the Bunn was leaving for good.

It had been only three days earlier that I heard about the "second ship." Perhaps the Bunn was being moved to it.

Only moments after Mueller walked down the gangway, *Democrat & Chronicle* reporter Rick Armon and photographer Carlos Ortiz stepped aboard for a trip to Toronto. Had the two come aboard only moments earlier, I would have asked them to take a picture of him leaving with the Bunn and to write a story about it.

It was not a good sign. It was a *rotten* sign. The "omenists" would have surely gone NUTS had they read about this in the newspaper.

Despite the departure of our dear friend, the day went on.

We left Charlotte with nearly a full boat: 760 passengers. There were 71 cars. Among this day's more notable events included:

A toilet paper dispenser disappeared from a stall in the starboard side men's room.

A large lady on high-powered, three-wheeled scooter spilled a cup of coffee all over the Bridge Deck unisex room creating quite a mess on the bulkheads, vanity mirror, and deck.

While cars were driving aboard in Toronto, I saw a man standing in his skivvies beside his vehicle. For some reason, he decided that he needed to change his pants on the spot, on the fully-loaded car deck, rather than wait until he could find the men's room.

Later, on the return trip from Toronto with 745 passengers and 164 cars, the missing toilet paper dispenser surfaced in the Fisher Price Kidz Room on the child's play table next to the Legos.

Who knows why people do the things they do?

This round-trip ended with two vehicle problems upon arrival in Rochester. One owner had locked his keys in the car and could not get in. Tech Director Bob Mansfield arrived on the car deck with a long piece of thin aluminum and jimmied it open. The driver got in and off he went.

Another owner had the rear parking brakes seize up on her minivan and they would not release despite all of the efforts by the ship's talented engineers. Mansfield resolved this problem by simply starting the engine, putting the van in "Drive", and driving it off the mezzanine deck with the two rear wheels locked. Squealing and leaving shiny black tire marks all the way down the aluminum deck, the car was finally off the ship. The *Spirit of Ontario 1* could now be cleared by U.S. Customs and begin loading.

Today was the last day of the August "half-price" promotion. The cabin staff had worked very hard during the month handling the needs of over 71,000 passengers. The promotion had brought out people who might never have otherwise ridden the ferry and, with it, more exposure and good, word-of-mouth advertising for the ship.

At the end of August, special events coordinator Jenny Lorenz needed to know what to do with her tentative spring events. For a month now she had been told to put them on hold and not to proceed. She went to her boss, Dave Killion, and asked what he wanted her to do about these huge events that she had worked so hard to make happen.

Killion went to DeLucia.

A short time later, Killion returned to Lorenz with word from DeLucia. She was told by Killion to cancel the spring events.

The end was near, but, still, no one suspected how bad it would become.

The first day of September found the deck officers studying for the U.S. Coast Guard pilotage exam after the *Spirit* was put to bed for the night. We all needed a Lake Ontario pilotage endorsement. After the evening run, deck mate Chris Coleman and I skipped any night work projects and concentrated on studying for the exam instead.

On Thursday, September 2nd, Lt. David Webb of the Buffalo U.S. Coast Guard office came to Charlotte to administer the "HSC Local Knowledge Lake Ontario" exam.

The test began at 1:45 p.m., shortly after the *Spirit* docked. The exam did not take much time and the ship had not been delayed when it left at 3:58 p.m. with 310 passengers and 69 cars onboard.

All of the deck officers passed the exam. Within the next few days, each of us would receive endorsements to our licenses which would say "This license is hereby extended to include First Class Pilot on the vessel HSV Spirit of Ontario 1 upon Lake Ontario between Rochester, NY and Toronto, Ont., Canada."

Within the week, the U.S. flag would be flying on our ship's flagstaff and we were now certified to replace the Seaway pilots. The expense of the pilots for CATS was just about to end.

The trip was uneventful. The engines were purring, the LIPS system was steering, and the equipment was humming. This put Chief Tony "The Croatian Sensation" Putnik in a very grand mood.

No problems today.

He looked over the top of his engine control console and out through the tall bridge windows at the blue lake and sky.

"It is so beautiful to be on the great lake of Ontario," he said with much gusto in his Italian-sounding, Croatian accent. He was so happy that day, he picked up the telephone, called the galley, and ordered a pizza for the entire bridge watch.

The Labor Day weekend was an enormously busy weekend for the *Breeze* and her crew. For most of the eight trips between Friday and Monday the ship had high passenger numbers.

On Sunday the 5th, U.S. Customs denied entry into our country to a middle-aged couple. The female detainee was a little school teacher from Long Island. She was with her husband. Her "visa-in-transition problem" story sounded similar to *Mamma Mia!* star Kim Huffman's problem.

On September 6th, U.S. Customs denied access to two Canadians. They included a middle-aged Canadian who was born in Poland and a young woman in her thirties.

During the *Breeze's* 80-day run we had detainees from both sides of the lake. Coming from Toronto to Rochester there were 80 detainees, or "turn-backs." This amounted to an average of one person a day for each of the 80 days that the *Breeze* operated.

On the average "Notice to Detain, Remove, or Present Alien" form from the U.S. Department of Justice that each detainee received from Customs, the reason a person was being denied entrance to the U.S. was commonly listed by the Customs officers as simply "Subject is inadmissible to the United States." No other reasons were ever given.

The Canadian Customs didn't offer much more in the way of explanations than their American counterparts, though, their reasons provided more intrigue. Encrypted phrases such as "No travel documents," "Inadmissible," "Wants to Withdraw," and "Improper documentation, no consent" were common.

Reasons such as "No proof of citizenship" and "Criminality" would definitely get you an overnight at the Hotel Breeze, as well as the strongly worded "Inadmissible, committing an offense upon entering," though I had never known of any offense upon entering being committed by any passenger (or crew) while on the *Breeze.*

And, finally, there was the cryptic "36(2)(b)" reason. Someday I must ask Charles Giunta what that means.

In the end, just as many Americans were turned-around in Canada as Canadians were turned-around in the United States, but because the ship always spent the night in Rochester, no one had to spend the night onboard in Canada.

The middle-aged Canadian couple who were detained on September 6th spent the night on the comfortable, blue leather couches in the *Breeze's* Business Class section. Unknown to everyone in the world, including themselves, they would be the last passengers to sleep on the ship for the remainder of the 2004.

Chapter 15
Tuesday, September 7th, 2004

Almost every morning for her last three months on duty, Purser Cheryl Wiemer had rubbed Tech Director Bob Mansfield's bald head for good luck. The morning of September 7th was the one morning the good-natured purser did not.

That afternoon CATS announced it was suspending service.

The crew meeting in the atrium with Captain Danny was now over.

As I looked out over the 138 passengers standing in a long line beneath a partly cloudy sky on the dock in Toronto, I wondered, did any of these people know they were taking a one-way trip to Rochester? Did they know they were possibly going to be taking their last ride on the *Breeze*? Had any of them considered an alternate way to get home to Toronto?

The ship was cleared to load passengers and cars. I, in turn, signaled to our ticket takers to let the people on.

Should I tell them? Or should I keep my mouth shut and play dumb?

As I churned over the right thing to do in my mind, as it turned out, I didn't have to tell them. They already knew. It had already been on television and everyone in Toronto knew. The last people in the region to find out this bad news was the good crew of the *Spirit of Ontario 1*.

The passengers began expressing their condolences to me as they filed by me. One by one, they expressed sorrow that the great ship was suspending service.

"That's terrible you're shutting down," said one elderly lady.

"I hope you're not down for long," said another with warm encouragement.

"I'll miss you. I hope you're back soon."

I am sorry for your loss.

Be strong. You'll get through it.

Several wished me well in my next endeavor.

Not a single person asked me, "How am I going to get back to Toronto?"

The compressed air starters in the engine room revved up. Its ear-piercing, jet engine sound shooting through the octaves, low-to-high, like an ascending forth of July rocket. They kicked over the ship's massive diesel engines and the 80 enormous cylinders thundered to life.

With 138 passengers and 15 vehicles aboard, the *Spirit of Ontario 1* began Voyage #330. We cast off our lines for the last time. Oddly, enough, after 80 days of mostly late departures and arrivals, we actually left on time for a change at exactly 7 p.m.

As the great ship backed away from the terminal and twirled in the channel, manager Kent Ehler and the Toronto CATS staff did their customary human wave. They had done the wave every day since June 18th.

This would be the last one.

Voyage #330 to Rochester was uneventful.

Only two days earlier, the *Democrat & Chronicle* proclaimed in an extensive story on the front page, **"Ferry steadies after rocky start."** Journalist Rick Armon's article spoke approvingly of the high passenger numbers CATS was enjoying due to the half-price promotion in August. He also wrote about the *Spirit of Ontario 1's* visibility in both the national and international press. There was no hint that things were suddenly about to change.

Prior to the arrival in Toronto, business class server Russel Schafer had received a call on his cell phone from a friend in Rochester. The suspension of service had already been announced on the local television news.

"The ship is done. Finished," he tried to tell his shipmates.

No one believed him.

Bartender Mike Masco was working in Business Class with Schafer and had heard his news. Masco didn't know what to believe. Before leaving Rochester, he had heard a rumor that the company was going to cut back to one trip per day.

Engineer John Enwright had said to ordinary seaman Macallister, "Captain Danny's going to have a meeting after we dock."

Macallister couldn't hear Enwright very well because they were outside on the stern and, between the engines, waterjets, and rush of the wind, it was noisy.

She would say later, "All of the ordinary seamen were sensing something uncertain about the future before we arrived in Toronto."

When Purser Chris Moore had announced over the PA, "Everyone needs to muster in the atrium," many of the cabin staff like Masco expected to hear about the reduction to one trip.

167

At 6 p.m., the families back in Rochester learned about the suspension of service from the television news while their spouses and relatives were on their way to Toronto. Very few calls got through as the crew was working.

For the crew, the news had provided an incredible contrast to the revelry and euphoria of June 18th when the *Spirit of Ontario 1* began operating.

After leaving Toronto, I found a cell phone message from my wife. She asked, "Hey, honey, did you know this is your last trip?"

What have you been doing since stepping down as CEO?
Working on the second boat, dude.

Had I known 10 days earlier that the company was going to pull the plug on service, I would have thought Dominick DeLucia's statement was totally bizarre and ludicrous.

To this day, I have no idea why he was thinking about the *Spirit 2* when the *Spirit 1* was on the verge of running aground in a sea of red ink.

Now, there we were, on the last run. Voyage #330. The easterly trip back was uneventful.

For Tonya Allen, the last voyage back to Rochester was really tough.

"Knowing that we were docking our boat indefinitely, we worked hard to keep up the morale of our coworkers. We did the extra stuff to leave the ship in good shape, like scrubbing the floorboards and bulkheads in the servery."

Allen was a young mother who was holding down two jobs. Besides the ferry, she was employed by the Riverside Convention Center in downtown.

"CATS and the ferry was my haven," Tonya would later tell me. "I like to feel like I've made a difference or my spirit would not have allowed me to stay, otherwise. There were regulars; people who rode the ship all the time. One rode 17 times."

I asked her if she would return. Like most of the employees I spoke with after the shutdown, most said they would. The shutdown had not dampened their enthusiasm for the project.

For my last watch as chief mate, I remembered it was pretty quiet on the bridge during the trip back to Rochester. A small, one-foot sea rippled out of the southwest. The wind driving it blew at a whispery five knots.

I had the conning officer's seat and kept a lookout for small boats and logs. Captain Danny manned the navigator's chair. Crossing the "Bone line," I made the call to the Rochester Coast Guard station.

John MacClean, the quiet Seaway pilot, made the last of the radio calls to the Lake Ontario traffic controllers. The ship was leaving Seaway Newcastle control and entering Seaway Sodus.

"Goodbye Newcastle. Hello Sodus."

"Sounds like a good name for a book," I said to the pilot.

Arriving in Rochester, it was now dark.

We took the speed off. As soon as the energy wake had passed and the bow dipped, Captain Danny ordered, "Hard right."

I shoved the joystick over to starboard and the *Spirit* swung smoothly over. Minutes later, I had the ship centered perfectly in the channel. Chief Bones was there and he escorted us in. Lots of people, as always, lined the piers. TV trucks with their satellite dishes reaching for the sky were gathered just like they had back on April 27th when the ferry first arrived in Charlotte to the cheers of hundreds.

In the dark, it was difficult to determine how many people turned out that night, but there were no cheers. Flashes from cameras sparkled along both piers.

The office and the press continued to say throughout the summer that our trip takes 2 hours and 15 minutes. Between running the engines at a reduced rpm, a bent port bow, the variation in vehicle number and weight, and a yet to-be-discovered bent waterjet, we rarely made our schedule.

On September 7th, it was 9:15 p.m. as we entered the Rochester jetties after the final trip from Toronto. Captain Danny quipped, "We finally made our schedule."

Light ships make their schedules.

The Texan docked the ship as smoothly and effortlessly as he had many times before. Both his and Captain John's skills had come a long way since the spring.

I went down to the gangway to line it up. Moments later, our passengers disembarked, leaving behind them countless compliments, accolades, and sincere hopes that we would return.

Purser Chris Moore did a final sanitary check of the passenger areas and cleared all of the money off the ship. The ship had carried extra change that night to ensure the bars and servery would not run out. He had to borrow a backpack out of the shop to carry all of the money, it was that heavy. He emptied the safe and took the money into the Link building for safe keeping.

In the aftermath of the shutdown, I asked many of the crew members what their best days were aboard the *Spirit*.

Purser Moore's best day occurred earlier on in the season when he was an ordinary seaman. He had gone to the bridge and Captain Danny allowed him to sit on the left chair. He watched the radar and did lookout duty with binoculars during the entire ride across the lake.

"Danny made you feel like a seaman," he reflected. "Captain Danny made people feel like they were more than someone who just emptied the trash. I enjoyed that. It was awesome."

Server Tonya Allen's best day on the ship was when the cast of *Mamma Mia!* rode over. A little girl with the tourism group (the daughter of the head of the group) came to see Allen every 10 minutes. Allen gave her pretzels; they were like gold to the girl. The next day, when the group headed back to Toronto, the little girl asked for and found her, and asked for her autograph. Touched by the girl's request, Allen signed one of the *Breeze* books and gave it to her.

Deck mate car-miester Chris Coleman's best day was when he escorted little first-grader Nicholas up to the bridge to present Captain John Williams with a toy ferry boat. Captain John had placed the ferry boat in between the throttles on the center console. Coleman enjoyed the passengers. He said to me after the shutdown, "The ferry in Rochester is like having a spaceship here. The passengers walk around with their mouths agape. Most people were thrilled. It was neat to be a part of it. You had a sense of ownership."

Duty-free shop attendant Carrie Cooper's best day was the Rotary Premiere Passage voyage. "There had been lots of excitement and everyone was dressed to the nines."

For engineer John Enwright, his best day was ironically his worst. The day that he was nearly killed in the engine room was also the day that his parents came aboard. He proudly gave them a tour. They were really happy and proud of what he was doing.

Deck mate Ian Sherwood's best day was also his worst day. "The ship had received word that there were going to be 185 cars and three buses waiting for us in Toronto. It was going to be an impossible situation. But with a little creative loading, we managed to pull it off," he told me later with great satisfaction.

The *Spirit* in Hawaii for Hawaiian
Superferry promotion, March 2004
Note the scale of person standing on top of wheelhouse
Photo courtesy of Asger Manoe, copyright 2004

Starboard side damage, New York City, April 1, 2004
Photo courtesy of Asger Manoe, copyright 2004

Atrium stairs and skylight
Photo courtesy of Petr Chudoba, copyright 2005

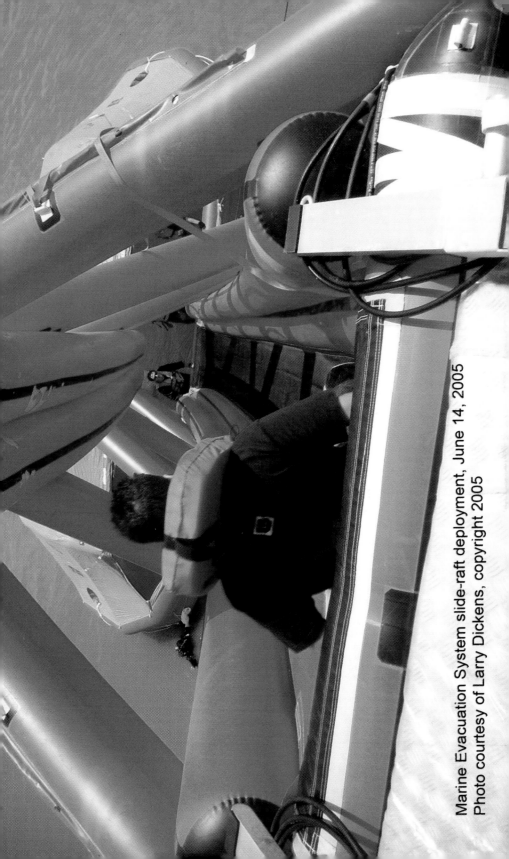

Marine Evacuation System slide-raft deployment, June 14, 2005
Photo courtesy of Larry Dickens, copyright 2005

Drydocked at Port Weller shipyard, May 22, 2005
Photo courtesy of Larry Dickens, copyright 2005

Cabin crew on Christening Day in Rochester, June 13, 2004
Photo courtesy of Beverly Rouse, copyright 2004

Rotary Premiere Passage, docking late in
Rochester on June 18, 2004
Photo courtesy of T.C. Pellett, copyright 2004

Engineer Bryan Hald's best days were during the major engine overhaul in Toronto. The young and curious engineer said, "Seeing the precision and pulling the cylinders. Not everyday you get to see an engine being torn apart and work with fourteen MTU techs from Germany. It was exciting, a blast, to be a part of it."

Chief Tony "the Croatian Sensation" Putnik expressed similar professional sentiments. His best days were every time that he started the engines, especially when an engine unexpectedly quit and he was able to fix and restart it.

Purser Delicia Hill's best day was September 6th, Labor Day. She had been one of the pursers during the extremely busy four-day weekend. A total of 9,378 passengers and 1,522 vehicles had come aboard the *Breeze*. She and her crew were exhausted and they were looking forward to things slowing down a bit.

"They were real troupers," she would later say. "They joked that if I was purser on duty, then the ship would always automatically be booked to capacity. I was pleased because I had managed to maintain a sense of calm and order on the passenger levels all weekend despite the busyness of so many people being on board."

Seaman Wayne Hickel's best day was "Every day," he reflected. "Seeing the rooster tale on the stern and it showing off rainbows; when it was a beautiful day; and when everyone got along and was happy."

Erin Macallister's best day was when "Captain Danny would hold a line-throwing competition on the dock. It loosened everyone up and created team spirit and camaraderie. Any day that ran smoothly was a best day."

For Purser Karen Marsh the big, gala Rotary event was the best day.

For Purser Cheryl Wiemer, "Every day!" but especially when her husband and her kids rode the grand ship.

Every day was a best day, too, for bartender Beverly Rouse. "I made every day good! I wanted everyone to leave the ship feeling happy."

As did the CATS employees on the north side of the lake.

The Canadian staff did their human wave every time the ship left. It began as act of spontaneity and represented an air of tremendous excitement on the part of those involved with this grand project. It became a ritual and continued every time. It was a metaphor for huge human energy.

It was a real tragedy that CATS had lost this energy. CATS would no longer link countries or people. The wave would be no more. Its employees were its best ambassadors.

Now, they were about to be dispersed and gone.

Spirit of Ontario 1 docked in Rochester, New York, 2004
Photo courtesy of Petr Chudoba, copyright 2004

Part III
The CAT'S Out of the Bag

Chapter 16
CATS stands for "Can't Answer That, Sorry"

"The directors created the Company but it was the captains and crew that gave the ships life. They performed the many tasks that enabled the Ontario No. 1 and Ontario No. 2 to operate for the economic benefit of the owners and for the benefit of their own well-being. Hundreds, even thousands, of times they repeated their duties allowing the ships to cross Lake Ontario in the service of the Ontario Car Ferry Company."
- Author Ted Rafuse in his book *Coal to Canada*

The suspension of service surprised all off-duty personnel, too. By the time I arrived at Windjammers Restaurant after the last docking, the placed was full of off-duty people. The dollar shelf had long since been emptied. I had begun the day by taking a company required drug test on Chili Avenue and ended it by being laid-off and going to Windjammers.

The Layoff Party at Windjammers. Employees continued to arrive and crowd the small bar. I remember playing a game of pool, hollering at a news crew across the street down at the terminal (they had some facts wrong as we watched the live newscast inside), and someone getting sick in the bathroom.

On-board and Terminal Services Manager David Killion bought a round of drinks for everyone in the place. He then climbed up on a shaky bar stool and called out for everyone's attention. When the patrons quieted down, he proclaimed in a reassuring voice, "Don't worry, everybody. This is what is called 'Posturing.' This is temporary."

As he climbed down from the bar stool I asked him if he had lost his job. He answered, "No."

Later, over a giant Windjammer hamburger, I talked to Bob Mansfield and asked for his take on the day's shocking event. He expressed optimism that we'd be running again by October 1st, only 24 days away, because it was shaping up to be a sell-out weekend.

The old *Ontario No. 2* ferry to Cobourg had departed Charlotte for the last time on April 30, 1950 and it would be over fifty-four years before any ferry service would resume on Lake Ontario. Mansfield was optimistic that the fast ferry would resume service much sooner than that.

The next day Dave Killion found himself laid off. This was, no doubt, thanks to "posturing." Like the rest of us, Dave had been postured right off the payroll.

Seamen are like actors, always looking for their next job. With shipping companies coming and going with irregularity, much like stage shows, the marine crew slowly got into that job-searching mind frame, something we were all quite used to doing.

However, tonight—lay-off night—was party time, no matter how dreadful the occasion.

The day after the ship suspended service, someone posted the ferry for sale on eBay for a buck.

A couple of days went by without a word to any of the crew.

The sudden loss of jobs created hardships. Deck Mate Chris Coleman's family had just arrived from Oregon. Chief Mate Neil's family had arrived from Louisiana a few weeks earlier and he had rented a house. Many others had taken leases on apartments. Everyone, both locals and out-of-staters, were facing a hardship.

At 9:45 a.m. that Friday, a large number of marine crew including the captains decided to converge on the office to hopefully get some answers. None of the principals were in that day. Only CATS attorney Adam Michael was available to speak with us.

Despite points presented to Mr. Michael regarding benefits cancellations, payroll cycle, more pay due, and the fact CATS will face difficulty recruiting new people in the future, we learned nothing from him.

Someone asked the CATS attorney, "Why was there such short notice about the shutdown?"

Michael answered, "The reason for the short notice was because the creditors on the Canadian side might seize the ship."

I looked up and asked, "What about this side of the lake? There are a lot of guys here who are owed money."

As the months went on, several employees would file claims for unpaid wages.

By Monday, September 13th, there was still no word regarding the fate of the *Spirit* and her crew. Annoyed, I sent a fax to Cornel Martin about the poor treatment of the crew in this matter. In it I had written,

"No one in management has called a meeting of all employees to explain the situation, nor was anyone told that their benefits would be canceled last Friday. The loyalty exhibited by management towards its employees is virtually nonexistent when compared to the loyalty put forth by the employees toward the operation of the ferry every single day. The employees are on the front line every day of the week facing the customer and providing service. The rave reviews the ferry has received is due primarily to the efforts of these hard working and courageous people."

Later that day, at Martin's direction, Captain John called and left a message telling me there will be a meeting at the terminal for the CATS crew tomorrow at 5 p.m. Sometimes you send a fax and don't receive a response. Sometimes you do!

I continued to be a believer that the ship was only temporarily sidelined. So confident was I in its return, I invited a vintner friend from the Finger Lakes to meet me at the terminal prior to the meeting. He had not yet seen the new facility and was searching for a possible wine tasting location. While he was there, I also gave him a tour of the *Breeze*, and introduced him to Captain John.

The crew meeting was held on the second floor terrace. A table with pizza and liters of soda had been set up. An estimated 100 employees were present.

The CATS president stepped up on top of a plastic milk crate beside the terrace's railing to address the gathering. He expressed genuine concern for the hardship that the current situation was causing everyone.

"We understand if you want to go out and find another job. We understand your need to have to work and we won't be upset if you look for work somewhere else."

Martin tried to explain several of the issues facing CATS; issues such as trucking, reflagging, Canadian Customs, and the Toronto terminal.

On a more hopeful and immediate note, he said, "Austal Ships does not want an economic failure." He added, "They look at this as the cornerstone of the emerging U.S. markets."

He then said CATS's startup goal is October 1st due to it being a sell-out weekend. He added, benefits would run through the end of month

177

and they would kick back in when rehired. He encouraged people to file for unemployment.

He then assured the group saying, "Dominick and Brian are committed. Brian is in New Orleans due to Hurricane Frances, to help move his family."

There were several questions, but not many. The meeting then ended and everyone began to disperse.

As people headed out of the terminal building, someone grumbled, "Kodak provides a placement service when they lay off people. CATS gave us a pizza."

Little did any of us know at that time, but Cornel Martin had just moved *his* family up from Louisiana only two days before the shutdown. The shutdown was as much a shock to him as it was to all of us. If only he had told everybody that afternoon on the terrace, everyone would have been more receptive, sympathetic, and supportive. Instead, many of the officers thought he had lied to them back at the job offer meeting on August 24th when he had been asked if the ship was going to run through the winter. That meeting had taken place only 14 days before the announced shutdown.

After the meeting, many of the employees walked across the street to Windjammers. The place was packed and it was difficult for late arrivals to get in through the door.

I was standing by the entrance talking to someone when reporter Jennifer Johnson of News 10NBC appeared. Standing outside the door, she asked me, "Are there any CATS employees in here?"

I turned toward the crowd and shouted above the noise, "HEY, everyone!"

There was a momentary lull as I had everyone's attention. I then hollered, "Are there any CATS employees in here?"

In unison, the crowd shouted back at me, "NO!!

I looked at Johnson, shrugged, and said, "I guess not."

In an effort to bolster people's spirits, on Saturday afternoon, September 18th, my wife, Sue, and I hosted what we called the "1st Annual CATS Marine Crew Cookout Party!" on a beach near my home on Canandaigua Lake. The day began with a great deal of southerly wind. Canandaigua Lake had a 2-3 foot chop. Later it would die down.

Many crew members made the 50-minute trip from Rochester. We grilled, there were coolers of soda and beer, and people brought dishes to pass. There was canoeing, boating, and tubing. The children built castles and dug canals in the sand. It was a good time. We even had a rescue at sea. Engineer Bryan Hald had taken the canoe out into an area of rough water and it capsized. Captain Danny's kids, OS Rick Marcellus, and I took the motorboat and plucked Hald from the water and towed in the swamped canoe.

During the party, Bob Mansfield continued to express optimism for an October 1st startup since that weekend had reportedly been sold out. The engineers at the party seriously doubted it.

"It'll take a week to start the ship up again," one of them said to me. "That means he'll have to call us tomorrow."

Toward the end of the party, we broke out a cake. I had purchased it from our local Wegmans bakery. I had the bakery place a large, icing photo of the *Breeze* on one side of the huge sheet cake. On the other side, I had them write the inscription, The *Spirit* will rise again!

On the morning of Tuesday, September 28th I had scheduled interviews for this book with former employees. Since I was going to be in Rochester, I called my friend Gary Mervis and left a message, inviting him to the ship for a tour. Gary is the founder and director of Camp Good Days & Special Times, one of the country's largest camps for children dealing with life-threatening illnesses. The organization had planned to ride the ship, but tickets had been sold out for the week they wanted due to the half-price promotion. Since they never had a chance to ride the *Spirit,* I wanted to, at least, provide him with a tour.

It is unfortunate he couldn't meet me because that very afternoon, three weeks to the day after service was suspended, a federal order was issued and the ship was impounded by the U.S. Marshals Service. No one would be able to have a tour of the ship for some time.

The armed U.S. Marshals arrived onboard on Tuesday, September 28th.

One colleague said, "Cool, CATS gets free security now."

Another colleague, who was a member of the skeleton crew that was required to be onboard the *Spirit* during this indefinite lay-by period, said, "They were a good bunch of guys. They had never seen a ship of that size before and they were in awe."

Once the marshals were settled into the ship, they would order a pizza from nearby Salvatore's and then watch a movie in the port theater for two hours with the skeleton crew.

As it turned out, the U.S. Marshals were not a free security service for CATS. It would eventually cost CATS $1,500 per day once everything

179

was sorted out. The company asked the judge if he would release the marshals and turn the security duty over to CATS. After all, the ship wasn't going anywhere. The judge agreed and the marshals were dismissed, though the ship remained impounded.

By the end of September, I had given up on the *Breeze* and had turned my attention to some serious job hunting. I contacted a group about work on LNG vessels, sent a resumé to Royal Caribbean Cruise Lines, and checked the employment ads in Rochester for writing work.

I even queried a former colleague who was working on a fast ferry that was crisscrossing the English Channel. He provided me with a couple of contacts. In the same email he also told me about a woman who had died due to injuries incurred on a fast ferry.

He had written, "We have just been canceled for over a week now...5-7 meters sea ....yikes....but they are sailing today on the limits, a 3.4 meter sea, so it's going be a bumpy ride. A couple of weeks ago we had an eighty year-old lady fall over in the cafe and she broke her hips and arm. But she died three days later from these injuries so you can tell it is rough in that type of sea."

The last place I wanted to be was the English Channel at this time of the year. I had been there and on the North Atlantic several times during the late fall and winter earlier on in my career and it was no picnic. My years on LNG ships traveling to equatorial climates cured me of winters in the North Atlantic.

I then looked through the pages of my old marine staple, the *Marine Log*. Perusing through the Employment section of the September 2004 issue, I came across an ad placed by "Maritime Recruiters" of Mercer Island, Wash. I had never heard of them before, but I noticed they were looking for a captain to command a high-speed Cat. I scratched my head, trying to think of what company operated HSC in that area and the only one I could think of was the Washington State Ferries system. It didn't make sense that they would be recruiting through this company since the WSF was unionized.

I called. A fellow answered the phone. "Hello," was all he said.

I thought I had dialed the wrong number.

I asked, "Is this Maritime Recruiters on Mercer Island?"

"Yes, it is."

"Okay, good. I'm calling about this captain's job on the high speed craft."

"Yes."

"Where is it located?" I asked.

"It's way out there in some place north of New York City, on Lake Ontario."

Oh. My heart quickly sank. "The one in Rochester," I said.

"Yeah, that's it," he said with a blip of enthusiasm.

I asked, "Did you know they shut down operations three weeks ago?"

"No kidding? I've been trying to get a hold of those people to find out what they want done with this ad, but they don't answer."

No kidding. Good luck, and good night.

In early November, CATS laid-off the remainder of its office staff. Only Cornel Martin, Bob Mansfield, and the two captains remained.

During the first week in November, WHAM-TV's Patrice Walsh reported, "Ferry terminal businesses are suffering. The businesses are sending a letter to Maplestar (their landlord) asking for a break in rent or advertising, or withholding their rent. Tommy Beaman (owner of California Rollin' Sushi Bar) just opened and says biz is lousy." They eventually did receive a break from their landlords.

I also visited the terminal in early November. It was a cold, partly sunny day.

It was a sad scene. Empty parking lots. Abbotts Ice Cream was closed. The gift shop had a few customers. Quiznos subs and the Bavarian Nuts shop did not. Cheeburger Cheeburger was open and was clean, bright, and cheery, but completely void of any customers. Five people were working, eager to serve a customer. As I looked in, the attractive waitresses were hungry for me to buy something.

The terminal was extremely quiet. There was no life.

Standing outside along the pier, I gazed at the grand ship through the tall, black wrought iron fence. She looked as though she was imprisoned. An innocent victim behind bars. She appeared small and diminutive. Almost nondescript as she hibernated, awaiting her fate.

Also, in early November, the Rochester community was embarrassed *internationally*—though no one here in Rochester knew it. World-renowned maritime magazine *Marine Log* held its annual "Marine Log Ferries 2004" event at Delray Beach, Fla., from November 8 through the 10th. It is billed as "North America's largest annual ferry conference and trade show." It was an embarrassment because no one was sent to represent CATS. The largest fast ferry to ever arrive in the United

181

States—to ever arrive in all of *North America!* —and it wasn't represented at the Fast Ferries conference.

It was, indeed, a sad scene.

Chapter 17
Swan Song

CATS founder Dominick DeLucia appeared on the cover of the *Democrat & Chronicle* on Thursday, November 10th. The headline read "The Breeze will sail again, says fast-ferry founder." This piece was a prelude to a bigger, follow-up story which was going to appear on Sunday. He admitted mistakes were made.

By this time, loyalty from former employees was at an all time low. Whatever sparks remained were extinguished on November 14th when the *Democrat & Chronicle* ran the huge, front page story in its Sunday edition entitled "Why the ferry foundered."

When reporter Rick Armon asked DeLucia the following question, "What are you most proud of?" DeLucia answered, "I'm extremely proud of the people that are sitting here with you now."

He was referring to three company officers: president Cornel Martin, chief financial officer Colby Amidon, and his attorney of the moment, Adam Michael.

He continued, "The people who have hung in there through thick and thin and could have been out there doing jobs that were maybe more low-profile and nondescript and certainly would have allowed them to sleep a lot easier at night and work a lot fewer hours. The management team at CATS has done a tremendous job, not only while the boat was operating but particularly the last two months to try to resurrect service."

"I'm also proud of the fact that the management team and founders created essentially an international border crossing in a post-9/11 era and I don't think that's inconsequential in any way."

"I am proud of the fact that the project has brought some significant profile to Rochester and we've proven with some hard work a substantial portion of the community can come together to get things done."

And so said DeLucia. All of it was true.

However, not a word was mentioned about his employees.

Not one word of gratitude was expressed about the sacrifices made by those who were on the front line every day, and the many who were still without work.

Wasn't he proud of the people who relocated from the four corners of the United States as well as those who were from the region? Those who came together and made this operation the success it was in the eyes of the public? Those many employees who still had not yet been paid?

183

The last spark of loyalty had been extinguished. Snuffed. Gone.

In December 2004, I said to a friend one night at Windjammers, "No one, not even Jimmy Hoffa himself, could have done as good a job at making the crew primed for union organization than the CATS management."

A year later, I'd be saying that about Rochester Ferry Company/Bay Ferries, but that story is still to come.

In the meantime, Captains John Williams and Danny Aycock wallowed aboard the *Breeze*, wondering about their fates.

They were going from pay period to pay period (which was every two weeks) wondering if they would receive their checks and if they'd still have health benefits for their young families. They were wondering if they'd have to pack up their families, load up a moving truck, and head back to Texas.

Despite the uncertainties in their lives, life wasn't treating them too bad compared to everyone else who had been employed by CATS. While other former employees had trouble collecting unemployment insurance, had no health coverage, faced eviction from apartments, wound up on public assistance, were late on their mortgage payments, or were simply grinding through their savings and 401Ks while job hunting, the two captains were the only two crew members still on the payroll at full salary. They each received $7,500 per month and retained their health benefits. Not bad pay for babysitting a dead ship.

This kind of "in limbo" sea duty is not what a seasoned and professional mariner signs up for and I understood the two captains' frustrations. Sailors always want to be going someplace. Anyplace. Moving. Being productive. Delivering cargoes. That's what we merchant mariners do.

Later on in November, they were given the positive assignment of writing up a Basic Safety Training curriculum for the next wave of new employees to be hired should the ship start up again in the spring. However, neither captain would ever see the *Spirit* run again for they would resign early on in 2005 and move on to different projects.

It is hard to understand why Dominick DeLucia and Brian Prince just didn't provide the cash themselves to save their own company after all of the years the pair put into it, and buy themselves the time to secure private funding from the business community.

On the Friday, November 19th—the Friday before Thanksgiving—Mayor Johnson and the city released its own plan to save—or takeover—the ferry.

Cornel Martin hit the roof in front of news crews and accused the city of stealing the company's business plan.

In an odd coincidence, CATS suddenly discontinued the rent payment on Bob Mansfield's apartment and took away his company rental car. Not to be deterred or intimidated by the loss of these creature comforts, the tech director immediately located a new, rent-free place to live: He packed his few belongings and moved onto the *Breeze* itself. The next day Mansfield became the first and sole resident of the coolest bachelor pad in the entire county.

He set up residence in the Fisher Price Kidz playroom and slept in the adjacent first aid room where there was located the only bed on the entire ship. In the first aid room there was also a sink, a wheelchair, and a closet full of aging Australian medical supplies. Probably a good thing. If the five years of ups and downs and stress over this operation ever blew out tough old Bob's heart, he'd at least be near an oxygen tank, a stretcher, and a bottle of aspirin until help arrived.

The ship's "Trucker's Shower" became his shower, and the popular Windjammer Restaurant across the street became his kitchen. He could be found there pretty much every night having dinner.

Bob Mansfield had designed a portion of the ship, he had overseen its construction for endless months in Australia, and he had watched his baby endure both physical and financial beatings. Now he was a permanent fixture onboard and didn't have to drive to work every day.

There's no place like home!

On Monday, November 22, WROC-TV Channel 8 reported: "The city is offering CATS about $42 million for the boat and other fixed assets. The ferry was a $57.5 million venture. The mayor says CATS founders Dominick DeLucia and Brian Prince, estimated to have invested $5 million in the ferry, want their money back."

"They want money. They want to try to minimize their losses. That's what this is all about. Nothing else," Mayor Johnson said. "There are going to be a lot of people without any money, but they want theirs. I think once the public understands that, they will have little sympathy for their position."

"CATS, through their confrontational style and selfish behavior will endanger the ferry deal for this community," the mayor said.

185

Sparks were flying.

The following Monday, 10 days after Cornel Martin's angry appearance on television, Dominick DeLucia began doing the public relations and press conferences by himself.

Alone.

It was sad to watch. DeLucia had spent the last five years of his life pursuing this tremendous, fantastic, and grand dream. His company had been basically neutralized, and he was alone in not realizing it.

Standing in front of TV cameras, he defended his company.

The CAT was left holding the bag.

December 8th brought another bad story. WHEC News10 had obtained a list of the creditors. $2.7 million were owed to a whopping 192 creditors.

The next day, the Attorney General's Office was offering a phone number for people who needed help getting their money back with their unused "Passport to Savings" tickets. This program had offered a miniscule discount on a one-way ticket when paid in advance.

More soap appeared in the *Democrat & Chronicle* on December 16th. Reporter Rick Armon had finally received word about Bob Mansfield's new bachelor digs. The edition presented this headline in the local section:

Idle ferry is one man's spacious apartment

On that day, I wrote this note to a friend in Australia about Bob's story:

"I don't know if this story was by design or not—Bob sometimes seems to know how to work the press, and is appearing on TV with greater frequency lately—but the timing couldn't be better. The day before CATS is supposed to come up with $30 million to save themselves in court, this story shows they can't even afford rent on an apartment!"

Friday, December 17th, 2004 was a crucial day in federal court in the life of Canadian American Transportation Systems. The deadline for it to produce $30 million had arrived.

December 17th was also the day of the Megamillions 11-state drawing. On this particular day, the prize amount was worth a hefty $25 million. Unfortunately, the CATS founders had not purchased any tickets and were not the winners.

"CATS is out! The City is in!" declared WHAM-TV13 anchor Don Alhart during the top of his local 6 o'clock newscast.

The next morning, the headline at the top of the *Democrat & Chronicle* front page said, "Australia offers city $40 million to buy ferry." The story also reported that a federal magistrate judge had decided "that the ship would be auctioned off on February 28th to repay creditors."

It was ironic. EFIC, the people that forced the foreclosure on the *Spirit*, were now, suddenly, the very people who were providing the city of Rochester with a $40 million dollar, low interest loan. This was clearly a no vote for CATS.

In the press, CATS attorney Adam Michael now blamed the city for interfering with CATS's efforts to resume service.

There is a simple lesson here: People who don't pay their bills lose their property.

It was the beginning of the end for CATS. As the company suffered this lethal, humiliating blow, the city prepared to evict it from its ferry terminal offices.

That night I took my wife to Charlotte to treat her to the world famous "Windjammer Burger" which I had been raving about to her for the last six months.

Entering the 'jammers, I experienced a sense of awe and magic. The bar had been transformed into a sort of Christmas heaven, for there was a dense sea of twinkly, colorful Christmas lights and decorations suspended from the ceiling.

The foosball game with the ATM standing next to it was unused. Across from the ATM, the pool table was also unused. The three booths with TV sets recessed into the wall were occupied, so my wife and I found a couple of stools at the bar and had our dinner there. As we ate our burgers, we watched an eternally well-preserved Vanna White flip over the giant numbers on the game show *Wheel of Fortune.*

I half-expected there would be a huge turnout of former CATS employees to celebrate the day's turn of events, much as there had been for the lay-off party back on September 7th. Sadly, less than a handful of former employees were present. One who was there was Bob Mansfield, the man with a ferry for a home and the *Spirit of Ontario 1's* sole occupant. He wasn't there to celebrate. He was simply there to eat.

Afterward, I walked my wife across the street to the ferry terminal. Inside, I showed her the warm and attractive Christmas decorations that adorned new walls and the Christmas tree near the departure hall.

Even the lonely *Spirit of Ontario 1* possessed a spark of Christmas spirit. She had been decorated, too. Members of her security crew had carefully strung white, miniature Christmas lights along the insides of her wheelhouse windows. Despite the cold she endured out there in the Genesee River, not having a clue about her fate, she looked warm and peaceful.

It was a dry, cold night and the roads were clear.

A light breeze blew across Lake Avenue.

CATS received *more* bad news the following week. On Monday, December 20th, it received notice that paperwork for its eviction from the ferry terminal was being filed in City Court by the city of Rochester.

Also on that day, the maritime consultant TranSystems (which had been hired by the city for $30 thousand) released its "City of Rochester Ferry Business Plan Review." Overall, it found nothing wrong with the city's plan to operate a ferry service which projected 385,705 passengers and 59,200 vehicles. These numbers were based on the annualized expressed demand from the CATS experience, and the general border crossing monthly seasonality adjustments.

In the TranSystems review's Executive Summary, it said, "Revenues as stated in the City Business Plan seem reasonable and conservative." It also stated "the service could see positive cash flows after debt service for the majority of the years of operation. At all times the year end reserve is positive and in Year 10 the projected reserve is over $9.5 million."

The next evening the City Council voted 8 to 1 in favor of accepting Mayor Johnson's plan to create a nonprofit corporation to try to bid on the ferry, and then to manage it. Later, it would be decided to form an LLC instead.

The world received bad news on Christmas Day. Shortly before 8 p.m. EST, while Americans were celebrating with their families and children played with gifts left by Santa, a magnitude 9.0 earthquake occurred off the coast of Sumatra and triggered a monstrous tsunami in the Indian Ocean. In a few short hours, over 150,000 lives were lost. The victims were from 50 countries. Tsunami relief efforts took center stage.

Aceh Province was the hardest hit area. Having spent 19 years hauling liquefied natural gas (LNG) out of eastern Aceh Province, I wondered if many of my old acquaintances had survived. I did hear from my former employer that one of the LNG carriers I had been second mate aboard in the 1990's just happened to be entering the Port of Arun near Lhokseumawe when the earthquake struck. He wrote,

"The *LNG Aquarius* was entering through the breakwater when the quake hit. They thought they had hit an obstruction or touched bottom which is extremely difficult to do at Arun, as you recall. They got inside and had all spring lines out with the first two head lines on the hooks when the tsunami came rushing. The Port lost about 10 feet of water rather quickly and whirlpools started inside with crazy currents all over the place. With three tugs alongside and only six lines out, the vessel was able to hang in there. The next scene saw the water rise about six meters and then the fun began. The ups and downs lasted about an hour and a half with the water going up and down about four times. The vessel was shifted out to anchor until the next morning, when they returned to the berth and completed cargo loading in just under 24 hours."

"The harbor saw the breakwaters just about submerged but no long term damage occurred. The scene downtown was a bit more dramatic, as well as deadly, but not as bad as the extreme western part of Sumatra. Looks like about sixty to eighty thousand killed but still counting. Figure we were very lucky since if the ship was either in the breakwater when the tsunami hit or alongside with all pumps going, it could have been a disaster with the Port closed for God only knows how long."

The high-speed catamaran *Westpac Express* with Captain Ken Kujala was dispatched on a 2,300 mile journey to Thailand with aid. Kujala had been our type rating examiner earlier in the year. The ship and her crew transported communications gear from Okinawa to Chuksamet, Thailand to support tsunami disaster relief efforts in the Southeast Asian region.

January 23rd, 2005 was "the day that television died" for it was the day that *Tonight Show* host Johnny Carson passed on.

The next day, former CATS COO Tony White returned to Rochester from Australia. The world-renowned fast ferry expert had been

189

personally asked by Mayor Johnson to come and prepare an extensive ferry start-up plan.

With Johnny leaving and Tony coming, the omenists could not determine if the signs were good or bad.

February 3rd, 2005 was my birthday. It was a sunny, snowy day with temperatures in the 30s. On the 6 o'clock news it was announced that an agreement was reached between CATS and the city. CATS was stepping aside and would not interfere with the upcoming foreclosure auction.

Chapter 18
Yes, We Have No Ferries...

Auction Eve.

On Sunday, February 27, 2005, RNews anchors were eagerly calling it "Auction Eve" on their daylong broadcasts. There was immense anticipation throughout the city and the surrounding region over the fate of the *Spirit of Ontario 1*.

Auction Eve was also the eve of the final episode of *The Bachelorette*. The community was as much abuzz about the impending outcome of the ABC reality show as they were the Bahamian-flagged ship sitting in Charlotte. A handsome, young 29-year-old man by the name of Jerry Ferris, a former native of nearby Brockport, was among the final two suitors seeking the hand of a lovely enchantress by the name of Jen Schefft.

Auction Eve was the night of the Oscars. Clint Eastwood had just cleaned up at the annual Hollywood awards event with his euthanasia film *Million Dollar Baby*.

Auction Day. Monday morning, February 28, 2005 was the big day, and a cold one. The temperature was in the low thirties. The sky was thinly overcast and the sun was barely visible. A Nor'easter was fast approaching. A complex low pressure winter system was moving north along the East Coast and spreading a wintry mix. Significant snowfall in the region was expected. The weather service had, for some inexplicable reason, dubbed the storm "Grapefruit." Grapefruit would arrive in Rochester by noon.

Patches of black ice lurked on the highways for those who ventured out to attend the public auction. The auction was to begin at 10 o'clock at the federal courthouse which is located in the Kenneth B. Keating Building at 100 State Street in Rochester. The courthouse is situated in close quarters to both the City Hall, just a block to the west, and the CATS offices, only four blocks to the north. Behind the courthouse and beyond what is known as the Genesee Crossroads Park flows the Genesee River. Sitting in the river to the north was the object of this day's attention. Seven miles away, the *Spirit of Ontario 1* awaited word of its new owner.

On Rochester's WHAM radio, U.S. Marshal Peter Lawrence was being interviewed by the popular morning talk show hosts Beth Adams and Chet Walker. He said he hoped he did not make any mistakes at the

191

auction, presumably referring to this being his first time ever conducting one. After all, it wasn't every century that a ship auction was held in Rochester. There would be only four bidders in the courtroom. The federal court had previously announced it was opening the ferry auction bid at $22.5 million.

In addition to the *Breeze* being auctioned, this was the day the $10 million winner of the Publishers Clearing House drawing would be announced. The lucky person would also receive a $39,000 Ford Thunderbird. The odds of an entrant winning the drawing would be 1 out of 330,000,000. The odds of the City winning would be one out of four.

From the outside, the federal courthouse in downtown Rochester resembles a small, but cheerful prison. A white, modern six-story building, its remarkably narrow windows resemble the slatted vent ducts on a computer and give the upper floors a jail cell-like appearance.

Outside of the courthouse, four local news "live" trucks were lined up nearly bumper-to-bumper, their "up periscope" telescoping satellite dishes standing as tall as the courthouse's four-story flag pole. Local channels 8, 10, 13, and RNews were all visibly represented. The flag was waving in the wind pointing north in the direction of Charlotte.

The row of buildings directly across from the federal courthouse were sparse in their business offerings. Many were vacant and seeking new tenants. Among the few businesses that existed was an adult book store called the "State Street Book Mart." The neon sign in its window glowed "Open." In fact, the neon sign never stopped glowing as the adult book store was open 24/7 according to the sign above its entrance. This same sign boasted "Adult Books, Magazines, Video Tapes, 8mm Film, and 25 Cent Video Arcade."

Up the street a short distance there was a pizza restaurant and the JS Pawn Shop where, according to the sign that overhung the sidewalk, they sold "Cigars and Guns." Further up the street and looming in the background stood the landmark Kodak office tower. It has been there since 1914.

The peregrine falcons residing on the top of the landmark building kept a watchful eye on the proceedings below. One circled above and contemplated landing on one of the extended news truck satellite dishes. The commotion on the ground kept him away.

Judge Jonathan Feldman's courtroom was located on the second floor. Court Room #1 had veneer-wood paneling on the walls. A wall clock over a side door was missing a minute hand. The courtroom's seating was sectioned off into thirds.

The largest section was closest to the door where my wife and I entered. This is where the interested public sat. It was packed. The local journalists sat in the front row left with notepads at the ready. No cameras or microphones were allowed, not even for the media. Everyone entering the building had to check their camera phones with security at the front door.

The middle was reserved for "Interested Parties." The City Council members, attorneys, Congresswoman Louise Slaughter, St. Lawrence Seaway Pilots' Association pilot Larry Hickey, Glenn Gardner, and various dignitaries were seated there.

The smallest section was close to the judge and to the right. Here the jury would normally sit; however, since this was an auction, this area was reserved for the representatives of the bidders.

I noticed a small and scattered contingent of my former CATS colleagues: deck officer Ian Sherwood, bartenders Beverly Rouse and Mike Miller, purser Chris Moore, and terminal duty officer Mark Cannon. Technical Director Bob Mansfield managed to get a seat in the front row right.

Tony White entered and sat down next to my wife and me. Since arriving in the Flower City in January, he had just completed an intense four weeks working on the city's ferry start-up plan.

Dominick DeLucia and his attorney Adam Michael then entered. The two walked forward and sat down in the Interested Parties section. I turned to Tony and asked, "Why is Dominick sitting there?"

No doubt, if Tony White had a newspaper in his hand, he would have baffed me over the head with it. In his usual candor, he dryly answered, "He's the owner."

I had completely forgotten! Ever since December 17th when CATS had failed to come up with the $30 million in court, and with the ship still impounded, I had summarily dismissed his ownership of the *Spirit*.

It seemed time to start and I glanced at the clock on the wall. Since the minute hand was missing, a backup clock was mounted below it above the Exit sign which said a little after 10. A glance at my watch confirmed it.

A short time later another person entered the courtroom. My friend Tom Hope appeared and was escorted to a seat in the "Interested

Parties" section. Tom is a noted writer and television pioneer. I asked him later how he happened to get a seat in that section. The cheerful 80-year-old told me they let him sit with the important people because those were the only seats remaining.

Finally, the room was completely filled. There was standing room only. Observers stood in the door and beyond into the voluminous hallway.

The event of the year finally began at 10:08 when Judge Feldman entered the room. Everyone stood up and silenced themselves as Feldman, a thin man in his 50s with a full head of hair and a long face, moved quickly behind the massive wooden bench.

The court clerk announced, "Judge Feldman presiding. You may be seated." As the observers sat down, she then read the case's name: "Amerada Hess Corporation versus Canadian American Transportation Systems, LLC, and others. 04cv6473Fe."

"Good morning, everyone," Judge Feldman began. "Welcome to federal court. We are here this morning to conduct a public auction for the vessel known as the *Spirit of Ontario*. The vessel was arrested by the United States Marshal on September 29th, 2004. Today's auction has been publicly advertised. Those interested in bidding on the vessel were granted access to inspect the vessel. Four parties have applied to bid and all four have met the bidding requirements established by this court. As I state your name, please identify for the United States Marshal your bidding identification party who will be responsible for the bidding, and please raise the paddle with the parties' name on it. Only one individual member from each bidding team will be allowed to bid on behalf of that team."

The bidders were assigned paddles, each numbered one through four. The paddles themselves were white foam core cutouts, cleverly in the shape of the *Breeze* and mounted on a stick. The four parties then identified the person bidding on their behalf.

Judge Feldman said he and the marshal had met with representatives of the authorized bidders last week and agreed to set the minimum bid increments at $10,000.

He continued: "It was also agreed that any bidding party may make a request for a short interruption of the bidding process—and I emphasize the word 'short'—and request a caucus among their bidding team. Finally, I would request that the high bidder assume the responsibility to file a motion to confirm the sale after the auction has been completed. That motion should be filed in federal court on notice to all parties."

Judge Feldman then asked, "Marshal Lawrence, are we ready to begin the public auction?"

"Yes sir, we are," Lawrence answered.

"You may conduct the auction," the judge said, turning the proceedings over to him.

The time was 10:11.

One baby in the back of the room was cooing and making small noises.

The U.S. Marshal took center stage standing in front of a podium located in front of the bidders section. He was a stocky, balding fellow with silver-rimmed glasses. He began by saying, "I apologize for any redundancy that I may have, but, we're going to get started and we're going to take this thing slow."

As Marshal Lawrence had promised on the Beth and Chet show that morning, he did not want to make a mistake.

"Good morning, ladies and gentlemen. Welcome to the Kenneth Keating Federal Building. My name is Peter Lawrence and I am the United States Marshal for the Western District of New York. Obviously, behind me is federal Magistrate Judge Jonathan W. Feldman, who has ordered and will preside over this auction. Also present today is Congresswoman Louise Slaughter and Mayor William Johnson. Present to bid on the vessel known currently as the *Spirit of Ontario* are representatives of the City of Rochester, identified as bidder number one. Representatives of the Export Finance and Insurance Corporation, identified as bidders number two. Representatives of MTU Friedrichshafen, bidders number three; and ABN-AMRO, bidder number four."

The bidders would be recognized by their paddles and titles.

After several lengthy opening obligatory remarks regarding the auction proceedings and payment, Marshal Lawrence began.

"Having been authorized by the court to commence the public auction for the *Spirit of Ontario,* I will now commence the auction. By order of the court, the minimum bid price for the vessel is $22.5 million. Do I have an opening bid?"

The time was 10:15 a.m.

EFIC, bidder number two, raised its ferry-shaped paddle.

The representative said, "The EFIC and ABN first mortgage credit bid is $29,635,400 US dollars."

With everyone understanding the bidding would be in $10,000 increments, I didn't understand how the $5,400 slipped in there.

"The bid is $29,635,400 dollars. Do I have a second bid?

There was dead silence in the room.

Tic...tic...tic..

After an interminably long, long, long three second pause, Marshal Lawrence repeated the question. "Do I have a second bid?"

When there was no other bid voiced, he continued, "The bid is twenty-nine million, six-hundred thirty-five thousand dollars, four-hundred. Going once..."

Everyone was on the edge of their seat.

Tic...tic...

Why wasn't the city bidding?

Suddenly, paddle number one was raised. Marshal Lawrence stopped and instantly recognized the bidder.

"Bidder number one, city of Rochester."

There was a collective moment of relief for everyone in the room.

A representative said, "The city of Rochester bids $32 million."

"The bid by the city of Rochester is $32 million. Do I have a higher bid?"

Dead silence.

"Thirty-two million dollars is going once...thirty-two million dollars is going twice... The city of Rochester is the highest bidder at thirty-two million dollars. Congratulations."

The room erupted into WOOs! CHEERS! and VIGOROUS APPLAUSE! They represented a collective sigh of relief in the wake of the cliffhanger moment when it appeared that EFIC was about to win the ship.

The time was 10:16 a.m. It was all over in just one minute.

Marshal Lawrence calmed the room down and then turned to the judge. "Judge Feldman, by the authority given to me by the court, I proclaim bidder number one, the city of Rochester, to be the high bidder for the vessel Spirit of Ontario. Judge..."

Judge Feldman took it from there.

"Thank you, Marshal. Just a few closing comments. Three and a half weeks ago many of us were in this courtroom placing a settlement on the record that resolved all of the differences between the parties. I said then that the only thing left in this case was to conduct a full, fair, and competitive auction. And, subject to the final confirmation, that auction has just taken place. I think it's important to note the fact that the city has won the auction allows the full benefits of the mediated settlement now to take effect. All ticket holders and gift certificate holders will now have the benefit of their purchase. The transition from CATS to the city will now be a smooth one under the terms of the mediated settlement agreement."

"And, finally, perhaps the most unique aspect of the mediated settlement: a fund of $700,000 will be created for the benefit of the unsecured creditors. Speaking as a lifelong Rochesterian, I share the views of many in our community. This case has generated enormous public interest and attention. And for good reason: that vessel, the *Spirit of Ontario*, is a one-of-a-kind vessel. Of course, reading the future is impossible and like many other major business operations, there are both risks and rewards to be encountered. But I do think it's important to say in this forum—and I will say it, and I will say it now: that in the many months that we have been working on this case and the many hours and meetings that we've had, we have had many disagreements among the parties, but one thing no one ever disagreed with, and that was that this vessel should be given a fair opportunity to succeed in this community. That was always the position of CATS, that was always the position of EFIC, that was always the position of ABN AMRO, that was always the position of MTU, and that was always the position of the City of Rochester."

"So, in a very real way, there are at least two winners at this auction: one is the city of Rochester and the community. But the second is the vessel itself, the *Spirit of Ontario*, which is now going to be given the opportunity to succeed in the community and for the community for which she was built."

Judge Feldman then looked over at a proud and beaming Mayor Bill Johnson and said, "Mayor Johnson, I don't want to rain on your parade, but you can't have the keys and take it out for a spin until we get the rest of the money."

The room filled with laughter.

Feldman continued. "And with that, I declare this public auction to be closed."

Bang! With one light blow of his gavel and another round of applause from all present, it was all over. The time was 10:19.

The *Spirit of Ontario 1* had been saved.

The easy part was over.

Later that day, a woman in Ohio won the $10 million and the $39,000 Ford Thunderbird from the Publishers Clearing House drawing while the City of Rochester won a fast ferry at a cost of $32 million dollars at the federal auction. The U.S. Marshals Service earned $50,000 for their role in the auction. Most everyone did well.

As the Nor'easter approached, a gentle lake wind blew across the decks of the still idle *Spirit of Ontario 1* as she patiently sat in the Genesee River. The expected snow began to fall. Weeks of snow lay ahead. CATS was now gone with the breeze.

Dominick DeLucia left the courtroom with visible tears in his eyes, according to one witness.

That night, former Brockport native Jerry Ferris also had tears in his eyes. A finalist in *The Bachelorette*, he was dumped by the lovely enchantress, Miss Schefft.

It was a bad day for both men.

Mayor Bill Johnson and the city of Rochester, on the other hand, were euphoric and ready to celebrate!

At the auction, Judge Feldman had said, "Perhaps the most unique aspect of the mediated settlement: a fund of $700,000 will be created for the benefit of the unsecured creditors."

The city of Rochester had agreed, if it were the successful bidder at auction, to set up a Creditors' Fund of $700,000 specifically in recognition of the fact that many of the creditors who did business with CATS were individuals and small companies. The establishment of a fund would help to offset the losses these businesses and individuals would suffer as a result of the forced sale for the vessel and CATS's insolvency.

The maritime liens, however, were to be paid first from the proceeds of the auction. As reporter Rick Armon wrote in the *Democrat & Chronicle* on February 12, 2005,

> More than $2 million worth of maritime liens have been filed in federal court against the *Spirit of Ontario*. The maritime liens—legal claims against a ship for nonpayment of goods or services supplied to the vessel—are paid first from the proceeds of the auction, according to maritime lawyers, meaning the amount can affect who ultimately recovers their money and who doesn't. For example, if the ship sells for $30 million and there are $2 million worth of valid maritime claims, there's

198

only $28 million left to be distributed to mortgage holders
and other creditors.

The liens and the amounts are: Amerada Hess Corp.,
$372,868; AP Safety and Security Corp., $7,971; Plant
Designs Inc., $16,481; St. Lawrence Seaway Pilots
Association, $25,836; Great Lakes Pilotage Authority,
$43,204; former ferry worker Asger Manoe, $6,283; MTU
Friedrichshafen GmbH, $338,268; former worker Richard
Czachur, $190,000; former worker Robert Mansfield,
$669,048; AAA Welding-Fabrication Inc., $20,557;
Netsmartz LLC, $99,953; California Maritime Academy,
$45,537; Hornblower Marine Services, $99,882; and
Horseshoe Hospitality, $105,670.

Germanischer Lloyd Inc. (GL) also filed a maritime lien against
the ship. The company provided inspection and documentation services
and claimed it was owed $8,198.

Even David's Gourmet Coffee of Rochester wasn't fully paid and
had to file a claim with the state Attorney General's Office. Well, at least
they got their Bunn Pour-o-Matics back.

As one former CATS employee remarked, "They didn't have to
take it up the Bunn like everyone else."

Winning a ship at auction is one thing. Operating it is another.
The next big questions facing the city and its citizens were: Can the city be
a marine operator, and who will manage it?

There were two operating bids on the table: AWARM (Anthony
White and Robert Mansfield) and Canadian operator Bay Ferries.

Many of the former employees assumed White and Mansfield
would be hired to manage it. After all, both men had extensive experience
with the *Spirit* and Mayor Johnson had personally invited Tony White to
return to Rochester and create a jump-start plan for placing the vessel back
in service. As the days after the auction dragged on with still no word
from the city about who was going to manage the ferry, suddenly doubts
began to swirl that the White-Mansfield proposal was not a slam-dunk.

Mansfield was getting frustrated. By HSC code, high-speed craft
are required to come out of the water annually for hull inspection. A
reservation had not been booked at either of the two suitable shipyards on
Lake Ontario and no one in the city would give him the authority to do so.

With the St. Lawrence Seaway about to reopen in March, the shipyards were quickly filling up their calendars. Mansfield had been staying in touch with the yard in Hamilton, Ontario. Tentative dates were discussed, but one date after another came and went. His hands were tied.

Finally, on Tuesday, March 8, 2005 the seemingly long wait was over. Bay Ferries of Prince Edward Island was selected.

Everyone was shocked, including Mansfield.

As he would say later, "The decision by the city to give the management of the vessel to Bay Ferries was among the lows in my career and I wanted to scream at them for the biggest mistake they were making."

Tony White had been reserved in his prediction of the outcome. When he and Mansfield weren't selected immediately following the auction, he sensed their proposal might not be a sure thing.

Among the reasons given by the city for this selection were that Bay Ferries had 40 years of experience in the ferry business, including their operation of the seasonal high-speed catamaran "The Cat" between Yarmouth, Nova Scotia, and Bar Harbor, Maine. Bay Ferries already had a marketing infrastructure in place, as well.

Another reason was that Tony White was only willing to commit himself to the project for one year due to other pending commitments. Given his experience in the fast ferry world, White really felt that one year was all the time the project would need his services, and, by the end of a year, the service would be in good shape and he would pass the reins onto someone else. Mansfield would remain with the project after White's departure thus ensuring a smooth transition with everyone concerned.

Friday of that week brought a 10 a.m. news conference with Mayor Johnson, city officials, and the introduction of Mark MacDonald, president of Bay Ferries. RNews carried 30 minutes of the press conference live from City Hall.

His job done, Tony White bade farewell to all of his friends and Mayor Johnson and left Rochester on March 29th. He was bound for Sydney and then home.

Bob Mansfield left soon after White.

While the flags at the Rochester ferry terminal flew at half-mast in deference to the passing of Pope John Paul II who had been promoted to glory only the day before, a huge, rip-roaring, "Good-bye Bob Party" was held across the street at Windjammers. The 'Jammers—forever Bob's kitchen—was packed with dozens of his former friends, employees, and colleagues. They all came to wish him well.

Two days later, the bald-headed Englishman walked down the *Spirit of Ontario 1's* short gangway for the very last time and flew away on April 5th. With the *Spirit's* sole resident gone, the area's most expensive apartment was now available for occupancy once again. It was the end of an era in the life of the *Breeze*.

A new and hopeful chapter in the saga of the *Spirit of Ontario 1* was about to begin.

The Epilogue That Wasn't

After the city of Rochester won the *Spirit of Ontario 1* at the jubilant public auction in federal court, it hired Canadian operator Bay Ferries to manage the vessel. In May 2005, the *Spirit* went to the shipyard for a shave and a haircut, an inspection, had a few minor repairs done to it, and then it went into service on Thursday, June 30th, 2005.

During the summer of 2005, the *Spirit* had a tremendously successful season, carrying more than its targeted number of passengers and showing all of the doomsayers and omenists—once and for all! —that the good ship could fulfill its myriad of promises to the community and the surrounding region.

If only the naysayers could see us now.

Everyone slept well and the grand ship and her proud crew and owners lived happily ever after!

~ The End ~

Well...not exactly.

That was the original epilogue I had written shortly after I was rehired in May 2005. I had wanted to conclude the story with the ferry's auction and then that would be it. Short and sweet, full of hope and optimism.

After all, what could go wrong?

As things eventually turned out, this was the Epilogue that wasn't. There would be no happy ending to this tale; at least, not for the city of Rochester and its taxpaying residents, nor for the 100 plus shipboard and shoreside employees.

The city of Rochester created the Rochester Ferry Company, LLC to operate the *Spirit of Ontario 1.* On January 20th, the City Council established an 11-member ferry board consisting of seven elected city officials or administrators and two "at-large" members who were non-elected, high-profile, business-savvy people from within the community. In addition, the mayor and council president would serve on the board as *ex officio* members.

As reported in the *Democrat & Chronicle* on January 21st, "the 11-person board, whose members aren't paid, includes two at-large community members: Charles C. Barrentine, director of Corporate Kodak Operating System, and Karen Noble Hanson, the finance director at the Episcopal Diocese of Rochester. The others are city officials: City Council President Lois Giess, Mayor William A. Johnson Jr., Budget Director William Ansbrow, Deputy Mayor Jeffrey Carlson, Environmental Services Commissioner Edward Doherty, Parks Commissioner Loretta Scott, and council members Benjamin Douglas, Wade Norwood, and Gladys Santiago."

All of the former CATS employees who wanted to return to work on the *Spirit* had to reapply with Bay Ferries and go through their interview process. I applied for a captain's position.

My interview with Bay Ferries was on April 13th. Present at the interview were Human Resources Manager Glenn Gardner (Rochester Ferry Company had rehired him), Bay Ferries Chief Engineer Gary Smith, and Vice President/Company Safety Officer Don Cormier. Cormier was a large, gentle man who bore a slight resemblance to the actor James Gandolfini. He was congenial, soft-spoken, and direct. The local press would later call him a gentle giant. He asked me many questions about my experience and my familiarization with the ISM code, or the "International Management Code for the Safe Operation of Ships and for Pollution Prevention."

He then asked me how I felt about working a 15-hour day. The U.S. Coast Guard was allowing a reduction to two crews in 2005. During the previous CATS year, there had been three crews: Two on-duty crews with one off-duty. The two on-duty crews would change out with each trip.

In 2005, there were several conditions the USCG attached to this two-crew allowance, the biggest one being that no crew member shall work more than 12 hours per day. This is not only a USCG requirement, but it is an international one.

I replied I did not have a problem as long as the rest period rules were truly going to be followed. With some companies, a wink and a nod replace observance of these rules. I was not about to be a front man for that type of operation nor did I want to see my crew fatigued.

I made my position quite clear to all present in the room by saying, "When it comes to the documenting of crew work hours, I'm not going to lie for you."

203

Cormier quickly assured me that Bay Ferries had every intention of following the rest rules.

On May 10th, I was hired as chief officer. Although it wasn't written into the job offer letter, Cormier told me that I was to be one of three masters-in-training candidates. In addition to myself, the company had hired Paul Greubel and Gerry Cooper to be chief mates/masters-in-training. Greubel was a former LNG vessel chief mate/relief captain (and a colleague) and Cooper was a retired Panama Canal pilot. Greubel would commute every week from his home in Connecticut, while Cooper would fly up from his home in Florida. Unlimited masters licenses were hard to find in Rochester.

Bound for the Port Weller shipyard located near the southwestern side of Lake Ontario, the *Spirit* left Rochester on Monday morning May 16th at 2 a.m. The ship was scheduled to be there for one week. As per HSC code, the *Spirit* was required to be taken out of the water annually for hull inspection. Among the work planned was power-washing the Ultrasleek coating on both hulls, the repair of the bent port bow tip, and the installation of the MES (marine evacuation system) units. They had been removed for inspection weeks earlier.

Danish captain Hädh had been hired to be master/training master. As I had written earlier in this book, Hädh had been a relief master for the month of July during the 2004 season. He had worked previously for Royal Caribbean Cruise Lines where he had been a deck and safety officer, and for Condor Ferries where he served as chief officer. In June, he would be joined on the *Spirit* by his Danish chief engineer/business partner. The two men would occupy the top two positions on the fast ferry.

The crew consisted of several crew members who had been rehired from the previous season as well as a few people brought in from Bay Ferries.

Engine builder MTU had been conducting engine upgrades and completed work on two of the four engines prior to the departure. With the ship bound for shipyard, the work on the remaining two engines ceased and the ship traveled west on just two engines.

We arrived at the Welland Canal before 7 a.m.

Port Weller Shipyard is on the Welland Canal. To go to the shipyard, the *Spirit* would have to transit only the first lock of the Canal. Due to the damage caused during the *Spirit's* delivery transit of the St.

Lawrence Seaway locks in April 2004, we focused on the fendering. As with the Seaway locks, the Welland Canal locks were 80 feet wide. With the *Spirit's* 78-foot width, there would be only 12 inches of clearance on either side.

Fendering materials were made. A dozen 4x4s were cut and hung down the sides of the ferry and off the bridge wings. About a dozen inflatable yacht fenders were purchased from West Marine and also hung over the side.

At each corner of the ship, inflatable fenders were attached to long pieces of line and manned. As the ship moved into the lock, crewmen would swing the fenders and cushion the bows and sterns when they appeared to be getting too close to the concrete lock wall.

Captain Hädh did an able job of driving the ferry into the tight No. 1 lock, especially with only two engines. There were no holes or dents like the last time the vessel went through Seaway locks, only a couple of minor scrapes on the forward MES doors and bridge wings.

Once through the lock there was a brief meeting with the shipyard personnel and then the *Spirit* was guided into the Port Weller drydock. It was just as narrow as the canal lock and the ship had to be delicately moved to avoid damage. Once in, the huge gates closed and the pumping out operation began. If all went well, we would be doing a hull inspection in the morning.

It was a little before 5 p.m. when the crew knocked off for the day. The ship would require a fire watch throughout the night. I volunteered for the first shift and the rest of the crew left for the hotel near St. Catherines. I was the only one onboard at the time.

Seated in a chair with castors in the ship's office, my chair suddenly flew aft and then shot across the room. The ship had dropped out beneath me. The *Spirit* had slipped off the blocks while the water was being pumped out. Though she bobbed around like a cork in a bathtub, she never banged against the bottom or the concrete sides. After a few long seconds, she settled down.

The departing crew had not passed through the front gate yet and were informed of the incident. They quickly returned to the ship and we began an internal hull inspection. Climbing up and down all of the void spaces and checking the engine and jet rooms, we were all relieved to find there was no damage.

The slippage, however, would cost two days. The drydock would have to be flooded, the ship would have to be removed, and then shipyard workers would have to reset the blocks. It would take the entire next day to do this.

Tuesday, May 17th there was a 10-15 knot cross wind and it was extremely difficult getting our lady out of the drydock. The ship's engines had been secured and we were a dead ship. Two tugs assisted. One tug pulled gingerly on the stern while the other stood by. The shipyard's winches on both sides of the drydock inched her backwards. Periodically, the winch cable leads would have to be changed to provide the proper leverage and control over the moving vessel. It was touch and go for awhile as the stern came within inches of scraping against the drydock's concrete walls. Though the *Spirit* had been built to fit through the Seaway's locks and Great Lakes' drydocks, they were not built for her soft aluminum skin. We were fortunate on that day and there was no concrete grinding into aluminum. Once clear of the drydock, both tugs gently pushed us over to a nearby mooring wharf for the night.

The drydock was pumped out, the blocks were reset, and it was flooded again. A lot of water had been moved in and out of the drydock since we arrived on Monday.

On Wednesday, May 18th, the *Spirit* returned to the drydock without a problem. This time the operation was successful. It was pumped out and the *Spirit* settled gently on her blocks. The work could now begin.

The first thing we did was perform an external hull inspection. Wearing rubber boots and carrying our digital cameras, Captain Hädh, several other officers, and I walked through the thin layer of mud that coated the drydock. As we surveyed the after part of the hull where the slippage had occurred, the only damage we found was a three-foot scratch in the hull coating on the port side.

However, as we walked around the ship examining the hull, it was discovered that one of the waterjet propulsion nozzles, or "bucket" as it is commonly called, on the starboard side was seriously bent. The worn paint and dull-looking scrapes were not fresh, an indication that this damage had occurred a long time ago.

Later on, the training master would tell officers and marine crew as well as company officials that the damage had occurred during the 2004 season. Most likely the ferry was backing up in Toronto when it had banged the bucket into the concrete pier.

A report on the incident had never been filed, most likely because it wasn't thought to be serious at the time. The nozzle had continued to function throughout the 2004 season. However, the bucket's deflection plate which reroutes the water stream forward and creates her astern thrust was not closing all of the way because of the damage. A bucket not "fully open" would impede the vessel's forward motion.

Between the damaged bucket and the bent-over port bow tip, a small amount of resistance through the water had existed throughout most of the 2004 season. There is no estimation how much additional fuel oil was consumed in 2004 due to these problems.

The good news was that the one-ton part was repairable. The bad news was the only shop approved by the classification society to fix this part at that time was located in Scotland. The bucket repair would eventually cost tens of thousands of dollars and two additional weeks of shipyard time while the part was removed, crated, and air-freighted to the U.K. The delay would also cost the city of Rochester two weeks of much-needed passenger revenue.

As Rob Hamilton, the type rating trainer and former chief engineer aboard the Bay Ferries Yarmouth-Bar Harbor ferry, told me in reflection one day after the discovery of the bent bucket, "Fast ferries...they're heartbreakers."

Some reporters in the local media blamed the additional two weeks on damage caused by the ship slipping off the blocks, though they never explained what this "damage" actually was. For its part in the misinformation, Rochester Ferry Company/Bay Ferries never explained the damaged bucket discovery to the press, and so in their eternal effort to connect the dots, the press made the assumption that the damage had been caused by the slippage. They continued to report this from time to time throughout the summer.

The bucket delay caused a ripple effect as it delayed the completion of the engine repair work on the last two engines. All of MTU's equipment and spare parts were back in Rochester sitting in large containers awaiting the ship's return. Moving all of their gear from Rochester to the shipyard was considered but determined to be impractical.

Work on the *Spirit* began. The bent tip of the port bow was removed and reconstructed. The hull's Ultrasleek paint coating was in excellent condition and needed no touch up, only a power washing. The entire exterior of the ship was given a new coat of white paint and the new company logos were applied. The CATS Maplestar logo was painted over. A blue logo of a pouncing cat was applied forward and a red Bay Ferries logo aft. The nickname "The Breeze" was replaced by a new nickname of Bay Ferries choosing, "The Cat." The words "THE CAT" were stenciled below the image of the pouncing feline. Also, on the starboard bow, the words "Toronto to Rochester" were also applied, as was "Rochester to Toronto" on the port bow.

The "omenists" took the new nickname as *another* bad sign. A letter to the *Democrat & Chronicle* editor said, "Did anyone consider the well-known fact that cats do not like water?"

The marine evacuation system units which had been sent ashore for inspection weeks earlier were delivered to the yard and installed. Also, a supply of rubber wheel blocks I had ordered finally arrived while we were in the yard. We threw away what little remained of the broken wooden blocks from 2004.

While we were away in the shipyard, contractors back in Rochester were busy converting the second level office space in the Rochester terminal's Link Building into a dormitory for the out-of-town crewmembers. During the 2004 season, CATS offered no living accommodations whatsoever for the crew—licensed or unlicensed. As mentioned earlier, many of the crew members had signed year-long leases on apartments or houses and wound up losing money on leases they couldn't break.

For this new season of the *Spirit*, the second level of the Link Building would now have a living room with a television, a kitchenette with a refrigerator and microwave, and several rooms containing bunk beds and single beds. Bunk beds for the unlicensed crew; single beds for the junior officers. For the senior officers, a small but comfortable house was rented on Madison Street, just a five-minute drive from the terminal. The Danish contingent, consisting of training master Hädh and his business partner/chief engineer, preferred to stay downtown at the Clarion Hotel. They would live at the Clarion for the next seven months at the city's expense.

The ship left Port Weller and returned to Rochester on Sunday afternoon, June 5th. The next three weeks flew by as last minute details were taken care of in rapid-fire succession. A brief summary follows:

Upgrade work on the remaining two engines was resumed immediately.

On Tuesday, June 14th we did a marine evacuation system deployment using the forward starboard unit for the U.S. Coast Guard. It was similar to the previous year's deployment. There was a small delay as

Marine Evacuation System slide-raft
deployment, June 14, 2005
Photo courtesy of Larry Dickens, copyright 2005

the crane that was hired to remove the evacuation system's door arrived late.

The deployment went off without a problem. The entire slide-raft arrangement took only 90 seconds to inflate and was ready for use. Crew members evacuated the vessel using the slide. Sheriff's divers were on hand to retrieve the two raft container shells. When the last crew member went down the slide and into the raft, it was cut free and towed over to the public boat launch where everyone disembarked. The MES specialists then trucked both the raft and the entire evacuation system unit back to their facility in Port Colborne, Ontario, for inspecting and repacking.

The growing optimism for the new season among the officers and crew was suddenly dampened on June 17th when Chief Engineer Barry Wood, two assistant engineers, and a QMED suddenly resigned. Rochester News 10NBC reported that

> Four key engineers have jumped ship. Among them was former Chief Engineer Barry Wood who says, "We can't do the work without union representation. Bay Ferries didn't share my sense of urgency about allowing unionization for all marine engineers in a timely manner."

Chief Engineer Wood and the other crew members had just recently completed the lengthy ship specific process of type rating. Now, with their departure, the process would have to be started all over again.

The majority of America's experienced mariners and engineers are unionized. The two largest unions are MEBA (Marine Engineers' Beneficial Association) for engineers/deck officers and MMP (Master, Mates, & Pilots) for deck officers. These unions have their own modern training schools, complete with engine labs and bridge simulators. They are up-to-date with the ever-changing international rules and requirements that affect mariners and offer courses which keep them current. They also offer pension and medical plans. Their members are the most capable, experienced, and qualified individuals in the country.

Rochester Ferry Company/Bay Ferries offered no pension plans and had no training facilities. They would farm out certain types of training to an existing school, sometimes even to one of the unions' facilities.

Since the ferry was supposedly going to reflag to the U.S. in the very near future, I did not understand why Rochester Ferry Company/Bay Ferries would not want to sign a union contract. In 2004, CATS had a difficult time recruiting licensed Americans to Rochester. The unions would have been able to provide a steady source of American manpower. Time would tell why.

On Thursday, June 23rd, the *Spirit* traveled to Toronto for the installation of the repaired bucket. It had just returned from Scotland. By that time, the marine evacuation unit was waiting on the dock, inspected and repacked. It, too, was installed. The bucket installation took longer · than expected and the ship and crew spent the night in Toronto.

Friday, June 24th. The bucket installation was completed and the *Spirit* left Toronto late that afternoon. It was an evening of celebration and Bay Ferries threw two parties for all of the employees. They had chartered the local dinner boat, the Harbor Town Belle—a small, mini-Mississippi paddlewheeler replica—for a sunset social cruise offshore, serving drinks and hors d'oeuvres. This was followed by a party at caterer Kurt Ritchie's Scuttlebutts bar and restaurant on River Street. Because of the *Spirit's* late departure from Toronto, all of us onboard missed the Harbor Town Belle social cruise, but we did arrive in time for the party at Scuttlebutts.

After 39 busy days of preparation to make Rochester's fast ferry ready to meet the expectations of the public, it was a good night to let loose with colleagues. Everyone was excited and pleased to be back at work on the boat again. The *Spirit* was special. It was a sign of Rochester's future. Each of us knew this and was proud to be a part of it. Scuttlebutts was packed with happy faces. Music and off-key voices blared from the sound system as people took a stab at karaoke. Against this backdrop, rehired crew members swapped sea stories of the previous year. Even the gentle giant, Vice President Don Cormier was present enjoying the festivities and talking to everyone.

It looked like a great new beginning with our new ferry operator. The optimism shared by all that night was stratospheric, despite the resignations of the engineering team earlier in the month. The future looked very bright.

The days continued to fly by quickly.

Saturday, June 25th, sea trials were conducted. Several high-speed runs offshore tested the newly upgraded engines. The results were satisfactory. The *Spirit of Ontario 1* was ready to go to work. There was time left in the day for some shiphandling exercises. Sitting five miles off the Rochester jetties, Captain Hädh let the chief mates—Gerry Cooper, Paul Greubel, and myself—one at a time, get our hands on the bridge wing maneuvering controls. We walked the ship sideways, both port and starboard, and then twirled it around both clockwise and counterclockwise. We then shifted to backup mode and performed the same maneuvers. This allowed us to begin getting a feel for handling the *Spirit*.

Sunday, June 26th, the *Spirit* was open to the public for viewing. Between 11:30 a.m. and 6 p.m., an estimated 5,000 to 6,000 visitors streamed into the ferry and toured the grand vessel's passenger areas along a taped-off route. Most of the people who visited that day had never seen the ship before except in the news. When they left the ship, most were impressed. Many commented on how grand our ship was and said they were very excited and anxious to ride the *Spirit*.

The next day, the ferry traveled once again to Toronto to celebrate the opening of that city's new International Marine Passenger Terminal. Both Rochester Mayor Bill Johnson and Toronto Mayor David Miller tied a rope knot to symbolize the linking of both cities. The Toronto terminal would be one of the few bright spots of 2005. It had been completed in January and turned out to be bright, comfortable, and efficient. Although there still were no shops to visit while waiting for a sailing, the thousands of future passengers would no longer have to stand outside on the narrow pier in the wind, rain, and snow, or be soaked by the mini-tsunamis kicked up by the ferry's powerful waterjets.

Tuesday, June 28th. At 9 a.m., the U.S. Coast Guard was aboard for inspection and to witness a drencher system test. The system was successfully activated and heavy spray poured from the drencher piping overhead. The car deck was awash with the chocolaty waters of the Genesee River. The Coast Guard was satisfied.

Wednesday, June 29th. The crew spent the day cleaning up and preparing the car decks for tomorrow's big day, the startup of service.

The *Spirit of Ontario 1* resumed service on Thursday, June 30th. Only one trip was made that day. Escorted out of the Genesee River, once again, by Chief "Bones" Mosgrober and his Coast Guard rescue boats, the *Spirit* had 287 passengers going to Toronto on that maiden voyage. Returning, we carried 259. It was a modest beginning, totaling 546 passengers; however, it was a much better start than our maiden voyage in 2004 in which we carried only 67 passengers over and 171 back.

The next day, the schedule offered two trips per day.

PART IV
Around the Lake
in 166 Days

Chapter 19
A Flawed Beginning

The passengers who rode the *Spirit of Ontario 1* in 2005 were filled with awe and expressed glowing compliments about the ship and her crew, just as they did during the CATS run in 2004. People enjoyed the service, the food, the comfort, and the spectacular views through the tall windows. Happy kids were entertained by the movies, the video game room, and the Fisher Price Kidz room.

Occasionally, when the ship was in port in Rochester, Human Resources Manager Glenn Gardner would bring a group of young students from one of the local schools onboard for a visit. In Toronto, Terminal Manager Kent Ehler or his assistant Debbie Knapp escorted groups of local firemen for visits.

Almost everyone who set foot aboard the *Spirit* had a thrilling world-class experience.

For the crew, the passengers and visitors were always the fun part of the job, the best part of the day. They were the reason we were there. We were proud of our ship and enjoyed showing her off.

Problems did exist behind the scenes; however we made certain the passengers and visitors never saw any of them. It was not a good year for many of the ship's officers as a dark cloud would descend over the bright ship. There would be many resignations due to frustration over the management and command of the vessel.

The training issue was troubling to my two colleagues, Greubel and Cooper, and to me. The three of us had been hired to be chief mates/masters-in-training, but we discovered we were not the focus of the necessary maneuvering training on the LIPS system. The LIPS system, as mentioned earlier, allows us to control the vessel: how we dock it and undock it; how we twirl it and walk the ship sideways. It is an absolute must that the masters be skilled in the use of this system, much like an airline pilot needs to be proficient in the use of a cockpit's maneuvering controls. Though we did receive some time on the LIPS joystick, the Danish captain was training all of the junior mates, too.

In a June 27th, 2005 interview Captain Hädh said as much to WROC-TV reporter Joylynn Whitfield. "I'm going to take all the officers. It goes from the lowest ranks to the highest ranks for the training program. It will be six weeks before I let them go by themselves."

This resulted in the three chief mates/masters-in-training having an opportunity to dock or undock the ship only once a day. With the ferry in service making two trips a day, there were only four opportunities to dock and four to undock. In addition, Hädh would not allow anyone to dock in Toronto initially until the officers could prove they could handle the docking in Rochester.

The ferry began running on Thursday, June 30th. A month later, there was *still* no focus on training the three master's candidates.

There was a total reversal in the way training was conducted when compared to the 2004 CATS season. Where the two CATS captains received intense maneuvering training during the first few days and the chief mates received none for weeks, now the masters-in-training were receiving little and the junior officers were receiving a greater share. It made no sense. In the usual order of things once the masters are trained, the training captain steps back and the American masters run the ship. Then they train the junior officers.

In 2004, the two CATS captains had each logged 24 dockings and undockings in both ports, day and night, in only 72 hours. Granted, this 72-hour period was time dedicated to touch and go training and was not conducted during actual ferry service, unlike the situation in 2005 where the only time training could occur was while the ferry was in service.

During the May shipyard the Danish captain had spoken of providing several days dedicated for touch and go training prior to going into service, however the extended two-week stay in the yard due to the discovery of the damaged bucket completely erased that prospect. This would have been all the more reason to concentrate the training on the three masters right away instead of spreading it thinly around to all of the other mates.

After 30 days under this training plan, I had logged only 22 dockings and undockings, with none in Toronto. This was true of my two colleagues as well.

Whenever I asked our training captain about receiving more "stick" time, he would say, "There's plenty of time. You'll have all kinds of opportunities."

Since it was late July and knowing there was only the month of August remaining before the reduced fall schedule would be implemented, I didn't see us as having "plenty of time," especially as the winds of autumn would be fast approaching.

In addition to the training issue, the Danish captain's management method was one of sternness and intimidation toward his three chief mates/masters-in-training.

Training master Hädh was a large man in his late 30s. He had Liam Neeson looks and his English, laced with an accent, made him sound like a Danish Arnold Schwarzenegger. He was a former body builder and, in his youth, a former participant in Strong Man competitions. He described one competition to me: it involved wearing a harness and towing a Mack truck behind him. The strong Dane continued to stay in shape through a weight-lifting regimen which he did religiously five nights a week in a Rochester gym near the Clarion.

The three masters-in-training were subjected to his numerous tirades and threats of being fired for insignificant reasons, not only face-to-face, but also over the ship's walkie-talkies. The ship's walkie-talkies shared the same frequency with the terminal personnel ashore.

On many occasions this man, who was being paid by Americans to train Americans, would refer to us as "lazy, American bastards."

In twenty-six years of sailing on commercial ships with dozens of captains and officers of different temperaments, I have never seen conduct as disrespectful as this by a master. It was not a pleasant time for many of the officers aboard the *Spirit* and, as a result, there would be a high number of resignations throughout the season.

On July 12th, only 13 days into service, three masters-in-training suddenly became two with the unfortunate resignation of Mr. Cooper. Cooper resigned as a result of the training master's conduct.

By that time, after 13 days, Cooper had been given the opportunity to perform only four undockings and one docking. The training records of Mr. Greubel and myself were similar in numbers. Training for the master's candidates was crawling along at a snail's pace.

Ironically, on that day, Cooper had just received his type rating as master endorsement for the *Spirit of Ontario 1* from Doug Wilson, the Transport Canada type rating examiner. In the eyes of Transport Canada, the former Panama Canal pilot was qualified to be captain of the *Spirit of Ontario 1*. Transport Canada is the Canadian equivalent of the U.S. Coast Guard.

Mr. Cormier's original plan for the masters called for three American chief mates/masters-in-training. Once trained, two of the masters would serve as the vessel's permanent captains, while the third master would serve as chief mate and be available as a backup master. Why he did not intervene and prevent Cooper's resignation is unknown.

If an American maritime union had been involved in this operation, none of the kind of treatment we were experiencing would have been condoned. However, in this nonunion, "at-will" contract setting, just about anything seemed to go. The working environment aboard this city of Rochester-owned, foreign flagged vessel was one of hostility and few of the officers looked forward to going to work in the morning. The work environment was a complete reversal of the 2004 season under CATS. Captains Williams and Aycock always treated their crew and officers with respect.

All of the officers believed the ship would be reflagged very soon and be turned over to the Americans. Only American licenses can fill the officer positions on an American vessel. With reflagging just around the corner, the officers expected the training master's departure was imminent.

On July 28th, after four weeks with no change in the master's training program, I sent an email to the company inquiring about the issue. Almost immediately the LIPS maneuvering training focus shifted to Paul Greubel and myself.

The month of August was already upon us. We had lost one valuable month of training.

Two weeks later on August 13th, Rochester Ferry Company/Bay Ferries fired assistant engineer John Enwright without cause or justification. Enwright was a highly competent engineer and a good instructor. He had been part of the *Spirit's* team in 2004 and was one of the first to be hired by Rochester Ferry Company/Bay Ferries. Enwright's knowledge of the ship considerably shortened the learning curves of many of the new Bay Ferries engineers when they were brought onboard.

Enwright would tell me later that the reason he felt he was fired was due to his repeatedly asking about the status of the American reflagging.

This dismissal prompted one of the American chief engineers-in-training to resign the same day. In addition to being upset over Enwright's firing, this chief felt Rochester Ferry Company/Bay Ferries was dragging its feet with its intention to make him a full-time chief engineer for which he was hired. He also did not care for the company's discouragement when attempting to report incidents to the regulatory agencies.

If an American union had been involved, Enwright would have been able to request a hearing and, without any valid company complaint against him, he would have been reinstated. As it stood, he had no recourse.

At this point in the season, the loss of American licenses was considerable. The operation had lost a chief engineer and two assistant engineers two weeks before service began. The operation then lost one chief mate/master-in-training in mid-July, and now another chief engineer-in-training and an assistant engineer were gone. All of these men had been type rated.

For a company that needed American licenses to reflag the ship to the U.S. right away, Rochester Ferry Company/Bay Ferries had many losses. This was surprising since American licenses are difficult to recruit to a startup operation in Rochester.

High turnover would continue to occur during the season. With each resignation, a replacement would have to be found, and then the time-consuming process of type rating training would begin all over again.

This turnover and the lack of trained American masters was contributing to the delay in the reflagging. The U.S. Coast Guard had only a few minor issues that needed to be dealt with and would take virtually no time (such as changing fire hoses to a different type). It was becoming the opinion of both the deck and engine officers that either the Danish contingent did not want to give up their jobs by relinquishing control of the *Spirit* to the American masters and crew, or the Rochester Ferry Company/Bay Ferries was intentionally prolonging the reflagging for some unknown reason.

Mr. Roger Paulus is president of the St. Lawrence Seaway Association. He is also an American pilot who served on the *Spirit of Ontario 1* many times during its two seasons. He told the officers on bridge watch on several occasions that a Bay Ferries vice-president had approached him early in the spring looking for a three-year contract with the Seaway pilots at a reduced rate.

Mr. Paulus told the vice-president that his Association could not provide a discounted rate due to the rates being federally mandated.

If the *Spirit of Ontario 1* was about to be reflagged, why would Rochester Ferry Company/Bay Ferries want to sign a long-term contract with the Seaway Association? Why would they wish to continue paying for the pilots, especially when the cost of the pilots and their limousines was one of the expenses that both CATS in 2004 and, subsequently, the city of Rochester were trying to eliminate?

In addition, CATS had gone to great lengths to ensure that their deck officers would be tested for a route-specific pilotage endorsement. This would allow the American officers to replace the pilots when the ship reflagged to U.S. During the entire 2005 season, the Rochester Ferry Company/Bay Ferries made no such effort. According to Lt. David Webb of the U.S. Coast Guard, no testing was ever discussed with the Buffalo U.S. Coast Guard office in 2005.

Chapter 20
Stories of the Summer

What would life be like on a passenger/vehicle ferry if there were no incidents? What would it be like if there were no "people versus people" or "man versus machine" conflicts?

It would be IDEAL.

The crew was always in pursuit of the perfect voyage, where nothing went wrong and our passengers were completely content and they and their vehicles reached their destinations unscathed. But, anytime you deal with the public there is bound to be an incident of some sort, no matter how hard you try or no matter what you do.

Down on the car decks, the incidents dropped dramatically during the 2005 season because of the fewer number of vehicles carried. Among the more memorable moments, there were several teary-eyed scenes with devoted pet owners who couldn't bear to be separated from their dogs for the length of the brief voyage. Due to health codes (and basic common sense and courtesy), pets, of course, were not allowed in the passenger cabin and were required to stay either in their owners' vehicles or in one of the ship's "Pet Porters." Periodically, each of the deck officers would have to trade-in our shoulder boards for our psychology hats and spend many patient minutes convincing guilt-torn owners that "Fluffy" would survive the brief journey across the fresh water lake.

The only exception to the "no pets in the cabin" rule was for special needs pets, such as seeing eye dogs.

One day a gentleman on the car deck was insistent about taking his dog to the cabin. He told me his dog was of the special needs category, claiming the animal could predict when the man was going to have an epileptic seizure. Being ignorant of this type of animal, I asked if he could show me any sort of documentation about this dog's rare ability. The man said "certainly" and began rifling through papers in his trunk looking for a certificate.

While the man searched, I noticed his little pooch was urinating red on the silver aluminum deck.

I said, "Excuse me, Sir. Your dog is peeing blood."

The man was very apologetic and said the dog was very old and had stomach cancer.

"Sir, I can't allow him upstairs," I said.

He quickly agreed to leave the animal in his vehicle.

Another time, a young lady who was hearing-impaired brought her special needs dog to business class with her. She laid out a blanket on the carpet for her little helper and assured me he would not be a problem.

While passengers were continuing to board, a small finch flew in through the side port, circled the atrium, and headed for the skylight.

I was on the bridge when Purser Wiemer called and asked for my assistance. She mentioned a dog was barking and a bird was flying around.

When I arrived in business class, the hearing dog was barking at the yellow finch which was now fluttering and slamming itself against the tall glass windows in the after corner, trying to escape. The young lady pulled her dog away by his leash and I reached across the blue leather couch, cupped my hands, and captured the small bird as he skittered across the window. I then took him outside onto the observation deck and released him.

No sooner had the bird flown away when the young woman appeared outside with her dog. He had been so revved up by the activity that he felt the need to relieve himself. She quickly cleaned up his droppings. The rest of their trip was uneventful.

Returning to incidents on the car decks, one female passenger walked into a support beam one day and bumped her head. The purser put ice in a bag and gave it to the lady to place on her head. She suffered no cuts and there was no blood or bruising. When asked, the lady could provide no details regarding the location of her encounter with the aluminum beam. In the report I wrote, "Passenger was apparently not watching where she was going. The recommended corrective action: Chief Mate to check beams and metal structures on the car decks to determine if any further painting with attention-getting yellow paint is necessary."

We had painted a lot of structures yellow on the car decks during the previous year. I sometimes wondered if we should just paint the entire space yellow.

Another lady was driving along the starboard side of the car deck when the right side of her van scraped against a bulkhead. Once she realized this, she attempted to back up. This caused a section of her vehicle's turn signal to tear off. Deck crew personnel rushed in and stopped her from going any further backward or forward and directed her away from the bulkhead. An approximately a one-foot long scrape occurred on one of the ship's fire panels. Apparently, the embarrassed driver had gone too far to the right.

In the "Once-in-a-Lifetime Experience" department, able-bodied seaman Rob Minnick was directing traffic at the top of the mezzanine ramp when, suddenly an older fellow drove his car up the ramp too far to the side and struck a ramp lift wire and flipper. The car then bounced off and the driver kept going.

Minnick, dressed in bright, red coveralls striped with wide reflective tape, used large, waving hand gestures, hollered, and tried to make eye contact with the oblivious driver to get the man to stop, but to no avail. With no time to jump either right or left, the AB was forced to hurl himself onto the hood. Even with a human being suddenly obscuring the view through the windshield, the elderly driver still did not stop. He made the 180-degree turn at the top of the ramp, pulled ahead, and then parked behind a line of cars. The rattled, able-bodied seaman then climbed down off the hood and asked the man what he was doing. Unable to come up with any rational explanation, the driver suddenly wanted to file for damage to his hood, claiming the seaman had caused scratch marks.

There were no major car crashes like the notorious "Runaway Volkswagon of 2004." Most people followed the crew's instructions and put their cars in "Park" and set their parking brakes. The new rubber wheel chocks were in full use. Gone were the makeshift homemade wooden jobbies from the CATS's days.

As in the previous year, when it came to the question of which suffered the greater damage in the endless saga of the ship versus the cars, the cars lost and the ship won.

During both seasons of the *Spirit*, there were occasionally injuries in the cabin as well. The most common one involved children running around the open air observation deck, unsupervised by their parents, who sometimes stumbled, fell, and ground their knees or hands into gritty, non-skid deck.

The pursers went through a lot of Band-Aids treating young people.

All of the smoke and fire doors in the ship were either spring loaded or had pneumatic door closers and we had a lot of complaints about children getting their fingers pinched when parents weren't keeping an eye on them. Sadly, one little girl even lost the tip of a finger due to a door pinching and an inattentive parent.

Many people have wondered about our long days on the fast ferry and where we rested.

The cabin staff would have a shift change with each trip on two-trip days, resulting in eight-hour days.

The marine crew, however, was onboard for the entire day from 7 a.m. to 10 p.m. Most of us arrived 15 to 30 minutes early to grab coffee, settle in, and be on deck and ready to go at 7 a.m. when passenger boarding and vehicle loading would begin.

Working on the ship for 15 hours a day was very long, although not uncommon in the maritime industry.

Due to international rules, a mariner is not allowed to work more than 12 hours a day. Rochester Ferry Company/Bay Ferries required an 80-hour work week, which equaled an 11.43 hour day. The remaining 3.6 hours were to be a rest period. The 3.6 hours was not continuous and was usually broken up into two segments of 1.8 hours each.

There was no place onboard for the marine crew to have a good rest. The only bed onboard was in the first aid room (Bob Mansfield's old "bedroom") and it was on a first-come, first-serve basis. Company rules forbid, and rightly so, the marine crew to sleep or rest in the passenger areas. The only other areas available for rest were the crew area, the forward mooring station, and in either of the two bridge wings or in the Navionics room.

The crew area was a tough place to rest. Its seating was upright, and the two security doors from the passenger areas were constantly opening and closing as people passed through, took breaks, ate meals, stopped for coffee, visited the ship's office, or went to the bridge.

Out on the bridge wings, there were two places in which one could find a remote place to rest. One was on the deck in the corner or the shelf on top of the cabinet which ran the entire forward length of the wing. The shelf would be my favorite. It was just wide and hard enough to allow a person to stretch out.

The most comfortable place to rest was down in the Navionics room, located directly beneath the control compartment (wheelhouse). The Navionics room was only four feet high and only accessible by getting down on all fours and crawling through cabinet doors located on either side of the navigation console. Once there, you had to walk around in a half-bent over position so as not to bang your head on the aluminum beams overhead. The space was crowded with ventilation ducts, electronic equipment, a big 10-gallon container and spigot for the windshield washer system, and cables *everywhere.*

Resting in the Navionics room was like resting inside an old television set, but unlike an old television set, it was air-conditioned and had a light switch. Plus, it could sleep two. At first, the officers used the long, athwartship ventilation ducts for beds, stretching out onto blankets and using foamy black pipe insulators for makeshift pillows. There was some floor space in the room and so, one day I requisitioned a single-sized Aerobed and took it down there. We plugged it in, inflated it, and—presto! —there was now room for three people.

During the warm summer days, several of the innovative ABs and OSs rigged netting and created a comfortable place to rest in the port side mooring station. The cool, summer air would blow in and the bow slicing through the water provided a tranquil background sound. When the temperatures dropped as autumn descended, this space was not as hospitable.

In the end, no matter how creative the crew was in finding a comfortable place, no one really got a quality rest period. At least, it was off-duty time for the marine crew and people could get off their feet.

None of the officers had any complaints about working a 15-hour day as long as we were allowed to take our rest periods. It was required under U.S. Coast Guard and international laws. It was also one of the conditions set by the USCG that would allow Rochester Ferry Company/Bay Ferries to reduce 2004's 3-crew system to a 2-crew system.

Our only near-miss collision in 2005 occurred on July 25th, when the *Spirit* had a close encounter with a windsurfer. As would be recounted later by a crewman, "On arrival Toronto between the first sea buoy and the "birds island" (a spit of land about a half-mile north of the entrance buoys that was covered with guano), a windsurfer was spotted coming across the fairway from starboard to port a half-mile away. The *Spirit's* speed was 10 knots. The Toronto Marine Police unit escort went up there to chase him away. Despite the huge catamaran bearing down on him, the windsurfer continued on the crossing course. The *Spirit* gave five short blasts (the danger signal) with the whistle. The windsurfer, suddenly, stopped and fell off his board in the water directly in front of the ship. This resulted in the *Spirit* having to go hard to port. At that point, the distance was about 400 yards and the speed was five knots. The Marine unit quickly cruised over to the surfer and plucked him out of the water. The *Spirit* had its engines going full astern because the ship could not go further to port due to risk of going aground. After the surfer was in the Marine units boat and clear, the ferry went to idle speed ahead, but we had to take the surfboard in between the hulls as there was no way of maneuvering around it. The *Spirit* then continued to the dock as normal."

Luckily, the owner or his surfboard did not go through the waterjets. The surfboard survived the passage between the ferry's hulls.

Sometimes passengers would inadvertently leave things behind and reclaim them later: Cell phones, books, passports, luggage, hats, keys, coats, wallets, toys, glasses, epipens, cameras. Sometimes passengers even forgot their cars.

The most unusual item left onboard by a passenger was discovered one morning on the rescue boat deck which is located aft and one deck below the observation deck. While inspecting the rescue boats, I discovered a pile of dirt, ash, and tiny smooth rocks dumped all over one of the rescue boat covers. Apparently, they had been dumped from the observation deck above. Naturally, I was puzzled at first. Usually, the things we find on the boat deck are things that blew off people who were out in the windy open space: eyeglasses, plastic cups, olives, swizzle sticks, pens, coins, candy wrappers, cigarette butts, cigars, ear rings, and chewed gum. But never ash, dirt, and tiny smooth rocks.

It then occurred to me. A week earlier a crew member had said to me that a passenger was asking about whom should they see onboard to get permission to spread their loved one's remains into the lake.

Click!

Someone had taken the cremated remains of a loved one out onto the observation deck and attempted to toss it into the fast-moving winds. The winds are, indeed, fast on the observation deck—sometimes tornadic—but there are also some wild, swirling wind patterns back there caused by the various structures and bulkheads deflecting and rerouting the wind stream. Most of the heavy stuff like the dirt and stone had gone straight down to the boat deck below, but the ashen remains must have swirled all around the observation deck and all over the passengers outside. The unfortunate individual who had been in the urn was now truly *gone with the breeze.*

I had a crew member sweep up the remains and quietly and respectfully deposit them over the side once we were out on the lake.

While leaving Toronto on the morning run on August 14th, the Danish captain, as was typical, ordered full speed ahead shortly after making the turn onto the 182-degree course. Within a minute the *Spirit* was flying down the Eastern Gap reaching 35 knots before the ferry even cleared the channel buoys.

Shortly afterwards, Constable M.J. Byers of the Toronto Police Service Marine Unit reported to the *Spirit* that two men had been thrown out of their rowboat due to the ship's high speed departure wake.

According to the Toronto Police Service Marine Unit and vessel incident reports, "It was reported shortly after departure from Toronto terminal, while exiting the navigational commercial channel, a small, 14-foot rowboat with two people in it experienced a wake from the vessel approximately two miles to the west of the channel. Their boat had pitched violently and threw the men overboard. One man bumped his head on an oar or the gunwale of the boat. The boat was in 4 to 4.5 feet of water. Both men are reported okay."

The ship's incident report stated the "Probable or determined root cause: Vessel caused a wake while exiting the navigational commercial channel. The rowboat was in very shallow waters, approximately 4 to 4.5 feet. The rowboat was not spotted due to distance."

The recommended corrective action suggested, by the master, was: "Slower speed exiting the channel." There was no mention in the report of the *Spirit's* actual speed as she charged down the channel.

Yippee-kai-yea!

The next day, a gentleman whom I will refer to only as Captain "D", ended up dealing with the Toronto Marine Police in regard to the incident. Captain D had just relieved the training master who said he was going on a Cuban vacation for 10 days.

Captain D struck an agreement with the law enforcement agency to not exceed 600 rpm, or about 15 knots, when leaving the port. Afterwards, the Toronto Marine Police boat went to the location where the rowboat incident had taken place after the *Spirit* left Toronto and observed there was no wake caused by the vessel when she departed at the reduced speed.

Don't dent the boat.

My old former LNG skipper, Captain Jack Donahue's words went through my mind on August 21st.

On that Sunday, after 22 dockings and 16 undockings in Rochester, and after eight dockings and 14 undockings in Toronto, I grazed the Toronto gangway during a docking and broke three windows.

It was the first time in my 27-year maritime career that I had caused any damage to a vessel. Mariners spend their lives striving to never touch anything with their ships. We live to avoid everything. Other ships, icebergs, rocks, containers, small craft, refugees, floating houses, and logs. We also live to avoid hitting piers *too hard*. Grazing the pier in Toronto and breaking three windows was my worst day at sea.

It was my nineth docking in Toronto. The winds were blowing at 20-25 knots from the port side, and blowing the *Spirit* onto the dock. I prematurely reduced speed as I approached the dock. The *Spirit* quickly lost headway and the wind began shoving her in the direction of the gangway. I attempted to counter this starboard motion with the joystick, pushing it sideways full to port, but it wasn't soon enough. The ferry's hydraulics response time is about five seconds. By the time the waterjets responded and began walking the ship to port and away from the dock, I had already grazed the gangway. Captain D quickly stepped in and took over.

As lousy as I had felt about it, many of my colleagues reminded me that I was not the first person in the world of fast ferries to break a window. Several, including Hädh (when he returned from his vacation) and fellow master-in-training Paul Gruebel, said that it could have happened to anybody.

For what it's worth, coming from the only man in history—so far—to bump it with a fast ferry, the gangway in Toronto is too close to the edge of the pier and, though it does not overhang the pier, the ship with its flaring bow does overhang the pier if she approaches too close or is at too steep an angle to the pier. Naturally, the moral of the story is don't approach it at too steep an angle.

The Toronto pier has been a tough place for the *Spirit* from the beginning. As mentioned earlier, last year another master-in-training hit the pier twice and bent the port bow tip over 180-degrees. Also, last year, one of the captains damaged one of the starboard water jets when he backed into the pier while departing. The city had lost two weeks of badly needed passenger revenue due to that incident.

Compared to this damage, my scrape was minor. My incident had caused only a one and half hour delay.

My first thought as the windows broke was the passengers sitting by those windows. The Staten Island disaster of 2003 raced through my mind.

My next thought was it was the end of the world.

I felt as bad as Captain B during the previous year when he nailed the port bow twice into the dock in Toronto. An average, non-seagoing person can not imagine how horrible it feels the first time. Bad, lousy, sick, nauseous. You want to hide from the rest of the world until the next century arrives.

Captain B had resigned after his bow-bending incident. He knew deep down inside that he would never tame the LIPS stick, and he had the courage to admit it to himself. The thought of resigning crossed my mind.

As I went through the day feeling horrible, I remembered Bob Manfield's words to reporter Berkeley Brean in New York City the day of that famous accident: "It's like when you bash the wing of your car. You think it's the end of the world."

Yes, I thought it was the end of the world.

On the dock there were 677 patiently waiting, fare-paying passengers, one of the largest loads in the month. 67 cars were lined up in the departure lot. Cancellation of the trip was not an option.

The marine crew and engineers worked quickly together and did a fantastic job of covering the windows with plywood and fabricating brackets to hold the plywood in place. I was still in somewhat of a depressed daze. I think the only constructive things I did was finding out what time the near-by Home Depot closed, sending people on a quest for plywood, and clearing the three window frames of the remaining shattered glass.

We were lucky. The Home Depot in Toronto closes at 7 p.m. on Sundays. The accident occurred a little after 6 p.m. Toronto terminal manager Kent Ehler, at home on his day off, was contacted by on-duty assistant terminal manager Debbie Knapp. Upon hearing the news, Ehler shot out of his house and went straight to Home Depot to get his foot in the door before it closed for the day. As he drove, the ship's crew put together a shopping list for him and relayed it via cell phone. A short time later, Ehler delivered the needed repair items to the ship and the crew went to work.

It was a warm evening and the cabin staff carried soft drinks out to the parking lot to the line of waiting drivers.

When the last window was buttoned-up, we began loading passengers and cars and then departed at around 8:30 p.m.

During the trip back to Rochester crew and colleagues were kind and supportive to me.

The incident made ridiculously big news in Rochester. *Anything* related to the ferry during those days made big news. Camera crews were on the pier when the *Spirit* returned. One news crew was in a small boat and shining bright and blinding TV lights into our wheelhouse. The flurry of coverage was so intense you'd think the ferry had crashed, sunk, and killed hundreds of passengers.

I decided that I was not going to quit. Resigning for me would be the same thing as "hiding" and I had no desire to hide. Nobody had remotely suggested that I was going to be fired. I thought about the incident and knew what I had done wrong in underestimating the wind factor. I would build from that experience and would not let this experience destroy me or my aspirations of becoming a fine, fast ferry shiphandler.

Hädh's relief, Captain D, a highly competent man with many years of experience on these high-speed machines, calmly said to me afterward, "Crap happens."

Captain D, more than anyone else onboard, would know. He had experienced the worst night of his maritime career on the other Bay Ferries THE CAT back in 1998. He was aboard the night that ferry had collided with the fishing boat *Lady Megan II* in fog and its captain had died.

It doesn't get any worse than that at sea, even if you aren't to blame and the other guy is. The *Lady Megan II* had been found at fault, not THE CAT or its crew. It doesn't change much how you feel, though.

Accidents happen every hour of every day on ships all around the world. Fast ferries are not immune to such situations, nor was the *Spirit of Ontario 1*.

"What Can Go Wrong?" asks the title of an article about fast ferry safety in the May 1, 2005 publication *Safety at Sea International* journal.

"Fast ferries have performed very well over the past 30 years and have carved out markets for themselves in many places where there is a need for a faster means of travel than that afforded by conventional displacement vessels," the article states. "Their safety record is generally regarded as good, but there is a small number of incidents that have provided clear warnings of things that can go badly wrong."

A sampling from various news sources and transportation investigation reports, as well as *Captain David Clark's Fast Ferry Web Site*, shows that things do sometimes go wrong:

In January 2001, the *M.V. Finest*, operated by New York Fast Ferries, ran aground off of Sandy Hook, New Jersey in New York Harbor. As reported by Elaine Van Develde in the Edison, N.J., Sentinal, as *Finest's* crew tried to maneuver the boat through ice to get an ill passenger to shore quickly, the vessel ran aground on a sand bar off Highlands in Sandy Hook Bay, stranding 257 commuters for more than five hours.

In April of 2001, the *M.V. Flying Cloud,* operated by the Woods Hole and Martha's Vineyard Steamship Authorities, ran aground off

Kalmus Beach after it left Hyannis enroute to Nantucket. All 12 passengers were evacuated and no injuries were reported. Reports indicate that the cause was navigation/operator error.

In March 1998, the high speed wave-piercing catamaran ferry *Condor 10* suffered damage to her bow visor. From a Transport Accident Investigation Commission of New Zealand report, *Condor 10* was proceeding out of Wellington Harbour into a moderate southerly swell, when the vessel encountered two short steep waves of approximately 4.5 meters in height. The master reduced speed as the ferry rose over the first wave, and the vessel dipped onto the face of the second wave. The resultant slamming displaced the bow visor and caused substantial damage to the surrounding hull structure. None of the 231 passengers and 22 crew were injured in the incident.

In December 2003, the *Katia,* a United Kingdom flagged, recently launched fast ferry, grounded at high speed during builder's sea trials. The U.K.'s Marine Accident Investigation Branch recounts that the *Katia* ran aground on Hurst Spit, in the western Solent, on the south coast of England while undergoing the first day of its sea trials. One person was injured and the vessel sustained some minor hull and propeller damage.

The MAIB reported that the accident was due to a combination of human error and poor operating compartment design. At the time of grounding, the vessel was being conned by the chief officer who was seated in the center pilot position. The sea trials' captain was in the co-pilot's seat to the chief officer's left and the trial engineer was at the engineer's position to his right. The accident occurred when the vessel was making 38 knots and approaching a turn on the most westerly section of a planned 32 mile circuit of the Solent. The MAIB noted that it happened at the end of a long day of trials: "The chief officer had become distracted by another person in the operating compartment, and a turn was started too late, causing the vessel to momentarily ground on a shingle spit."

On fast ferries you cannot take your eyes off the road for a second, unlike on slow moving conventional vessels where you can make a sweep of the horizon with your binoculars and then walk back to the coffee corner and pour yourself a quick cup.

As mentioned earlier, Bay Ferries' Bar Harbor-Yarmouth high speed ferry THE CAT was involved in a tragic accident.

In September 1998, THE CAT collided with a fishing boat, the *Lady Megan II*, resulting in the death of the skipper of the smaller vessel. From the Marine Investigation Report summary:

> The fast ferry catamaran "INCAT 046" left Yarmouth, Nova Scotia, for a scheduled crossing to Bar Harbor, Maine, U.S.A. Visibility was near zero in thick fog. Meanwhile, the fishing vessel "LADY MEGAN II" was approaching Yarmouth Harbour after a fishing trip off the Nova Scotia coast. The navigating personnel of both vessels were using radar as the primary instrument to position their vessels. A few minutes after having agreed on a port-to-port passage in the area of a fixed light commonly known as "Bug Light," the vessels collided in the narrow Main Channel. The master of the fishing vessel sustained fatal injuries.

It was determined that the fault of the collision rested with the *Lady Megan II*.

One of the most horrific incidents of the past few years was the *M.S. Sleipner* disaster off the coast of Norway in November 1999. Traveling at 35 knots, the high speed craft ran aground, slamming into the Store Bloksen rocks. After a time, the bow broke off and the craft moved off the rock. The damage to the hulls was very extensive. Just over 30 minutes after running aground, the main section of the craft went down. Those on board ended up in the water.

Of the 85 persons aboard, 16 lives were lost. A special commission of the Norwegian Government was established to investigate and report on the accident. The inquiry put most of the blame on the master and first officer who were in the control compartment at the time. The craft ran straight onto rocks because the bridge team did not realize exactly where they were.

The new Austal-built ship had been delivered three months earlier in August.

Sometimes just *working* on a fast ferry can be hazardous to your health. In March 2006, a BYM (*Boats, Yachts, and Marinas*) News Service headline read, "Crew member killed at sea on Italy to Corsica ferry."

"One crew man has died and another has been seriously injured, following an accident on board Corsica Ferries' *Mega Express*, from Savona, in Italy to Bastia, in Corsica. The men are of Italian nationality. At about 9 a.m., two crew members of the fast ferry were working inside a lifeboat, carrying out maintenance work, when it suddenly fell into the sea. The mono-hulled ferry put about and, after numerous maneuvers, hampered by rough seas and a violent wind, was able to recover the two men. One was found to have been killed and the other had multiple fractures, caused by the shock of the lifeboat hitting the sea. He has been evacuated to Bastia hospital."

After working on the *Spirit of Ontario 1*, I can not imagine why anyone would be outside working inside a lifeboat on a fast ferry on a *nice* day, much less on one "hampered by rough seas and violent winds." We always saved our on-deck work for our layover days.

Sometimes fast ferries collide with whales. As the catamarans with their sharp dual bows cut through the water, they sometimes cut through the whales. It is reported that sometimes whale heads float ashore. This is happening with greater frequency with the proliferation of fast ferries in the world. As Teri Shore of *Earth Island Journal* wrote in the fall of 2001, "In the Canary Islands off northwest Africa, a new high-speed passenger ferry system instituted in 1999 has taken a major toll on pilot whales, sperm whales and dolphins. During the first three months of operation, four whales died from collisions. The impact of one collision was so strong that a ferry passenger was also killed."

On April 10, 2006 Kyodo News reported that 49 people were injured, 13 seriously, when a high-speed ferry collided with a large marine animal off the coast of the southern Japanese island of Kyushu. One of the crew members was quoted as saying the ferry "collided with a whale-like marine animal."

The news story said, "The Toppy 4 ferry with 109 passengers onboard was heading from Yaku Island to the city of Kagoshima when the accident occurred off Cape Sata, the southernmost point of the four main Japanese islands, Kyodo reported citing the Japan Coast Guard. The ferry was seriously damaged, but was not in danger of sinking. Similar collisions between ferries and animals, off the western coast of Japan, had been reported earlier in the year."

When fast ferries are not delayed due to bridge, engine, or manning problems (or collisions, fires, groundings, or other catastrophes), they can be stopped simply by the weather, too. This was the case several times with the *Spirit of Ontario 1* in 2005. High winds and tall seas can make catamaran shiphandling extremely difficult and risky.

As Bob Mansfield had once said, "The wind factor would need to be coordinated with the captain's experience."

The *Spirit of Ontario 1* does have limits. It is not allowed to operate in sea heights of 4.5 meters (just under 15 feet) due to the possibility of slamage and damage to the tunnel (the area between the hulls).

Besides, the ride would be terrible for the passengers, one that most would never want to repeat.

In the world of fast ferries, the *Spirit of Ontario 1* did have her own share of incidents where she was damaged by coming too hard against a pier. Most have already been described in this book. The majority were small and unreported in the local press. In 2004, there were four "dings." In 2005, there were four, two of which were caused by the Danish training master. They were all relatively minor compared to other incidents that have occurred on the world's fast ferry stage.

Not that all of this is meant to be any sort of acceptable excuse for my own accident, but "Crap happens."

And who knows? If the Danish master's training program had been focused on the three masters candidates during the tranquil month of July instead of sharing the "stick" time with all of the junior officers, my accident might not have occurred. I continue to wonder about this today.

On August 29th, Hurricane Katrina devastated the Gulf Coast.

Two days later, Katrina blew through the Lake Ontario area.

Reporting to work that day, I found that the winds were blowing 44 knots from about the north-northeast straight down the mouth of the Genesee River. The ship was bobbing up and down like a cork as it sat along its berth. It was raining hard and visibility was a mile or so. With this much wind, I could only imagine what the conditions were like out on the lake. I thought, "No way is this trip going today. This is a day to cancel!"

The Danish training master thought otherwise. Experience had shown him worse conditions during his years crossing the English Channel. He said, "We go."

Yippee-kai-yea!

That morning trip we had 257 passengers and 28 cars aboard. The cars were strapped to the deck. This was the roughest trip the *Spirit* had in its two seasons on the lake. The seas were three to four meters in height. We went through a lot of motion sickness bags.

The food in the servery flew across the deck and was trashed. Half the crew became seasick and disappeared into whatever hiding place they could find. Some disappeared into the passenger areas.

As I made a round through the cabin, I assisted a young lady crawl her way to the women's room. It was so rough and the ship was pitching and bouncing so badly, I had to crawl along on the deck beside her to help guide her.

After delivering the poor woman to the ladies room aft, I continued my round, holding tightly on to handrails as I headed forward to the Panorama Lounge. At the exact moment I entered that lounge, the ship was coming up fast, the buoyancy in her twin hulls and the crest of a swell driving the bow of the ship rapidly upwards. My timing couldn't have been worse for I found myself in a small open area on the starboard side of the Panorama Lounge, completely out of reach of handrails or seats just as the *Spirit* plunged downward into the next swell.

In my entire maritime career, I had never experienced zero gravity before on a ship. I was weightless, the ship had dropped out from under my feet, and I was floating like an astronaut training in a KC-135A aircraft. When the ship plunged into the next swell and stopped falling, I hit the deck hard, but somehow I managed to keep my balance and land on my feet.

Continuing with this eternal round of the cabin, I saw people getting sick and enduring the rough ride. There was nothing that I or anyone could do for the passengers except hand out motion sickness bags and stick it out until we arrived in Toronto.

At one point, a passenger told Purser Delicia Hill that there was a man lying on the floor of the men's room. I went to investigate and found there were actually *two* men lying on the deck. Both were locked inside two of the tiny restroom stalls and were dealing with seasickness by staying close to the porcelain bowls. Through the space under the doors, I could see that both men were lying on their backs in the narrow stalls, apparently with their feet propped up against the walls.

I asked each of them if there was anything I could do for them. I asked this more for the purpose of making sure they were conscious rather than offering assistance since there was nothing I could do for their seasickness. Both gentlemen moaned, "No."

Oddly enough, I did not see a single bad Letter to the Editor show up in the local newspaper.

Seasickness is an odd thing. Not everyone suffers from it. Ever since I made my first sea voyage as an 18-year-old cadet at the maritime academy, I have never been bothered by motion sickness. In fact, upon returning to the wheelhouse and resuming my watch in the conning officer's seat, I found that the effort of making a round in the cabin space had given me quite an appetite. While the *Spirit* continued to shoot upward and then plunge downward in Katrina's swells, I asked my watch partners if the caterer was serving hot chili and apple cider.

My watch partners groaned at the thought of such a combination.

The return trip to Rochester was not as bad. The winds were now following us and they were beginning to die down. Steering the ship himself, Captain Hädh tacked back and forth in the swells to minimize the rough ride.

Katrina blew through the area quickly and by the afternoon trip to Toronto and back to Rochester, lake conditions had settled down considerably. The ship rode well and no one became seasick.

The day ended on a bad note when the Danish master accidentally punched a hole in the back of the ship while maneuvering into the berth in Rochester. The damage, though minor, would cost thousands of dollars to repair.

During the middle of September the ship lost another master's candidate. A gentleman who I will refer to as Mr. Donner had been hired in mid-August. He resigned after only twenty-eight days. Donner had found a better employment opportunity elsewhere and, reportedly, had had enough of the way the *Spirit* was being commanded. He had expressed to me his dismay with the operation.

Paul Greubel and I, the only remaining master's candidates, continued to receive the occasional threats of being "sacked," as the training master would say. It was not a whole lot of fun for any of the officers to come to work every day and wonder if this would be the day when these idle threats would become real.

On one particular day, the training master was unusually loud and agitated as he threatened to fire me over some insignificant, unmemorable issue relating to a purser. A few short hours later, in a complete turnaround of attitude, he came to me and asked if I'd be willing to return to work early on September 26th so that he could go to a Rolling Stones concert in Toronto. One of the Seaway pilots had managed to purchase a ticket for him.

One minute I'm about to be fired; the next I'm being asked to do a favor.

The Dane explained how this curious situation would be engineered. The plan was that I would relieve Greubel as chief mate so that he could sail the ship as captain.

Now, up until this moment, neither Greubel or myself had been deemed fit by this man to be in command of the ship, and, though Greubel was not being *promoted* to captain, he was being asked to *be* captain for one night so that our training master could go to a rock concert.

The logic was baffling.

It should be noted here that both myself and Mr. Greubel had already received our type rating endorsements from Transport Canada. In the eyes of this agency, which was the Canadian equivalent of the U.S. Coast Guard, we were competent to sail as master.

I agreed to return early for no other reason than to ensure that Paul Greubel sailed as captain and, thus, put an end, once and for all, to this nonsense that there were no American masters capable of assuming command. The Rochester Ferry Company/Bay Ferries was delaying the reflagging of the ship and continued to use the lack of trained Americans masters as an excuse in the press.

Chapter 21
A Night to Remember

On Saturday, September 24th, the most significant event in the life of the *Spirit of Ontario 1* occurred.

During the evening run as the fast ferry made its way back to Rochester from Toronto, the smoke detector in the port engine room of the *Spirit* sounded an alarm on the bridge. There were 241 passengers and 41 vehicles aboard that night. A monitoring camera in the engine room was not functioning and the assistant engineer was sent to investigate. Within minutes, the bridge received his urgent call to shut down both main engines and generators. A high-pressure fuel oil leak had occurred on one of the engines and the entire space was permeated with combustible, atomized diesel oil. The *Spirit's* engine room was in danger of exploding.

The chief engineer immediately shut down the machinery in that space. The chief mate quickly mobilized the marine crew and firefighting equipment was deployed. Although this would have not done any good to prevent an engine room explosion, it would have provided protection in the event of a fiery aftermath.

The chief mate and engineer cracked open the door to the engine room and saw fine white mist. The idea of opening the door and allowing oxygen to enter crossed their minds, but they decided if it was going to blow, it would have blown by now. At that point the mixture was too rich. After opening the door, the smoke and white vapor began to clear out. The smell of diesel oil had already traveled up the stairs and was noticed by passengers in the Stern Lounge. The fans on the car deck, normally used to expel vehicle exhaust, were activated and sucked the fumes out through the stern vents.

When the air was clear enough, five marine crew members were sent in with absorbent pads to clean up the mess. Diesel oil was all over the place—on the hot engines, bulkheads, decks, touch screens, and equipment. It was difficult to walk because the deck was slippery. The space reeked. It was hard for the crew to breathe and the oil irritated their throats.

Once enough of the cleanup was completed, the other engine that had not suffered a fuel leak was then restarted and the ship continued on its way to Rochester.

No sooner had things settled down for the crew when, 40 minutes later, a similar leak began shooting diesel oil into the starboard engine room. By now, the ship was 20 minutes from the Rochester jetties and it was decided to continue to run the starboard engines despite the leak.

The *Spirit of Ontario 1* needs a minimum of three engines in order to maneuver at the dock. It was decided to allow the engine to leak and get the ship with its passengers to the dock ASAP rather than shut down the engine. Fuel oil continued to spray and run down the bulkheads. The chief mate and the chief engineer stood by just outside the engine room with extinguishers in hand, peeking in through the door to keep an eye on it and making sure that atomized fuel oil was not filling the space.

Fortunately, the ship made it safely through the Rochester jetties. With its three running engines, the catamaran was then able to do its 180-degree turning maneuver in the yacht basin and then back into the dock at the Rochester terminal. The vessel was half an hour late.

That night repairs were made. Holes and cracks were discovered in the fuel oil pipes that were connected to a fuel pressure relief valve. The piping was replaced.

Days later when I joined the ship and heard the accounts from crew members, one of the senior officers said to me, "We were this close to having a catastrophic event." He held his index finger and thumb only a hair apart.

The fuel oil system in the MTU 20V 8000 M70 diesel engines operates at an extremely high pressure of 1400 bars, or 20,300 pounds per square inch (psi). As explained to me by an MTU representative, some of the fuel oil system's relief valves were opening prematurely and allowing high-pressure fuel oil into a pipeline not designed for that pressure. The relief valves were sent to MTU in Germany so that it could be determined why this was happening and what type of upgrade would be needed to correct the problem.

In the meantime, I was told, there were "no assurances that it won't happen again."

Aside from the leaks themselves, the most troubling aspect about the September 24th incident was that Rochester Ferry Company/Bay Ferries did not report it to the U.S. Coast Guard and the Bahamian Maritime Authority as required by law, or to Germanischer Lloyd.

With an uncertain fix to the high-pressure fuel oil systems in both engine rooms overhanging the *Spirit of Ontario 1* and the possibility that trouble could reoccur, this did not alter the plan for the training master to attend the Rolling Stones concert only two days later.

On September 26th, I returned to work a day early and relieved Paul Greubel as chief mate. He was made captain just for that evening's one-way trip back to Rochester.

The approach to Rochester was no picnic that night. The winds were up and the ship was being pushed around as she approached the jetties. Greubel did a proficient job piloting the ship in and then turning her around and docking her.

Thursday, September 29th was the first day of the reduced fall schedule. Several ABs and OSs were cut. One of the unpleasant aspects of a seasonal job occurs when people have to be let go due to the schedule being scaled back. The Rochester Ferry Company/Bay Ferries did something even worse: They kept the unlicensed marine crew in suspense and did not let any of them know who was going to be retained until the day before. There was no forewarning and four crew members found themselves suddenly unemployed.

On October 4th, a week after the Rolling Stones concert, Mr. Greubel was finally promoted to captain: however, the training master remained onboard every day that he was in command.

On October 6th I was called into the office. Two weeks earlier I had written a strong letter expressing my concerns about a safety issue that involved undocking procedures in Toronto. I thought the purpose of this meeting was to discuss my letter. Instead, and to my surprise, I was informed that I was no longer going to be considered for one of the top two positions on the *Spirit,* citing reasons of concern over my shiphandling skills and the August 21st gangway incident in Toronto which, by now, had occurred over 6-1/2 weeks earlier. Following that incident, I received very little additional training from the Danish captain; however, I was allowed to dock and undock the ship several times in both Toronto and Rochester, though with less frequency than before, each time without incident.

There were no other American masters candidates. Four had come, two had gone, one had been promoted. I had been neutralized. The *Spirit* would not be reflagged any time soon.

For three consecutive days in mid-October, the fast ferry suffered more high-pressure fuel oil problems.

On October 16th, *three* of the *Spirit's* engines developed high-pressure fuel line leaks during the course of its return trip to Rochester.

Though the leaks never filled the engine rooms with atomized fuel as they did on September 24th, it was a tense trip all the way to the dock as we didn't know from one moment to the next how bad it would get or if we would have enough engines to dock.

Once in Rochester, repairs were made during the night.

Despite the repairs made the night before, we experienced another fuel line leak on the return trip to Rochester. Fuel mist was discovered coming from the front of the #4 main engine. The engine was secured and the assistant engineers were sent to investigate the problem. They reported that the fuel line from the pressure relief valve was cracked and misting atomized fuel into the engine room.

The engine was secured for the remainder of the voyage and then restarted for the purpose of entering the Rochester jetties and docking the vessel.

The broken line was replaced and the engine was tested that evening.

Incredibly, the *Spirit* experienced *another* fuel oil leak the next day on October 18th during a highly publicized promotion cruise. There were 432 passengers and five vehicles aboard. Half-way into the trip to Toronto, the ship was forced to return to Rochester.

All four of these fuel oil incidents initially went unreported to the U.S. Coast Guard and the Bahamian Maritime Authority.

That afternoon, after the cancellation of the promotion trip, Rochester Ferry Company President Benjamin L. Douglas released the following statement:

> This morning, a fuel line to one of the four engines of the fast ferry loosened, causing the engine to lose power. The captain, recognizing that the combination of that loss of power and the potentially rough waters, decided not to sail across the lake and turned back to port in Rochester.
>
> Such weather related occurrences happen from time to time in every kind of travel. Our passengers' comfort is our primary concern and as is the case with airlines, we sometimes will cancel crossings if the situation calls for it.

"Loosened."

"A fuel line...loosened."

According to an MTU representative and several of the engineers onboard, the fuel lines on the relief side of the fuel system were being eaten away from the inside by the high-pressure fuel oil in the system, just as they had been on September 24th and during the previous two days. This was the fourth incident in three weeks.

The fuel oil problems did not appear on the radar screens of the regulatory agencies until the next day on October 19th when the story about the cancelled promotion trip appeared in the Rochester *Democrat & Chronicle*. The story prompted a U.S. Coast Guard official to call Rochester Ferry Company/Bay Ferries and inquire about it. They also requested that the company file a form CG-2692 to report the incident. A CG-2692 is a common form used by all U.S. flag vessels and vessels operating in U.S. waters to report marine accidents, injuries, or deaths, as well as propulsion and steering-related failures.

With incidents involving atomized fuel oil filling an entire engine room, diesel oil spilling down bulkheads, and the potential for an engine room explosion, there is no question that a CG-2692 would be required at the end of the day. Carrying a foreign flag on a city of Rochester-owned vessel does not exempt her or her operators from following the reporting requirements in U.S. waters.

An American master or chief would have reported these incidents without fail because their licenses are issued by the very organization to whom we are required to report, the U.S. Coast Guard. The "thou who giveth can also taketh" policy provides a strong incentive to play by the rules. Another reason an American master or chief would report incidents without fail is because most American officers belong to maritime unions. In a union setting, an officer who follows the laws and does what is right, does not have to worry so much about company retribution. If a company attempts to punish a man for obeying the rules, the union will step in and defend him.

In the nonunion Rochester Ferry Company/Bay Ferries environment, with its "at-will" contracts, company retribution was a stark reality. We already had seen one engineering officer unjustly fired, and Greubel, myself, and several other crew members were frequently threatened with being fired for non-issues by the training master. He was the Rochester Ferry Company/Bay Ferries on-scene representative. His immediate supervisors were at the company headquarters in Charlottetown, Prince Edward Island, most of the time. Without any type of labor representation, none of the employees had little, if any, recourse.

The *Democrat & Chronicle* article about the fuel oil leak, either directly or indirectly, also made the Bahamian Maritime Authority aware of the problem. The BMA would not know about it for at least a month. On November 22nd, 2005, BMA wrote a letter to Bay Ferries Management requesting that they file a report about the incident.

It is never good when your regulatory agencies, the ones that can pull the plug on the show, have to read about an incident in the newspaper.

While these shipboard problems continued to raise questions with the ship's officers about the integrity of the Rochester Ferry Company/Bay Ferries, on October 22nd the ferry operator submitted its first quarter financial report to the Rochester Ferry Company Board. Though the board had expected that the initial projection of a $725,000 loss would be higher, the progress report showed a whopping $4.2 million loss. Half of the three-year, $8 million cushion had been expended.

The financial report would be made public the following week on October 27th.

The fuel oil system was not the only system posing problems for the *Spirit*.

On October 26th, the LIPS maneuvering system suddenly quit during docking in Toronto. The vessel was only 10 meters off the dock when the joystick no longer responded, forcing Captain Hädh to quickly shift to back-up mode. Two days later, the day's trip was cancelled due to the LIPS problem as the engineers worked feverishly to diagnose and correct the problem.

On Sunday, November 27th, there was both a fuel oil leak in the port engine room *and* a hydraulics leak in the jet room. The port engines had to be shut down while the leaking hydraulic line in the jet room was repaired. After the engine was restarted, the fuel oil system had reset itself, stopped leaking, and was back to normal.

On December 2nd, another hydraulics leak in the port jet room and strong winds nearly sent the *Spirit* skittering across the Genesee River and into the Rochester Yacht Club's swimming pool.

On that evening, the weather was terrible, with snow squalls and 35-40 knots of wind off the pier. The ship entered the Rochester jetties with higher than normal rpm to counter the effects of the westerly winds and swell. In the turning basin, the *Spirit* was spun around and backed in as usual, but when she was 15 meters off the pier, Hädh discovered he had lost all steering on the port side. He immediately shifted to back-up mode.

243

Fortunately, at that point, two mooring lines were already ashore; a spring line aft, and a head line forward. The captain attempted to back the ship into her berth, but due to the high winds, the ferry drifted nearly thirty meters off the pier before holding. With steering available only on the starboard side, the captain and the mooring crew managed to bring the *Spirit* close enough to put out two more lines ashore forward and then worked the stern in.

After approximately ten minutes of wrestling with the ship, the leak in the jet room was repaired, the port engines were restarted, the control was shifted out of back-up mode and returned to LIPS mode. The docking was then completed using LIPS control.

It was a hell of a docking for the *Spirit* and her crew.

Chapter 22
The City of Rochester/Bay Ferries Season

Following the summer season, passenger numbers between September and December were dreadful: 39,349 passengers and 5,573 vehicles.

None of the ship's officers could understand why the Rochester Ferry Company/Bay Ferries allowed the ship to operate on extremely light passenger days. The *Spirit* was burning about 6,600 gallons of diesel fuel per round trip at a cost of roughly $16,000. A passenger number threshold for canceling a voyage was never established, although the terminal managers had asked about it. They needed to know at what point to order a bus to take the passengers to their destinations.

To offer an example, on Monday, October 31st, we had a remarkably bad day. Only 36 passengers and six cars went to Toronto. On the return trip, we carried 37 passengers and seven cars.

At 6:50 a.m. I called the Rochester terminal on my radio and asked if the trip was still on. The duty manager answered, "No one has called to cancel it."

I even called the training captain on his cell phone as he was driving in. He said no one had said anything to him about canceling, adding, "That is not our decision to make. We go."

During the fall, we had 14 days where we made voyages with fewer than 100 people per trip.

It was reported in the media that the Rochester Ferry Company was broke by the end of October. That was when the $8 million cushion that was established after the federal auction was exhausted. The Rochester Ferry Company/Bay Ferries was losing money at a rate of $1 million a month.

An October 30th "Letter to the Editor" in the *Democrat & Chronicle* seemed to succinctly sum up the situation: "Ferry eats money as whale eats krill."

On October 27th, an odd story appeared on Rochester's WROC-TV. Entitled "Bay Ferries to begin using boat for parties," the city's chosen ferry operator was only now announcing a plan to use the *Spirit* for private parties while the ferry was docked at the port. It was definitely a little to late to try to sell this idea. This type of program should have been conceived, prepared, and promoted during the summer in anticipation of the planned reduced voyage schedule; not *after* the reduced voyage schedule began. Most business and group organizers need weeks, if not months, to plan their events. The story added, "Package specifics available in two weeks."

The October 31st editorial page of the *Democrat & Chronicle* criticized the publicly-owned Rochester Ferry Company for its secrecy. It said,

>   "Even worse than the dispiriting numbers from the ferry's first report to the city's ferry board is the lack of sufficient openness and public accountability. The report given to the press and public is extremely sketchy.
>
>   There is no line-item accounting of spending over this period, according to the document made public. The ferry spent way more than its revenues could support, but the details about that divergence are nowhere to be found in what the taxpayers have been provided.
>
>   That has to change. Immediately. A line-item accounting of expenses, a breakdown of when costs soared and when they evened out, details about vendors and contracts and maintenance and fuel—something that can feasibly be called a budget—has to be made public now."

Originally scheduled to run through December 31st, the ferry service was shut down early on Monday, December 12th, due to mounting costs and dwindling passenger numbers. Many of us were actually grateful. Now, the city wouldn't be wasting any more taxpayer dollars on fuel oil, pilots, and everything else.

Our passenger numbers that last day were truly embarrassing. Leaving Rochester we had carried 27 passengers, seven of which were local TV newscasters and journalists who were onboard to cover the last day of service. The reporters had to look hard to find our passengers for interviews or risk interviewing each other. We also carried six vehicles.

On the return trip from Toronto, we carried 36 passengers and 10 vehicles. Deck mate Kris Werner and his skilled crew found themselves busy directing traffic...for less than a minute.

Left lane. Right lane. Middle lane.

Zoom-zoom!

Clank-clank! Bang-bang!

The 10 cars were off the ship in seconds.

Little did any of us know at the time, we had just made our final voyage to Rochester aboard the *Spirit of Ontario 1,* much like the final CATS run on September 7th, 2004.

We had crossed the "Bone line" for the very last time and would never again be calling the Rochester Coast Guard to let them know of our arrival time.

The next day, we began the *Spirit's* winterization. It was a clear, cold, but nice day with little wind to accomplish the outdoor tasks. Among the many jobs, we moved the rescue boats down to the car deck, installed plywood over several ventilation intakes, and covered the atrium skylight with protective plywood and tarps. The ship's atrium would never see Rochester or Toronto passengers again.

On December 14th, Rochester Mayor Bill Johnson asked the City Council for authorization to allow the Rochester Ferry Company to sell $11.5 million in bonds, backed by the city, to keep the ferry afloat.

Shortly afterward, former Rochester police chief and now Mayor-elect Robert Duffy weighed in. Since his incoming administration would be inheriting the ferry, he asked for a postponement of the City Council bond vote so that his team could assess the ferry situation.

December 14th was my last day of employment with the Rochester Ferry Company/Bay Ferries. My crew and I had completed the majority of the deck winterization tasks. It was also the day of the Bay Ferries Christmas party.

The party was held at Jack's Place located in nearby Durand-Eastman Park. In the wake of a very rough season for the officers and crew, it was a nice gesture. Besides the ship's crew, shoreside staff and terminal security personnel were all invited. People were dressed nicely and enjoyed themselves.

Despite the holiday cheer had by all that night, there would be much bitterness afterward.

The stars and stripes of the American flag never made it to the tiny Bahamian territory that floated on the chocolaty waters of the Genesee River in Charlotte.

When asked about the lack of reflagging, former CATS technical director Bob Mansfield told reporter Rachel Barnhart in October 2005, "It's almost as if everybody thinks it's (the ferry) not going to survive and they're protecting their interests by not putting it under the U.S. flag."

Perhaps that was so. At the time of this writing, this author does not fully know the truth behind the failure to reflag the *Spirit of Ontario 1*.

When the *Spirit of Ontario 1* had completed its first season under the new Rochester Ferry Company, 110,692 passengers and 17,367 vehicles had been carried.

As my colleague had said back in the shipyard, "Fast ferries...they're heartbreakers."

No truer words were ever spoken.

Chapter 23
"Killing cat was 'act of mercy,' owner says"

In a story that appeared in the January 16, 2006 Rochester *Democrat & Chronicle,* reporter Patrick Flanigan, wrote, "Tracie Stear didn't want to kill her cat. But she thought that under the circumstances, it was the right thing to do."

The story was about a cat that was in declining health and was "suffocated by its owner after a friend allegedly broke its neck in a failed attempt to euthanize the sick animal."

Had the story appeared on January 10th instead of the 16th, the above headline could have easily doubled for the fast ferry, too, for on that day, newly-elected Rochester Mayor Robert Duffy made an announcement that would do pretty much the same thing to the *Spirit of Ontario 1.*

Shortly after sunset at a 5 p.m. press conference at City Hall, Mayor Duffy stepped up to the microphones and podium on his way to a City Council meeting. The council meeting was to decide whether or not to approve the bonding of $11.5 million to keep the *Spirit of Ontario 1* alive.

The fast ferry was still a very big story in the community and still commanded the airwaves. Carried live on many of the local news stations, Mayor Duffy said,

"First of all, we asked ourselves can we afford to operate the ferry? Number two: is there a sound business and marketing plan? Is there a likelihood for success? And, is this the best way that we can spend $50.5 million? And the answer to each of those questions is 'no.' My answer tonight at the City Council meeting will be this: I will not authorize the bonding of the $11.5 million to continue the operation of the fast ferry. The city of Rochester will no longer be in the ferry business."

With those few words, the *Spirit of Ontario 1's* fate had been sealed. The next day's newspapers summed it up in a couple of words. In large block letters, the *Democrat & Chronicle's* headline said "**SUNK AGAIN**" while the Messenger Post Newspapers read "**ABANDON SHIP!**"

For what it's worth, CATS and the city of Rochester were not the first fast ferry operators to go out of business. In a political scandal in British Columbia, Canada, that is known as the FastCat Fiasco, the government at the time commissioned the construction of three BC Ferries PacifiCats for the purpose of improving ferry service, but, more so, to

249

spark the dying British Columbia shipbuilding industry. Neither goal was accomplished. These three huge vessels were built between 1995 and 2000. They were 402-feet (122.5 meters) long, had a service speed of 37 knots, and could carry 1,000 passengers and 250 cars. The third ship was completed but was never commissioned because the fast ferry program had already gone out of business.

Issues that contributed to that operation's failure (besides politics) included high fuel consumption, frequent engine breakdowns, flotsam getting sucked into and damaging the waterjets, a wake problem that damaged shoreside property. In addition, it didn't save as much travel time as originally anticipated.

Built at a cost of $450 million dollars ($150M each), taxpayers received almost nothing for the entire fleet which was auctioned off in March 2003 for a paltry $19.3 million dollars ($6.3M each).

They're heartbreakers!

That evening during its newscast, WHAM-TV13 displayed a picture of the *Spirit of Ontario 1* with a red circle and a slash over it. The caption beneath it read "Ferry Finished."

A project that had been in the public eye for many long years, the ferry had meant great hope for many citizens in the community. At the conclusion of the broadcast, longtime anchor Don Alhart and his news team created a poetic "A Look Back at the Ferry" through video and verse. It captured the sentiments of the community.

SHE WAS BORN DOWN UNDER
OUR PRIDE IN HER BIRTH
BUILT IN AUSTRALIA
IN THE CITY OF PERTH

WE WATCHED HER TAKE SHAPE
A HALF WORLD AWAY-
KNOWING THAT SOMEDAY-
SHE'D BE SAILING OUR WAY

THAT DAY FINALLY CAME-
SHE LEFT WITH A BLAST
FAST FERRY SERVICE
FOR US - AT LONG LAST

THROUGH PANAMA CANAL
AND ON UP THE COAST
THE PROBLEMS BEGAN
A FEW MORE THAN "MOST"

UP TO THE BIG APPLE
SHE CRASHED INTO A DOCK
THEN SCRATCHES AND SCRAPES
IN A ST. LAWRENCE LOCK

THEN WE GATHERED ON SHORE
NO MORE WOULD SHE ROAM
ROCHESTER'S FAST FERRY
HAD FINALLY FOUND HOME!

PREMIERE PASSAGE DELAYED
BUT THEN CAME THE DAY
WHEN ROTARIANS AND GUESTS
WOULD PARTY AWAY

BUT ALL OF THE GAIETY
IN TIME WOULD BE GONE
THE ORIGINAL OWNERS
WOULD NOT BE HERE LONG-

AN AUCTION ENSUED
ON THE LINE WAS IT ALL
AND THE ONE HIGHEST BID-
OUR OWN CITY HALL!

LAUNCHED AGAIN WITH A FLARE
WE COULD NOT RESIST
BUT FINANCIAL PROBLEMS
INDEED, WOULD PERSIST.

FROM MAYOR TO MAYOR
A REQUEST WE SHOULD NOTE
TO BORROW MORE MONEY
TO KEEP IT AFLOAT!

BUT TODAY FINALLY CAME
AND THE STORY WOULD FLIP
"CAPTAIN" BOB DUFFY SAID-
"ABANDON THIS SHIP!"

SO TONIGHT- IT REMAINS
ALL ALONE AT CHARLOTTE
WONDERING WHY--
OR PERHAPS WHY NOT--

WHY DIDN'T IT WORK
WHAT'S WRONG WITH THE BOAT
IS THERE ANY WAY
WE CAN KEEP IT AFLOAT?

QUESTIONS TO PONDER
IN SHOCK AND IN SORROW
IS THERE ANY HOPE LEFT?
WELL- THERE'S ALWAYS- TOMORROW!

Photo courtesy of T.C. Pellett, copyright 2004

The Real Epilogue

The *Spirit of Ontario 1* was not to be auctioned again.
A little under four months after Mayor Bob Duffy made his announcement to end ferry service, the *Spirit of Ontario 1* was sold to Euroferries Ltd. of England on May 3, 2006.

"I'm very pleased to come today and announce the ferry is sold," Mayor Duffy said at a 5 p.m. press conference at City Hall.

At the time of this writing in late June 2006, the *Spirit* was still docked in Charlotte and the city of Rochester and Euroferries were close to concluding the sale. The two parties had agreed on a price of $29.8 million. Euroferries plans to operate the ship between Dover, England, and Boulogne, France. The *Spirit's* new name is not known.

Both CATS and Rochester Ferry Company/Bay Ferries failed to realize that one of the best tools in their public relations kits were their own employees.

The crew of the *Spirit of Ontario 1* was rarely recognized in the local press for its efforts, except for the occasional "Letters to the Editor" sent to the *Rochester Democrat & Chronicle* by pleased and grateful passengers. One of the reasons for this book is to pay tribute to the crew, especially those who stuck it out for the two seasons.

Two-hundred and forty-three thousand passengers crossed the *Spirit's* gangway. The crew members were the frontline people. Sure, the ship is fantastic!, high-tech!, and world class!, but it was the *people* who worked onboard that gave the ship its heart and had a direct hand in creating the rich and forever-lasting memories that those passengers carried away with them. Without a good, caring crew, the most astounding ship in the entire world can be just a cold and empty shell, unworthy of any memory.

On occasion I'd have the pleasure and rare opportunity of talking with people who had ridden the old Cobourg ferries. As they recount their trip aboard those vessels of yesteryear, the memories are always warm, sometimes having been a childhood once-in-a-lifetime thrill.

Shortly after the city of Rochester announced the *Spirit's* shutdown in January, friends who had ridden the ship would speak of her with the same fondness and warmth as those who had ridden the previous ferry service of 50-plus years ago. The *Spirit* was now slipping into that category of becoming a ferry of yesteryear.

One of the great things the *Spirit of Ontario 1* would leave behind is the hope for another, yet smaller and private ferry operation to pick up where she had left off, one day soon. She clearly had demonstrated that a market for a ferry service between the two cities does exist.

As she passes quietly through the Rochester jetties one last time and heads northeast for the St. Lawrence Seaway, she will leave behind a beautiful new ferry terminal that would patiently wait for another ship to replace her and to grace her pier with a new wave of travelers who would pass through its newly constructed corridors.

Inside the terminal, a lone *Mamma Mia!* poster which had been hanging since 2004 would watch along with the hundreds of well-wishers as the *Spirit* sails into the next life, goes to her last reward, is promoted to glory, books her final passage, casts off toward eternity, reaches the end of the line, steams into the sunset, motors to the great beyond, sets course for calmer waters, journeys into the wild blue yonder.

Finished with Engines. Over the Bar.

The *Spirit* will rise again.

AUTHOR'S COMMENTS

The prospect of several of our country's ports being managed by Dubai Ports World gained global attention in 2006. A much larger problem that has been overlooked in the United States for a very long time is American merchant ships changing their registries to flag of convenience countries and outsourcing American jobs. When a ship flies a foreign flag, the hiring of crews is open to multinationals. Vessels entering U.S. ports flying an American flag are manned only by American crews. This provides another layer of security for our country's ports.

This is especially true where the *Spirit of Ontario 1* was concerned. This vessel was the fastest one of its size on Lake Ontario and could pose a serious security threat if it fell into the wrong hands. An American flag would have meant a higher level of security to the vessel, her passengers and crew, and shoreside assets (such as the nearby Ginna Nuclear Power Plant).

In addition, American crews pay U.S. federal and state income taxes. Foreign crews generally do not. In addition, depending on a country's rules for their citizens who work abroad, foreign crews sometimes do not pay any income tax to their home country.

Registering the *Spirit of Ontario 1* to the United States would have allowed the Rochester Ferry Company to apply for financial aid through several federal programs, such as the Maritime Security Program, programs within the Department of Homeland Security, the Ferry Boat Discretionary Fund, and others.

The difficulty in finding both licensed and unlicensed American mariners would have been solved by tapping the resources of the U.S. maritime unions, unions which offer their own pension and health plans, as well as their own training facilities.

The daily costs of the expensive lake pilots and their transportation would have been eliminated.

Many of the *Spirit's* officers believed Rochester Ferry Company/Bay Ferries did not seem to be interested in bringing the *Spirit* under the U.S. flag in 2005, despite the prominence of the issue. The indicators we saw included:
- The St. Lawrence Seaway Pilots' Association president had been approached in early 2005 by a Bay Ferries vice-president seeking a three-year, reduced rate contract for the continued services of the pilots.
- Focused training for the masters-in-training did not begin for over a month after service began, and only after this chief mate/author wrote a letter

i

to the company questioning this lack of training. Valuable training time was lost.

- One American master-in-training was driven to resign only 13 days after service began. Later in the season, two other American masters-in-training eventually resigned for similar reasons.
- Without American licenses, there can be no American flag to displace the Bahamian flag. The turnover in American licensed officers was incredibly high in 2005. Three chief mates/masters-in-training, three chief engineers, and four assistant engineers resigned at various times throughout the brief season. There was also one unjustified firing. Total: 11 American licenses lost. The company seemed cavalier in allowing these difficult to recruit licensed officers to resign.
- There was no effort on the part of Rochester Ferry Company/Bay Ferries to arrange for a route-specific pilotage exam for the new mates and masters-in-training like CATS had aggressively done in 2004. In December 2005, a representative of the U.S. Coast Guard told me that they were never contacted about it.
- The Danish training master frequently told the officers that the *Spirit of Ontario 1* would never have an American flag on her stern.
- After seven months of costly training and four American masters candidates to work with, only one American was allowed to be captain. Even so, the training master never entirely relinquished control of the vessel to the American master. Two American masters were needed to reflag the *Spirit of Ontario 1* to the U.S.

Under CATS management in 2004, there had been no accommodations for out-of-town marine crew and meals onboard the *Spirit* cost the crew 50% of retail. Despite these hefty living expenses, CATS experienced only two resignations; neither of which was related to management issues. In 2005, lodging ashore and meals for the marine crew were provided under Rochester Ferry Company/Bay Ferries. Despite these valuable perks, 11 American licenses resigned.

I observed other issues that hurt the *Spirit's* chances of survival.

There were no big and noticeable promotions in 2005. There was no visible marketing plan.

The wall space inside the ship and in the terminal was not utilized for advertising in 2005. The *Mamma Mia!* poster that was hung in the departure hall in July 2004 continued to hang in the terminal throughout 2005 and into 2006, even though the Toronto show had closed in May 2005.

There were no special events coordinators like Jenny Lorenz in 2005. Under CATS, there had been over two dozen excursions and events during the *Breeze's* short 80-day run. Thousands of people were served. Tens of thousands of dollars worth of revenue were generated. During the entire five-and-a-half months of Rochester Ferry Company/Bay Ferries service, there was only one corporate excursion. Forty-six people were served. Amount of revenue generated: insignificant.

The Rotary Clubs of both Rochester and Toronto had successfully staged the Premiere Passage in 2004. The event was the most elaborate, exciting, and memorable event to take place on the *Spirit of Ontario 1* during her two short years of service. It is surprising that no other groups or businesses ever followed Rotary's example and utilized the ferry to hold other huge, orchestrated events and/or fundraisers. It was surprising that no one at Rochester Ferry Company/Bay Ferries attempted to cultivate events such as this.

In 2004, the *Spirit* had been able to take diesel fuel in Rochester twice a day in between trips using the two in-ground fuel tanks at the terminal. These tanks had been specifically installed in early 2004 for this purpose. During the 2005 season, for some reason, the in-ground tanks were not used. Instead, the fuel oil was trucked in all the way from the Buffalo area and loaded once a day. As a result, the *Spirit* had to lug around two trips worth of fuel oil which added more weight to the ship and resulted in higher fuel consumption.

Bibliography

The Rochester *Democrat & Chronicle* coverage of the fast ferry project, 1998-2006.
The following articles were referenced:
"Analysts say ferry estimates too high," September 17, 2002, written by Rick Armon and Gary Craig.
"Aussie is top gun in world of fast ferries," February 26, 2003, written by Rick Armon.
"Local workers sought for ferry," October 25, 2003, written by Todd Grady.
"$85,000 gift to Habitat earmarked for rebirth," January 2, 2004, written by Rick Armon.
"Coast Guard team travels to Australia, praises ship's quality," February 6, 2004, written by Rick Armon.
"Canadian gala to greet ferry," March 31, 2004, written by Rick Armon.
"Sparsely populated ferry leaves," June 18, 2004, written by Jeffrey Blackwell and Lara Becker Liu.
"Ferry engine woes put hundreds onto buses," June 27, 2004, written by Enid Arbelo.
"CEO and president of ferry to step down," July 7, 2004, written by Rick Armon.
"Ferry steadies after rocky start," September 5, 2004, written by Rick Armon.
"Founder discusses ferry's future," November 10, 2004, written by Rick Armon.
"Why the ferry foundered," November 14, 2004, written by Rick Armon.
"Idle ferry is one man's spacious apartment," December 16, 2004, written by Rick Armon.
"Australia offers city $40 million to buy ferry," December 18, 2004, written by Rick Armon and Gary Craig.
"Ferry carries $2 million in liens," February 12, 2005, written by Rick Armon.
"City sets up ferry oversight group," January 21, 2005, written by Rick Armon.
"Ferry reverses course midtrip," October 19, 2005, written by Brian Sharp.
"Letter to the Editor," October 30, 2005. "Ferry eats money as whale eats krill."
The Editorial Page, October 31, 2005.
"Killing cat was 'act of mercy,' owner says," January 16, 2006, written by Patrick Flanigan.

COAL TO CANADA—A History of the Ontario Car Ferry Company by Ted Rafuse, Steampower Publishing.

"A Look Back at the Ferry," poem courtesy of Don Alhart and WHAM-TV, copyright 2006.

Marine Log, January 2004, pg. 37. Hornblower Marine Services advertises internationally for marine crew.

Marine Log, May 2004, pg. 39. CATS advertisement, "NEW Passenger/Auto Ferry Design and Build Contract, Request for Proposals."

Marine Log, September 2004, pg. 53. Employment section. "Fast ferry captain wanted."

Marine Log, October 2004, pg. 13. Marine Log Ferries 2004.

Marine Log, May 2005, pg. 7. Article "Guilty pleas in Staten Island ferry disaster case."

Rochester Business Journal June 11, 2004, article *Fast Forward: Spirit of Ontario 1* by Will Astor

"History of Human Error Found in Ferry Accidents," *New York Times*, November 1, 2003, written by Mike McIntire.

Captain Clark's Fast Ferry Web Site

Kevin Williams, WHEC-TV Meteorologist, and Weather-Track

National Weather Service in Buffalo, New York

WHEC-TV, Rochester, NY, April 1, 2004, Ferry collision with Pier 17, interviews conducted by reporter Berkeley Brean.

WROC-TV, Rochester, NY, June 27th, 2005, "Ferry crew gets up to speed" by reporter Joylynn Whitfield.

WHAM-TV, Rochester, NY, August 2, 2005, "Flagging An Expensive Charge" by reporter Jane Flasch.

RNews, Rochester, NY, July 2004. Interview with CATS President Cornel Martin. Reporter Rocco Vertuccio.

PacifiCats, FastCat Fiasco, article Wikipedia.

Earth Island Journal, Autumn 2001, Vol. 16, number 3. "Watch Out for Whales!" by Teri Shore.

Transportation Safety Board of Canada, Marine Investigation Report Collision Between The Fast Ferry Catamaran "INCAT 046" and The Fishing Boat "LADY MEGAN II" Yarmouth Harbour, Nova Scotia, 4 September 1998 Report Number M98M0061.

Transport Accident Investigation Commission (TAIC report 98-204), available from TAIC's web site www.taic.org.nz.

University of Rochester web site, November 12, 2002. "University Receives Multi-Million-Dollar Commitment From Under-40 Alumnus."

Many thanks to...

Many thanks to George Monagan, Tony White, Bob Mansfield, Asger Manoe, Anonymous, Cliff Babson, Neil Shanahan, Chris Coleman, Ian Sherwood, Kris Werner, John Enwright, Bryan Hald, Tonya Allen, Delicia Hill, Wayne Hinkel, Mary Howard-Lawrence, Eugenia Lavigne, Erin Macallister, Rick Marcellus, Karen Marsh, Mike Masco, Chris Moore, Eric Mueller, Roger Paulus, Kurt Ritchie, Beverly Rouse, Cheryl Wiemer, Carrie Cooper, Frank Cranmer, Peter Schuffels, Tony Putnik, and Jenny Lorenz.

A very special thanks to Susan Dickens, Tom Riley, Beth Flory, Bob Anthony, Rick Armon, Captain Mike Blanton, and Ed Hanley for their invaluable comments and time.

Many thanks to Don Alhart for allowing me to include his poem "A Look Back at the Ferry."

Also, I wish to express my appreciation to Captain John J. Donahue, Paul Tracy, Tom Hope, Dominick DeLucia, Cornel Martin, John Waggoner, Captain Ken Kujala, Captain Paul Greubel, Captain Gerry Cooper, Captain David Doucet, Kent Ehler, Debbie Knapp, Adrian Chagoya, Valerie Knoblauch, Lindsey Dickens, Adam & Hillary Ferrante, Ted Rafuse, Kim Huffman, Elaine Verstraete, David Love, Glenn Gardner, Spyglass Studio, Susan Larysz of S&G Imaging, and Nicole Vanpraag of Austal Ships of Henderson, Western Australia. Also to the Greater Rochester Visitor's Association, Inc. and T.C. Pellet, Patti Donoghue, and Ed Hall.

Many thanks to Rick Armon and Brian Sharp of the Rochester *Democrat & Chronicle*. Also to the *Democrat & Chronicle*, Messenger Post Newspapers, Allison Cooper, David Wheeler, Patrice Walsh, WHAM-TV13, WHEC-TV10, RNews, Berkeley Brean, Brother Wease, Windjammers, Scuttlebutts, and Marine Engineers' Beneficial Association.

Photos courtesy of Beverly Rouse, Asger Manoe, Petr Chudoba, T.C. Pellet (Assistant Communications Director, Greater Rochester Visitor's Association), and Austal Ships of Henderson, Western Australia (Thank you, Nicole Vanpraag). Map/route graphic of Lake Ontario courtesy of Tom Riley.

About the Author

Larry Dickens graduated from the Massachusetts Maritime Academy and holds an unlimited oceans master's license. He spent most of his seagoing career aboard liquefied natural gas supertankers operating in the Orient. He writes purposeful, young adult novels (*Mrs. McGillacuddy's Garden Party, Forever Ten, Hillary's Wish*), as well as contemporary sea novels (*Tropical Depression*). He lives in the Finger Lakes region of New York State with his wife, artist Susan Prislopski Dickens.

Mr. Dickens welcomes your thoughts about his books. Visit his web site **www.LarryDickens.com** for contact info as well as his latest book releases, press, and useful links.

Other books by Larry Dickens

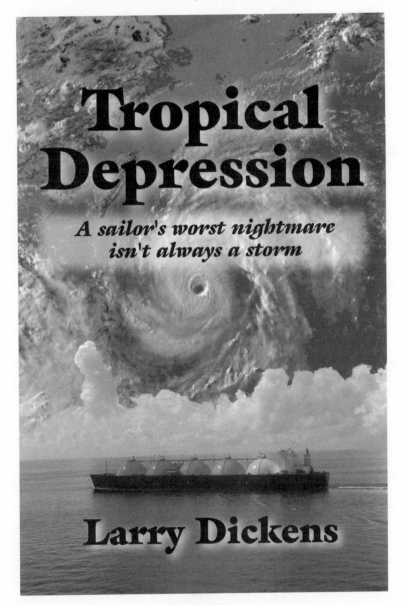

General Fiction
Tropical Depression

Order your copy at www.LarryDickens.com

Young Readers Novels by Larry Dickens

When being nice isn't enough!
Mrs. McGillacuddy's Garden Party
For everyone 10 to 110 years

A tale of what might have been for a little boy.
Forever Ten
For ages 12 to 120 years
Order your copy at www.LarryDickens.com